Boston
April 1989

FROMMER'S

BOSTON

FAYE HAMMEL

assisted by Rita Pollak

GW00691941

□

1989–1990

Published by Prentice Hall Trade Division
A Division of Simon & Schuster, Inc.
Gulf + Western Building
One Gulf + Western Plaza
New York, NY 10023

ISBN 0-13-047929-2
ISSN 0899-322X

Design by Levavi & Levavi, Inc.
Manufactured in the United States of America

*Although every effort was made to ensure the accuracy
of price information appearing in this book
it should be kept in mind that prices
can and do fluctuate in the course of time.*

CONTENTS

MAPS

INFLATION ALERT: We don't have to tell you that inflation has hit the United States as it has everywhere else. In researching this book we have made every effort to obtain up-to-the minute prices, but even the most conscientious researcher cannot keep up with the current pace of inflation. As we go to press, we believe we have obtained the most reliable data possible. Nonetheless, in the lifetime of this edition—particularly its second year (1990)—the wise traveler will ad 15% to 20% to the prices quoted throughout these pages.

CHAPTER I

AN INTRODUCTION TO BOSTON

□ □ □

More than anything else, it is the lure of history that draws visitors to Boston. From all over the country, and the world, they come—to follow the path of Paul Revere, to visit the shrines where long-haired radicals like John Hancock and Samuel Adams incited the colonists to revolution, to pay homage to the one city that is, more than any other, the birthplace of these United States.

But there is a lot more about Boston to enchant and excite the visitor than the memories and monuments of the past, important as they are. Boston is very much a metropolis of the '80s, a unique town that combines big-city excitement and sophistication with a pace that is positively relaxing. Boston has long prided itself on being the "Athens of America" (America's Florence rather than its Rome, its Leningrad rather than its Moscow), and the cultural vibrations are strong; Bostonians are justly proud of the great Boston Symphony Orchestra, the superb Boston Museum of Fine Arts, Harvard University, and the Massachusetts Institute of Technology (the latter two are actually in Cambridge). There are schools, colleges, and medical centers, research and cultural institutions wherever one looks. Boston is the big city which draws bright young people from all over the world to live and work here. In fact, employment recruiters for New York and other big-city firms often get flat refusals from Ivy League college grads; they all want to move to Boston instead!

Boston is a modern city where the old still lives and is cherished. Centuries-old meeting houses sit almost side by side with some of the most modern architecture and grandiose civic projects in the world, all part of contemporary "New Boston." Boston has some of the best hotels in America; scores of exciting restaurants, both old world and daringly new, serving perhaps the best seafood in the country; a host of attractions and amusements for children; a vast complex of museums, parks, an aquarium, and flower gardens; and a shopping scene that is irresistible. Boston has its Back Bay brahmins and its students, the Old Money of Louisburg Square and the blacks and Hispanics of Roxbury and the South End. Its population is a fascinating mix of *Mayflower* settlers, old families, vast quantities of Italians and Eastern European Jews who came to work in its factories and mills around the turn of the century, Asians, and, most prominently, Irish— the Curleys and Kennedys and Fitzgeralds and Cushings—who have given Boston a full share of both raffish history and glory.

Boston itself has a population of 571,000, but as the hub of the Greater Boston area, which numbers some 2¾ million people spread out in 83 cities and towns, its importance is far-reaching. The most diversified city in New England, with electronic equipment, computers, machinery, fishing, banking, and insurance, all big business, it has big-city know-how plus small-town charm. It is a particularly pleasant city for walking and ambling about. Fruit and flower stands can be found on corners, especially in the downtown shopping area and around Copley Square. Newbury, Charles, and Boylston Streets abound with inviting shops, antique stores, and galleries.

Best of all for the traveler, Boston is ideally situated as the starting point for all sorts of New England holidays. Even if you just stay in Massachusetts you can, within an hour, drive to the beachy, boaty North Shore resort towns of Salem, Marblehead, Essex, Newburyport, Gloucester, and Rockport, each filled with more than its share of historical and contemporary interest. Head south, and within 90 minutes you're at Plymouth, where it all began, and in another hour you're on that fabled peninsula called Cape Cod, one of the best summer vacation areas in the world. Turn west and Sturbridge Village, a re-creation of an 1800s rural village, is just about 90 minutes away. Fly, ride the rails, or drive to Boston to start your holiday. Rent a car there and explore the state of Massachusetts—that is, if you can bear to leave the absorbing sights of the city.

BOSTON'S HISTORY

Boston's history and American history practically started together. Settled ten years after the Pilgrims landed in Plymouth, the marsh-covered Shawmut Peninsula (later to be named Boston) quickly became an important shipbuilding center and fishing port, and, very early in the game, the British began pressing for laws to restrict the trading activities of the colonies, which were cutting into their own profits. By the middle of the 18th century, "taxation without representation is tyranny" had already become a battle cry for revolution, and after the Boston Massacre of 1770, in which five men were killed by British soldiers after a petty row, the colony was ripe for action. The famous Boston Tea Party started it. Paul Revere's ride took place on April 18, 1775, the Battle of Bunker Hill on June 17 of that year, and by the fall Boston was a military garrison, with Gen. George Washington taking charge of the colonial army. The British were sent scurrying home and the city was free.

By the close of the century, trade was picking up; the population was pushing 25,000; Charles Bulfinch's architecture was gaining an international reputation; and many of the fine houses of Beacon Hill (which are still lived in today) were being built. In the 19th century, Boston became a shipbuilding and manufacturing center as well as an important stop on the "underground railway" via which the Abolitionists smuggled slaves into Canada. The city continued to expand and has done so until the present. Not only has the population swollen, but much of the marsh area has been filled in. The original Back Bay behind the tiny Shawmut Peninsula is now the midtown area (although still called Back Bay); all of South Boston, with its docks and marine park, is on land reclaimed from the bay; and what had been Noddle Island, across from the bay, is now the vast Logan International Airport, also built on landfill. Either from here or from one of the fine highways that lead into the city you begin your explorations of the "Hub of New England"—Boston.

CHAPTER II

FINDING YOUR WAY AROUND BOSTON

□ □ □

Boston is an easy city to find your way around, once you get the "lay of the land." Contrary to the general impression, Boston's streets were not built on existing cattle paths. The settlers carefully copied the procedures used in old England for laying out streets (which, come to think of it, were probably based on following cattle paths). We'll orient you with some views from the top, then show you how to get about on ground level. Let's start at Logan International Airport in East Boston.

ARRIVAL

Boston's Logan Airport may be the most accessible of any in the country, situated just across the bay, only three miles from the downtown area (via tunnels under the harbor). Taxis (around $7), hotel shuttle buses ($3 to $5, depending on the hotel), and the subway (60¢) run into the heart of the city. If your destination is not Boston or Cambridge, you can share a cab with other passengers headed in the same direction; check the Share-A-Cab stand at each terminal. Try the subway if your luggage is light. A shuttle bus takes you to the MBTA (Massachusetts Bay Transit Authority) Airport Station which borders the terminal. From there it's seven minutes to downtown Boston. For specific information, check the subway kiosks at all the airline terminals. (More details on the "T" later.) There is also limo and bus service north, south, and west of the city. And on a fine day there is nothing better than the Airport Water Shuffle, big comfortable boats that get you to the Boston waterfront in ten minutes. A free shuttle bus takes you from the terminal to the Logan boat dock for trips downtown. Fare to Boston is $5 adults, $2.50 children one way. For more information call 800/23-LOGAN.

THE VIEW FROM THE TOP: Our favorite way to survey any new city is from the top, and Boston obliges with three skyscraping observation points: the John Hancock Tower, the Prudential Skywalk, and the Air-Traffic Control Tower at Logan Airport. If you've come by jet, try the **Logan Tower** for your first look at the city, the harbor, and the beaches you'll be touring later. Take the elevator in the center of the parking garage to the 16th floor where you can listen to piped-in control-tower talk while you enjoy the view. There's no admission fee and it's open from 9 a.m. to 6 p.m. (summer hours until 9 p.m.). Or try the picture-windowed lounge, one floor up, where you can watch the planes, the ships, and the city traffic from 3 p.m. to midnight Sunday through Thursday, and noon to 2 a.m. on Friday and Saturday.

A popular high point in Boston is the **John Hancock Observatory** at Copley Square (tel. 249-1977). Take the "T" to Copley Station, walk one block to the Observatory, where elevators whiz 60 floors in 30 seconds. Try to time your visit to just before sunset. The view can be spectacular, and it's always fun to watch the city light up at night. Admission is $2.75 ($2 for children ages 5 to 15 and senior citizens), and includes a 15-minute sound-and-light show focused on a diorama of Boston 1775, a film of present-day Boston, a taped description of the city by the late historian Walter Muir Whitehill, and a display of color slides of Boston and New England. There are free adult- and kid-size "funscopes" to focus on Boston landmarks, and telescopes (25¢) that can zoom you in on objects 740 feet below or miles crosstown. Hours are 9 a.m. to 11 p.m. Monday through Saturday and noon to 11 p.m. on Sunday. Open daily with the exception of Thanksgiving and Christmas.

The **Prudential Center Skywalk,** located on the 50th floor of the Prudential Tower, 800 Boylston St. (tel. 236-3318), offers the only 360° view of Boston and beyond. From the enclosed observation deck you can see for miles, even as far as the mountaintops of southern New Hampshire, or south to Cape Cod with the help of one of the coin-fed telescopes. The Skywalk hours are Monday through Saturday from 10 a.m. to 10 p.m. and Sunday from noon to 10 p.m. Admission is $2 for adults, $1 for senior citizens and children ages 5 to 15. On the 52nd floor the view

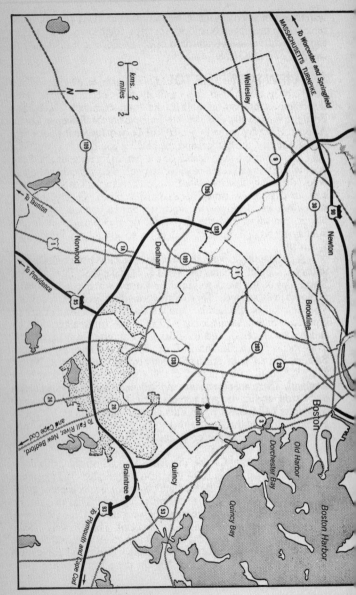

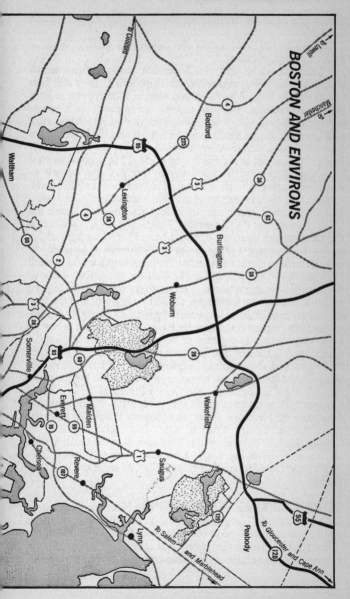

comes with food and drink at the Top of the Hub Restaurant and Lounge.

From any of these towers you can get the general layout of Boston, described below.

Face the ocean and you'll see the wharves from which Boston's fishing fleet and merchant ships sailed. They still bear names such as India Wharf and Commercial Wharf, but now hold luxury apartments, marinas, hotels, restaurants, and urban-renewal projects. In front of you is the Aquarium, which you must visit later, and across the harbor, the airport and the North Shore beaches. As you turn counterclockwise, you see the Mystic River Bridge leading out of the city to the north. (The original town is on a peninsula, and is connected by bridges and tunnels to surrounding areas.) To the left of the bridge is Bunker Hill Monument; to the right is the site of the Charlestown Navy Yard (now decommissioned and home to luxury apartments), where the U.S.S. *Constitution ("Old Ironsides")* is docked. Now, look across the panorama of Boston—the Old State House, wedged in between the skyscrapers of the banks and insurance companies; the new Waterfront Park; the Faneuil Hall Marketplace and Faneuil Hall; the new City Hall; and in the distance, the golden dome of the State House. In the center is a long stretch of green (in season) which marks Boston Common, the Public Garden, and the tree-shaded expanse of Commonwealth Avenue. To the right of Commonwealth Avenue is the Charles River, which separates Boston from Cambridge. The park area bordering it is the Esplanade, where locals sunbathe and jog and the Boston Pops and other orchestras and dance groups perform at the Hatch Memorial Shell. To the left is the vast complex of apartments, hotels, smart shops, and restaurants known as Copley Place and the Prudential Center. And in between is Back Bay, with the art galleries and boutiques of Newbury Street, the Boston Public Library, the Romanesque Trinity Church, and Old South Church at Copley Square. Beyond is the Christian Science Center, with its beautiful reflecting pool, Kenmore Square, Fenway Park; and in the distance are the Blue Hills (where there is winter skiing).

YOUR WALKING TOUR BEGINS: Now come down to earth and we'll give you instructions on how to reach the places you've just seen. Let's go to the **Boston Common** first. This is the oldest people's park in the United States, dating back to the 1630s. (The pigeons came later.) It was from here that the British redcoats marched to Lexington, and it is here that the Freedom Trail starts. And so will we.

Begin at the **Visitor's Information Center** on the Common. You're standing on Tremont Street, a busy shopping center. Across the Common is Beacon Street with the gold-domed State House designed by Charles Bulfinch. This is also the start of Beacon Hill, with Louisburg Square, the last outpost of the Proper Bostonians, at the top; and Charles Street, with boutiques and antiques at the bottom. Between them are rows of steep little streets, stretching back toward the Massachusetts General Hospital.

Park Street forms the right-hand side of the Common (the Park Street subway is here) and then gives way to the rest of Tremont Street, which leads to Government Center, Faneuil Hall Marketplace, and the waterfront. Beyond that area is the North End. Boylston Street runs along the left side of the Common and leads to the Public Garden, the Back Bay area, Copley Place, the Prudential Center, John B. Hynes Convention Center, and the Christian Science Center. Massachusetts Avenue, behind the convention center, divides this area from the cultural and educational zone on the other side, which includes Symphony Hall, the Museum of Fine Arts, the Gardner Museum, Northeastern University, and Simmons College. Boston University is beyond Kenmore Square.

If you're still standing at the Information Center, behind you is the shopping district—Downtown Crossing, with Filene's department store and its famous Basement—and Chinatown. (See our sightseeing section for more complete descriptions.)

Remember, there is no real pattern to Boston's streets. They just happened. You only need to be aware of the general arrangement. And if you get lost, well, sometimes you find the most interesting shops and restaurants that way.

Note: On the whole Boston is a safe city for walking, but there are some areas that we would avoid at night: Tremont Street from Stuart Street to Boylston Street; and Boylston Street where it crosses the Combat Zone at Washington Street. The Combat Zone, an area of bars featuring nude dancers, peep shows, and erotica, is the reincarnation of the famous Scollay Square. The original Scollay Square is now a Boston landmark and home to Government Center and City Hall. But with the construction of new office buildings and the renovation of existing properties, the Zone is shrinking. As "adult entertainment" is squeezed out, the Combat Zone will probably become a choice area in the near future. Until then, do your strolling in daylight.

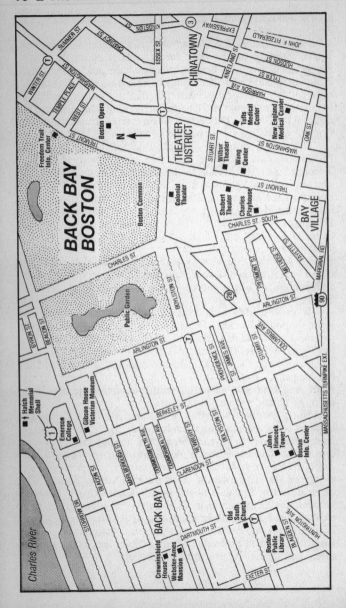

BOSTON'S WEATHER: New England has never been known for ideal weather. Winters can get cold, very cold, with snow on the ground for months. Summers can be hot and sticky, with temperatures soaring into the 80s and 90s during July and August. Spring is usually mild and beautiful; fall is crisp and clear, with the kind of Octobers that the poets used to write about. But it can be hot in fall and breezy in summer and cool in spring, so when you pack for your visit to Boston, be prepared for anything. The city, though, is "on" whenever you arrive. Winter is high season for theater, symphony, and the like (and you can get off to the mountains and ski for the weekend); and a summer vacation is fun because you can always mix a boat trip or an afternoon at a nearby beach into your sightseeing.

To get the weather report, dial 936-1234, 973-6620, or 787-7372. And if you're in Boston itself you can check the weather by looking up at the lights on the old John Hancock Insurance Company in the Back Bay. (The new Hancock building is the glass-paneled one.) A steady blue light means clear; flashing blue, cloudy; steady red, rain; flashing red, snow—except during the summer when flashing red means the Red Sox game has been cancelled.

BOSTON: AVERAGE MONTHLY TEMPERATURES
(in degrees Fahrenheit)

January	29.9	July	73.7
February	30.3	August	71.7
March	37.7	September	65.3
April	47.9	October	55.0
May	58.8	November	44.9
June	67.8	December	33.3

ABOUT THAT BOSTON ACCENT: Yes, it's true. In Boston, they don't have horses, they have "hosses"; they drink "watah"; and they "pahk" their cars. So strong, in fact, is the Boston accent that it takes natives about ten years of living away from town to overcome it. But don't worry, you'll catch on quickly, and when you get back home, your own accent may sound awfully hahsh (we mean harsh) to the eardrums.

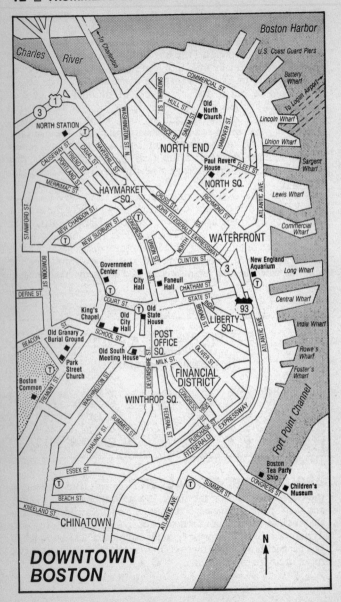

DOWNTOWN BOSTON

GETTING AROUND

The subways and your feet are your most practical means of transportation in Boston.

TAXIS: They're expensive and not always easy to find. But when you do get one, this is the fare arrangement: the first two-sevenths of a mile costs $1.10 and the first mile costs $2.10, with a charge of 20¢ for each additional one-seventh mile. "Wait time" is $12 an hour; and there is a charge for tolls for the tunnel, turnpike, or bridges.

Boston's taxi drivers may be among the most literate in the country—many students work their way through college by cabbying. They're probably the best dressed, too, since Boston has a "dress code" for the drivers—they must wear shirts, be hygienically clean, and keep their beards (if they have one) neatly trimmed! Most of the cabbies, no matter what their backgrounds, are full of opinions, ranging from critiques on politics to hotels, restaurants, the architecture of the "New Boston," and "the syndicate." A good way to get informed.

SHOPPER'S SHUTTLE BUS: Those big, red, double-decker buses that you see going through town are a great way to get from one shopping area to another, and get a bird's-eye view of the city (from the top deck) at the same time. They make a loop connecting Back Bay, Downtown Crossing, and Faneuil Hall Marketplace with stops at stores, hotels, and historic sights. You can get on at any one of the 25 stops marked with the sign of a big red bus and get off anywhere along the loop for only 50¢ for adults and 25¢ for children and senior citizens. Some hotels will even give you a free pass. The shuttle runs every 15 minutes from 10 a.m. to 6 p.m. daily.

THE MBTA: These code letters stand for the Massachusetts Bay Transport Authority, "T" for short, which runs both the subways and the trolley buses. It's the oldest subway system in the country, and some commuters feel they're riding the original 1897 trains. But the system is being modernized. If you avoid the rush hours, a subway ride is not at all traumatic and it's then that you can get a look at the murals adorning the station walls in the historic districts. The scenes are both of Boston's past and of the parks and buildings you'll see when you emerge to the surface. And if above the roar of the trains you think you're hearing music, don't panic—that's just what you are hearing. Entertainment is now provided along with the subway crush. Local musicians perform on the station platforms from 7 to 10 a.m. and 4 to 7 p.m. Helps make the commute a bit more pleasant!

Route and fare information and timetables are available at the Park Street subway station (under the Common) which is the center of the system. Each line is shown on subway maps in color— Blue, Red, Green, and Orange. For quick reference: the Red Line goes to Arlington, Cambridge, Park Street, South Station, Ashmont, Mattapan, Quincy, and Braintree; the Blue, to Government Center, Aquarium, Airport, Revere Beach, and Wonderland; the Green, from Lechmere, Science Park, and North Station through downtown Boston to Prudential Center, Symphony, Kenmore, Brookline, Brighton, and Newton (you'll probably use this line the most); the Orange, from Malden and Charlestown through downtown Boston to Chinatown, New England Medical Center, on to Forest Hills. "Park Street Under" is on the Red Line; Park Street and Fenway Park, on the Green.

Note on transfers: Don't try to switch from an inbound to an outbound train—or outbound to inbound—at Copley. There's no pedestrian walkway joining the two. Make the transfer at Arlington.

Fares are now a 60¢ token for underground (rapid transit) lines, and extra for some surface line extensions. For specific information on the subway system, call 722-3200, Monday through Friday from 7 a.m. to 6 p.m. Transfers between lines and for suburban buses can be made at various stations. Exact fares are required on the trolleys and connecting buses, no paper bills are accepted, and change can be made in the stations. All of the "T" lines close down by 1 a.m.—some earlier—so be sure to check time schedules so you won't be stranded.

DRIVING AND PARKING: If you're a motorist staying in one of the motels on the outskirts of town, it may be easier to leave the car in the lot and come into town by public transportation. Driving can be confusing since the streets have no logical numerical or alphabetical order, and one-way streets and construction sites pop up at you unexpectedly. Also, parking is expensive and inadequate to the point that locals paraphrase the title of the popular multimedia show *Where's Boston?* to "Where's Parking?" On-street parking spaces are hard to find, and the metermaids are always on the job to ticket drivers who violate the no-parking, no-standing signs, or

BOSTON RAPID TRANSIT LINES

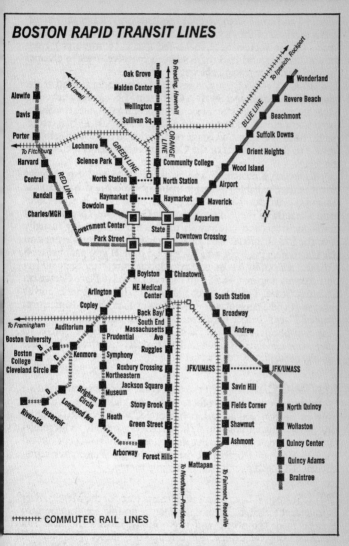

Oak Grove
Malden Center
Wellington
Sullivan Sq.
To Reading/Haverhill
To Lowell
Alewife
Davis
Porter
To Fitchburg
Harvard
Central
Kendall
Charles/MGH
Lechmere
Science Park
North Station
Haymarket
Bowdoin
Government Center
Park Street
GREEN LINE
RED LINE
ORANGE LINE
Community College
North Station
Haymarket
State
Downtown Crossing
BLUE LINE
Wonderland
Revere Beach
Beachmont
Suffolk Downs
Orient Heights
Wood Island
Airport
Maverick
Aquarium
To Ipswich, Rockport
N
Boylston
Arlington
Copley
Auditorium
To Framingham
Boston University
Boston College
Cleveland Circle
Kenmore
Symphony
Prudential
NE Medical Center
Back Bay/ South End
Massachusetts Ave
Ruggles
Roxbury Crossing
Northeastern
Jackson Square
Stony Brook
Green Street
Heath
Arborway
Forest Hills
Chinatown
South Station
Broadway
Andrew
JFK/UMASS
JFK/UMASS
Savin Hill
Fields Corner
Shawmut
Ashmont
Mattapan
North Quincy
Wollaston
Quincy Center
Quincy Adams
Braintree
To Needham-Providence
To Fairmont, Readville
B
C
D
E
Brigham Circle
Longwood Ave
Museum
Riverside
Reservoir

++++++++ COMMUTER RAIL LINES

who allow their meters to lapse. Read the hieroglyphics on the meter carefully. In some areas parking is allowed only at certain hours; in others there is no charge after 6 p.m. or on Sunday and holidays, and some streets are for residents only. Rates vary in different sections of the city, so have a supply of quarters and dimes ready. (Some meters have to be fed every 15 minutes.) Even though garages and parking lots are expensive, they're cheaper than a $50 fine or towing charge.

Boston's two largest garages are hidden underground at the **Prudential Center** and **Boston Common.** The garage at the Pru has entrances on Boylston Street, Huntington Avenue, the Sheraton Boston Hotel, and near Lord & Taylor and Saks Fifth Avenue. At the Boston Common Garage on Charles Street, round-trip bus service to the other side of the Common and back is included in the fee.

Rates keep escalating and we hesitate to give any definite prices as they're liable to change from the time you drive in to the time you drive out. City-owned garages such as the Boston Common Garage and the Winthrop Square Garage (near Summer and Franklin Streets and a short walk to Downtown Crossing) usually have the lowest prices. The garage near Government Center and the Haymarket pushcart area has a good deal. If you park before 8 a.m. and are out by 6 p.m. you get a special rate; after that you pay hourly rates. Figure $4 to $5 an hour at Lafayette Place Garage on Chauncy Street, Dock Square at Faneuil Hall Marketplace, and at garages at the Transportation Building at Park Plaza, Aquarium, Copley Place, Prudential Center, John Hancock Building, and near Symphony Hall. The best advice we can give you is to leave your car at your hotel and take a cab, the shuttle bus, the subway or walk.

RENTING CARS: When the time comes for those out-of-town excursions, you can find offices of all the major car-rental firms both in Boston and at Logan Airport. If you've rented a car to drive to Boston and plan to fly home, check carefully about return facilities. Some of the smaller firms don't want to accept out-of-state cars or will implement drop-off charges. Have your rental agency call ahead to confirm the arrangements.

TOLLS: Boston has a one-way toll structure for the Mystic River Bridge and Callahan Tunnel. You pay a double fee coming into Boston from the north, and pay nothing leaving the city: 50¢ when crossing the bridge, 60¢ through the tunnel. There are toll booths on the Massachusetts Turnpike extension from Newton into Boston. Keep a supply of quarters, dimes, and nickels handy.

BUSES: Boston's major bus terminal is the **Greyhound/ Trailways Terminal** at 10 St. James Ave. (tel. 423-5810). The **Plymouth and Brockton Bus Company** (tel. 773-9400) goes to Hyannis on the Cape; and **Bonanza Bus Lines,** to Woods Hole, Newport, R.I., and Providence, R.I. They're located at the Greyhound Terminal and Bonanza uses the Greyhound phone number. **Peter Pan Bus Lines** (tel. 482-6620), at 555 Atlantic Ave., services Boston-New York and western Massachusetts.

RAILROADS: There are three rail centers in Boston—**South Station** on Atlantic Avenue, **Back Bay Station** at 145 Dartmouth St., and **North Station** on Causeway Street. Amtrak (tel. 482-3660) has arrival and departure points at South Station and Back Bay Station. The MBTA (tel. 722-3200 weekdays, 722-5000 nights and weekends) operates trains to Ipswich, Rockport, and Concord, N.H., from North Station, and commuter lines to points south of Boston from South Station.

AREA CODE: When you're dialing Boston from out of state, use area code 617 or 508 (check our listings). For some calls beyond the metropolitan area you must dial "1," followed by the phone number.

EMERGENCY PHONE NUMBERS

Ambulance	911
Fire	911
Medical Hot Lines	
Beth Israel Hospital	735-3300
Boston Evening Medical Center	267-7171
Eye and Ear Infirmary	523-7900
Massachusetts General Hospital	726-2000
Pharmacy open 24 hours	
Phillips Drugs, 155 Charles St.	523-4372
Poison Information Center	232-2120
Police in Boston/Cambridge	911
State Police	523-1212
Travelers Aid Society	542-7278

TRANSPORTATION INFORMATION

Airlines (Logan International Airport)   561-1800
Bus Terminals
    Greyhound/Trailways   423-5810
MBTA (Rapid Transit)
    Services and Schedules   722-3200
Taxis
    Checker Taxi   536-7000
    Red Cab   734-5000
    Town Taxi   536-5000
Trains
    Amtrak   toll free 800/USA-RAIL
    North Station   227-5070
    South Station   482-3660

VISITOR INFORMATION

Boston Chamber of Commerce   367-9275
Center for International Visitors   542-8995
Convention and Visitors Bureau
    Recorded Information   267-6446
    Visitors Services   536-4100
Disabled Information Center   727-5540
Musical Events
    Concert Line   353-3810
    Jazz Line   262-1300
National Park Service   242-7286
Travelers Aid Society   542-7286

OTHER USEFUL PHONE NUMBERS

Directory Assistance   411
Postal Information   654-5083
Shoe Repair (Filene's Basement)   357-2978
Sports Teams Information
    Baseball (Red Sox)   267-8661
    Basketball (Celtics)   227-3200
    Football (Patriots)   262-1778
    Hockey (Bruins)   227-3200
Time   NERVOUS (637-8687)
Weather   WE6-1234
                                        973-6620
                                        787-7372

BOSTON RADIO AND TELEVISION SHOWS

Radio Stations

WEEI (news)	590 AM
WRKO (talk)	680 AM
WGBH (Public Radio)	89.7 FM
WJIB (popular music)	96.9 FM
WCRB (classical music)	102.5 FM
WBCN (rock music)	104.1 FM

TV Stations

Channel 2 (WGBH)	Public Television
Channel 4 (WBZ)	NBC
Channel 5 (WCBV)	ABC
Channel 7 (WNEV)	CBS
Channel 38 (WSBK)	Sports

CHAPTER III

HOTELS IN BOSTON AND CAMBRIDGE

□ □ □

Where to stay in Boston? That depends on your taste and the style in which you're accustomed to traveling. Boston offers an excellent range of accommodations from luxury hotels in the finest European manner to the gracious style of "Old Boston" and the sleek modernity of "New Boston." There are moderately priced motels and inns, and budget lodgings, with a total of 43 hotels with 14,000 rooms in Boston and Cambridge. And more hotels are under construction or on the drawing boards.

The hotel industry in this exciting city is geared for convention groups and tourists, and you're bound to benefit from all the attention and services they give to their guests. The suburbs also offer charming inns, guesthouses, and bed-and-breakfast homes.

Even in the key vacation months of July and August, you should have no trouble getting a room, but it's always advisable to reserve ahead (the telephone area code is 617, and many hotels have a toll-free 800 number). Reservations are imperative in spring and fall when conventions descend upon the city. Most of the hotels do not charge for children sharing rooms with their parents, and some offer special rates for students with ID cards and senior citizens with AARP or NRTA cards (these are noted in our listings). Parking is available at most hotels (usually at a fee) and motels, and others have arrangements with nearby garages. If you must leave your key with the car, check on the liability of the hotel and garage in case of theft. Better yet, find a place where you can lock the car and keep the key.

The City of Boston has a strict fire-protection code, and fire alarms, smoke detectors, and sprinkler systems are mandated. Many hotels have their own fire brigades and security patrols.

And, oh yes, there is a 9.7% tax on all hotel bills (5.7% for the state, the rest for the city) which must be added to the price —sorry! Not all cities in the suburban areas have imposed a local tax, so you may only have to pay the 5.7% state tax in some towns.

To help you in making your own choice of a Boston hotel, we've divided our recommendations into categories by price and area: **Elegant and Expensive,** hotels in the Back Bay, downtown, Faneuil Hall Marketplace areas, and the waterfront ($175 to $275 double); **Super Star,** the large, exciting, mostly new convention-type establishments ($160 to $240 double); **Deluxe** ($100 to $150 double); **First Class** ($85 to $130 double); **Moderate to Budget** ($75 to $120 double); **Hotels in Cambridge;** and **Resort Hotels.** (Note: Less expensive hotels are listed in Chapter IX, "A Student's Guide to Boston.") We've concentrated on those hotels that are convenient to historic areas and transportation, that offer special touches of luxury or service or just plain good value for the money. Our listings are mainly for Boston, Cambridge, and some of the suburbs on the rim of the city. Accommodations on the North and South Shores and on the "Paul Revere Trail" (Lexington and Concord) are listed in the sections describing those areas. We've also listed resort hotels with easy access to the city and points of interest. Some of the hotels, even the top-quality ones, offer special package deals from time to time. Check when you call for reservations. You may get a bonus of free meals or even an extra night's stay. Rates are subject to change if operating costs rise.

If you call a toll-free 800 number and find that all the rooms are booked, try the hotel's local number. Most of the hotels have a number of rooms that they rent themselves rather than through the parent company's headquarters.

So now let's begin with the grandest of the grand. . . .

ELEGANT AND EXPENSIVE HOTELS (DOUBLES, $175 TO $275)

Although several new elegant hotels have been built in the past few years, the **Ritz-Carlton,** 15 Arlington St., Boston, MA 02117 (tel. 617/536-5700, or toll free 800/241-3333), is still the standard for luxury in Boston. Overlooking the Boston Public Garden in the Back Bay, the Ritz has a tradition of gracious service and charm that has made it famous for over a half century, attracting both the "proper Bostonian" and the celebrated guest who seeks excellence the world over. The service and attention to detail are legendary. The Ritz-Carlton has the highest staff-to-guest ratio in the city, including white-gloved elevator operators. (You don't even have to press a button.)

The 277 guest rooms, including 41 suites with wood-burning fireplaces, have classic French-provincial furnishings accented with imported floral fabrics, and crystal chandeliers. Each room has a refrigerator, well-stocked honor bar, color TV concealed in an armoire, clock radio, message phone, and individual climate-control unit. The bathrooms, which are surfaced in Vermont marble, also have a telephone. Additional amenities include hair dryers, complimentary shoe shine, twice-daily maid service, nightly turndown with an orchid on the pillow, flowers on the table, and a morning newspaper. Soft terrycloth bathrobes hang in the closet, and you may purchase one to take home, along with a thick bath towel. All the guest-room closets lock; and all the windows open, the better to enjoy the view. Room-service pantries are on each floor to provide immediate service 24 hours a day, and complete concierge services are available, of course. In addition, complimentary chauffeured limousine service is offered for service within the city weekday mornings.

The Ritz-Carlton rooms on the 15th and 16th floors have a panoramic view of the city. Guests on those floors are also invited to relax in the Ritz-Carlton Club, a pleasant lounge, open from 7 a.m. to 11 p.m., serving complimentary breakfast, afternoon tea, hors d'oeuvres, and after-dinner sweets.

While maintaining all its traditional services, the Ritz has added something new—a health club with an eight-station Universal machine, exercise bicycles, computerized treadmill, weights, sauna, and massage room.

Rates for rooms at the Ritz are $175 to $275 for singles, $200 to $300 for doubles, and $275 to $300 for the Ritz-Carlton Club. Suites are $375 to $1,500, and the most luxurious of all, the Presidential Suite, is $1,700. Valet parking in the hotel's garage is extra. You can experience all this luxury on weekends at a special price with the Vintage Weekends packages. Included in the arrangements are champagne, flowers, fruit basket, and a gift certificate for shopping on Newbury Street, depending on which package you choose. Vintage Weekends are based on double occupancy for one or two nights.

The Ritz is also noted for the superb Ritz-Carlton Dining Room (described in Chapter IV), and the very popular Ritz Bar, located off the street-floor lobby (see Chapter VII). The second-floor Lounge is famous for lunch and afternoon tea, and evenings from 5:30 p.m. until midnight, cigar and pipe smokers can relax there over cognac, rare cordials, caviar, and desserts. The Ritz Café is open for breakfast, lunch, and dinner from 7 a.m. to midnight.

The **Four Seasons Hotel,** 200 Boylston St., Boston, MA 02116 (tel. 617/338-4400, or toll free 800/332-3442), is a small hotel with a grand concept. Located across from the famed Public Garden, it has 288 guest rooms and suites; an elegant restaurant, Aujourd'hui; and the popular Bristol Lounge. Striving for an ambience that is luxurious and elegant, yet at the same time relaxed and informal, it has no strict dress code but does set very high standards of service and attention to detail. Chinese and Japanese urns and an antique mahogany clock are focal points of the lobby; and a 60-inch crystal chandelier highlights the grand stairway and picture window framing the Public Garden.

The elegance of the public areas is carried over to the guest rooms and suites, which are patterned after a traditional guest bedroom in a Beacon Hill home. The cherry furniture is designed by Henredon; the drapes and spreads are in floral print patterns created by the London firm which makes chintzes for the queen. Beds are large and comfortable, and breakfronts conceal the remote-controlled TV with movie channel, and the refrigerated mini-bars. The suites range from 64 Four Seasons Rooms, which have enlarged alcove areas for entertaining or business meetings, to luxurious one- or two-bedroom arrangements. All rooms have the nice touch of bay windows that open plus individual climate control, digital alarm clock radios, and two phones—one of them in the bathroom. Amenities also include full-length mirrors, hairdryers, terry bathrobes, and flowers in the bathroom. Also featured is twice-daily maid service, 24-hour valet and room service (with hot meals available at any hour), individual safe-deposit boxes, and an attentive concierge. A number of rooms are available for nonsmokers. Small pets are accepted.

Topping off the luxury, on the eighth floor of the hotel are an indoor swimming pool and whirlpool with a view of the Public Garden from the large window wall, and a health spa with weight room and sauna. The pool and spa are shared with the residents of the ultra-expensive condominiums that occupy the upper floors of the 15-story brick-and-glass hotel.

Rates start at $160 single and $180 double for the moderate room category and move up with the view and additional luxuries to $225 single or $245 double for deluxe Four Seasons rooms. Suites are $250 to $795, and the Presidential Suite is $1,200. Weekend package rates are available.

The **Copley Plaza,** the grande dame of Boston hotels, 138 St. James Ave., Boston, MA 02116 (tel. 617/267-5300, or toll free 800/225-7654), has been synonymous with elegance since it opened in 1912. Now the mosaic floors, rich wood paneling, and original works of art on the walls have been restored by master craftspeople to the splendor that attracted Caruso, Churchill, and scores of political, royal, and entertainment celebrities over the years. Gilded ceilings, Waterford crystal chandeliers, marble-topped tables, and antique furniture grace the lobbies and function rooms (home to so many diplomatic receptions and grand balls). The gracious ambience extends to the guest rooms, which have quilted floral bedspreads, mirrored triple closets, plush velvet chairs, thick rugs, and marble-topped night tables. All rooms have color TV and push-button telephones, and 24-hour room service is available.

Rates are $140 to $195 for singles, $160 to $195 for doubles, and $250 to $700 for suites. Children or an extra person under 18 are free, and a rollaway bed with a full mattress is $20 extra. You can park in the nearby Hancock Garage for $14 a day or use valet parking for $18. Weekend and other package rates are available.

The Copley features outstanding dining and drinking facilities: the gourmet Café Plaza (see Chapter IV); Copley Restaurant, with traditional New England cuisine; Copley's Bar, where the "beautiful people" meet; the renowned Plaza Bar; and the Copley Tea Court, open for breakfast, lunch, and authentic afternoon English set tea.

The Colonnade, 120 Huntington Ave., Boston, MA 02116 (tel. 617/424-7000, or toll free 800/323-7500), creates an aura of stylish elegance from the moment a derby-hatted doorman greets you at the entrance and escorts you into the lobby famed for its exquisite chandelier. This is a European-style independently owned hotel where every guest is given personalized VIP service, and the staff can cater to you in 18 languages.

The 294 rooms all have an L-shaped floor plan with distinct sitting, sleeping, and dressing areas. All rooms have double beds and are big, bright, attractively decorated, and furnished with color TV, a large dressing table and makeup mirror, soft carpeting, and even tinted windows to prevent sun glare. There are bathrobes for guests to use, and an amenities package that includes bubble bath and sea shell soap, luffas, sewing kits, flowers in the room, and complimentary Godiva chocolates. Every room has two phones, including one in the bathroom. The luxury suites also have honor bars. Some rooms have special accommodations for the disabled.

There is a seasonal "rooftop resort" with pool and nine-hole putting green. At night you can dance or just listen to soft jazz at the Bar at Zachary's. And if you're hungry, room service is available 24 hours a day. Or try one of the hotel's restaurants: Zachary's, expensive and elegant (see Chapter IV), or the Café Promenade, an attractive restaurant serving breakfast, lunch, and dinner from 7 a.m. to 11 p.m., plus Sunday brunch and afternoon tea.

Rates are $125 to $175 single, $140 to $190 double, $195 to $210 for mini-suites, and $275 to $575 for larger suites. There is a charge of $15 for an extra person, but children under 12 stay free with their parents. (Babysitters are available through the hotel's concierge service.) Parking is included in the tariff.

In the downtown area, the Marketplace, the financial district, and the waterfront, you will find these elegant hotels: the Lafayette, the Meridien, the Bostonian, the Omni Parker House, and the Boston Harbor Hotel.

Creating a luxury hotel in the heart of Boston's Downtown Crossing shopping district sounds like a revolutionary idea, but it has worked perfectly for the new **Lafayette Hotel,** 1 Avenue de Lafayette, Boston, MA 02111 (tel. 617/451-2600, or toll free 800/992-0124). The 500-room Swissôtel rises 22 stories above Lafayette Place, a three-level shopping complex of boutiques and restaurants. Guests arriving at the Concourse entrance are whisked by private elevator to an elegant lobby worlds away from the bustle below. Designed in colonial Jeffersonian style, the hotel is beautifully decorated with both antique and contemporary furnishings, Waterford crystal chandeliers (even in the elevators), and imported marble columns. The upper floors offer sweeping views of Boston's waterfront and Beacon Hill. Logan Airport is 15 minutes away, and the Financial District, Freedom Trail, Quincy Market, Boston Common, and Government Center are within easy walking distance.

Guest rooms are grouped around four atriums, each with semiprivate lobbies on the 6th, 10th, 15th, and 19th floors, creating the effect of a small hotel within the hotel. Decorated in warm color schemes of green, mocha, or rose, with chintz spreads and drapes and plush carpeting, the rooms feature a sitting area with writing desk, settee, and king- or twin-size beds. Fifty-three luxurious suites feature either L-shaped rooms with sitting areas or living rooms with connecting bedrooms. One complete floor is reserved for nonsmokers; 25 rooms are designed for the disabled; and several rooms are equipped for the convenience of women travelers with hairdryers, makeup mirrors, and extra personalized touches. Each unit has remote-control color TV with in-house movie channel, individual air conditioning and heating, a mini-bar, direct-dial phones with message signal, plus a second phone in the marble-countered bathroom. Amenities include full-length mirrors, imported toiletries, plush bathrobes, twice-daily maid service, and nightly turndown with Swiss chocolates. The Lafayette also features a 52-foot-long indoor swimming pool with sun terrace, health club with saunas and exercise room, 24-hour room service, and same-day laundry and valet service. For added security, door locks have a preset computer code that is changed for each guest. A special feature of the Lafayette is the "Swiss Butler" floor, where guests are pampered from check-in to express check-out. The butler performs traditional butler functions, acts as a private concierge, and even runs errands at no extra charge above the room rate.

Rates are $160 to $190 single, $180 to $210 double, with a $22 charge for an extra person. Suites range from $250 to $400, and the Presidential Suite is $2,000. On weekends, children under 18 are free with their parents. Special weekend packages are available.

The Lafayette also houses two great restaurants: Le Marquis de Lafayette, considered by many as the finest French restaurant in Boston; and Café Suisse, which features a continental menu and a theme buffet on the weekends.

The **Hotel Meridien,** 250 Franklin St. at Post Office Square, Boston, MA 02110 (tel. 617/451-1900, or toll free 800/543-4300), has the unique distinction of being a historic landmark. Located in the old Federal Reserve Bank building in the financial district, the Meridien has incorporated some of the bank's elegant architectural details into its own grand scheme. The original marble staircase leads to the dining areas and the coffered gold-leafed ceiling now tops the elegant Julien restaurant and bar. Two grand murals by N. C. Wyeth grace the walls of the bar, and ornately carved marble fireplaces and floor-to-ceiling arched windows are reminders that the original building was patterned after a 16th-century Roman palazzo. For the 20th-century touch, there's a six-story glass atrium creating a perennial garden court for the Café Fleuri which serves breakfast, lunch, dinner, and Sunday jazz brunch.

While the Meridien is especially convenient for business guests, the great attention to detail and excellence makes it ideal for anyone who loves to be catered to. Special luxury touches include a mini-bar in the rooms, 24-hour room service, candy on the pillows at night, and marble bathrooms with French soap, shampoo, and shower caps. The 326 rooms involve 153 different styles and shapes, including dramatic loft suites with first-floor living room, a bedroom in the loft area, and bathrooms on both levels, priced at $275. Two decorating schemes are used: traditional, with chintz and floral patterns; and modern, with ebony, beige, and oyster white. All rooms are soundproofed and air-conditioned, with color TV, HBO, and ESPN, and have the special touch of two telephones—one in the bathroom. For extra security, a plastic card with a lock combination that can be changed for each guest replaces the traditional door key. Valet parking in the connecting garage is available at an extra charge.

Rates are $175 to $205 single, $195 to $225 double. An additional bed is $20. Parlor/bedroom suites start at $375. The Meridien has some very special weekend packages from $99 to $199 for one night that include use of the swimming pool and health club plus free parking. Each weekend there is an art show and reception, hosted by Merri Goyette, displaying the works of local artists, with complimentary tea, coffee, pastries, and a classical string quartet.

The **Bostonian Hotel,** 4 North Street, Boston, MA 02109 (tel. 617/523-3600, or toll free 800/343-0922), is a picture-postcard red-brick building with flower-decked balconies overlooking Faneuil Hall Marketplace. Though small in comparison with some of Boston's other hotels, it's big in charm and has all the amenities that create a top-rate hostelry.

Located in Dock Square, a site that was part of the waterfront in colonial days, the Bostonian has 155 rooms including 11 suites spread over two wings. One wing features contemporary rooms; the other, a renovated 1860 building, is traditional in style. On the fourth-floor rooftop is the glass-enclosed Seasons Restaurant, one of Boston's finest (see Chapter IV), reached by its own glass elevator.

The interior of the hotel is designed with a variety of architectural plans and decors, including small stairways, working fireplaces, and oval bathtubs and Jacuzzis. All the suites have mini-bars, and refrigerators are available on request. Throughout the hotel, the soft colors and floral patterns of the spreads, drapes, and upholstered pieces blend with the traditional or contemporary styles of the tables and armoires. Some suites have double vanities and separate dressing areas (with terry robes in the closet). All rooms have radio alarm clocks, color TV tucked into the armoire, and two phones—one of them in the bathroom. Bathrooms are equipped with heat lamps, and with both overhead and European-style hand-held shower sprays. Chocolates and mineral water are included in the evening turndown service, plus a complimentary shoeshine, if desired.

If you are a light sleeper or want to sleep late in the morning, you might prefer a room facing away from the bustle of the market since marketplace activity begins almost at dawn. If you do get up early, it's fun to watch all the activity in the area.

Rates range from $190 to $220 single, and $210 to $240 double. Suites go for $255 to $500. There is no charge for children under 12 occupying the same room as their parents. Overnight parking in one of the hotel's lots is $18. The Bostonian also provides scheduled complimentary limousine service to the airport and parts of Boston.

Weekend packages are also available at $275 that include continental breakfast and a gift basket. One-night packages are $175.

Located right on the historic Freedom Trail, the **Omni Parker House,** 60 School St., Boston, MA 02107 (tel. 617/227-8600), is regarded as the oldest continuously operating hotel in America. But there's nothing antiquated about this member of the Omni hotel chain. Recent renovations have restored the elegance that made it a favorite hostelry in the days of Longfellow and Emerson. The guest rooms are decorated with soft colors and thick carpeting, modern art on the walls, and of course, color TV. Rooms have views of Old City Hall or the new Government Center.

Rates are $150 to $185 for singles, $165 to $200 for doubles. You can have a mini-suite for $185, or a truly elegant large suite for $255 to $500. There is no charge for children under 16 sharing a room with parents. Room service is available. Special weekend packages are offered.

Eating and drinking facilities are excellent. Parker's has superb food served in a gracious style and Sunday brunch. Parker's Bar is on the site of the "Saturday Club" of 1860s fame, where Emerson, Longfellow, Oliver Wendell Holmes, Whittier, and James Russell Lowell met. On the lower level of the hotel is the turn-of-the-century-type room, the Last Hurrah, a favorite of the local pols from the State House and City Hall for lunch and dinner; and a busy late-evening spot for drinks and dancing to an "in-house" swing band.

To reach the **Boston Harbor Hotel,** Boston's newest luxury hotel located on the waterfront, you can be conventional and drive *or* you can make a grand entrance by sailing (in just seven minutes) across the harbor from Logan Airport to the hotel's on-site ferry pavilion (see below for details).

Conveniently located near the downtown area, Boston Harbor Hotel, 70 Rowes Wharf, Boston, MA 02110 (tel. 617/439-7000 or toll free 800/752-7077), is within walking distance of Faneuil Hall, the New England Aquarium, and the Financial Center. A magnificent central archway topped by a copper-domed observatory (where weekday lunch is served) accents this traditional Boston red-brick building. Most of the public spaces share the magnificent view across the harbor, including the Rowes Wharf Restaurant and Café and the Harbor Lounge, which serves afternoon tea daily in addition to standard lounge fare. A museum-quality art collection of more than 100 paintings, drawings, and prints decorates the public spaces of the hotel. It includes views and maps of old Boston, paintings of sailing ships, and works by prominent Massachusetts artists.

The 230 guest rooms have either a view of the harbor or the Boston skyline, and all have operable windows so that you can open them and enjoy the fresh ocean air. Two floors are designated for nonsmokers and 18 rooms are equipped for disabled guests. All the rooms are luxurious living and bedroom combinations, decorated in rose-and-white color schemes with mahogany furnishings that include armoire, desk, TV, and soft lounge chairs. Suites are even more elegant, with floral drapes and spreads and a few with private terraces. Amenities include three phones (one in the bathroom), mini-bars, hairdryers, bathrobes, complimentary shoe shine, and fresh flowers. There is 24-hour room service, twice-daily maid service, and an attentive concierge to fill any and all special requests. Naturally, each room has individual heat and air conditioning and state-of-the-art life safety systems.

Rates range from $190 to $215 for singles; $200 to $225 for doubles. One-bedroom suites start at $350 and two-bedroom suites at $550. The Presidential Suite, with two bedrooms, whirlpool bath, and a superb view, is $975. There are some good weekend packages available on Friday and Saturday nights at substantial savings.

Hotel guests may also use the facilities of the **Rowes Wharf Health Club and Spa,** which include whirlpool, sauna, steam and exercise rooms, and a 60-foot lap pool, open from 6 a.m. to 10 p.m. seven days a week. Also available is a salon for facials, hair styling, and manicures. There is no charge for use of the pool, sauna, and whirlpool, but the exercise equipment is $10 extra. (You can buy aerobic or swim attire, if you didn't pack your own.)

If you're driving to the hotel, be prepared for Boston traffic. Take the Southeast Expressway exit at South Station, stay in the right lane and follow Atlantic Avenue, past the Northern Avenue bridge to the entrance of the hotel. There is 24-hour valet parking. If you come by plane, take the free bus at your terminal to the water shuttle. It leaves every 15 minutes from 6 a.m. to 8 p.m., Monday through Friday, and every 30 minutes from 12:15 to 7:45 p.m., Saturdays and Sundays. (And of course the ferry returns to the airport.) One-way fare is $5 for adults, $2.50 for children under 12.

THE CONCIERGE ADVANTAGE: In line with classic European tradition, many luxury and first-class hotels now have a concierge desk in the lobby. Wonder what in the world that suave, sophisticated person behind the desk does? Here's our miniguide to help you use the services the concierge offers.

First, do not be intimidated or shy—the concierge is paid by the hotel to serve the guests. (Of course tips are appreciated.) To name a few services, he or she makes and confirms reservations, checks street maps and local phone books, and may even order flowers. The concierge will also do simple tasks such as getting stamps and checking the weather forecast, or perhaps do the "impossible" and get tickets for a sold-out play or sporting event. Don't hesitate to ask questions. Remember, the concierge has probably heard and answered all types of inquiries before.

SUPER-STAR HOTELS
(DOUBLES, $160 TO $240)

Dominating the busy corner at Dartmouth Street and Huntington Avenue, the 36-story **Westin Hotel**, 10 Huntington Ave., Boston, MA 02116 (tel. 617/262-9600, or toll free 800/228-3000), is an eye-catching concrete-and-glass exclamation point at the gateway to Copley Place, Boston's mecca for shops, restaurants, and theaters.

The glamour starts with the two-story-high twin waterfalls cascading into flower-banked pools at the glass pedestrian entrance opposite the Boston Public Library. And it continues via moving staircases soaring between the falls to the Grand Lobby and the Lobby Lounge, a relaxing spot for drinks and conversation.

The 800 guest rooms are spacious and airy with excellent views from the large bay windows—you might request a view of downtown Boston, the airport and harbor, or the Charles River and Cambridge when making reservations. Furnishings are oak on the even-numbered floors, and natural mahogany on the odd-numbered ones. The quilted spreads and drapes are coordinated to blend in warm tones with the wood finishes and all the pillows are luxurious goose down! (Synthetic fibers are available for allergy sufferers.) Each room has a round table or a combination desk and table, comfortable chairs, individual climate control, windows with operable sashes, clock radio, push-button phone, cable TV, and pay-movies.

Forty rooms are designed for the disabled with wide doors

and tubs, hand-held shower sprays, and phones in the bathroom. These adjoin regular rooms to accommodate guests who may be traveling with the disabled person.

Single prices range from $170 to $210 and doubles run $195 to $240. The one-bedroom suites are $410 to $510, and the two-bedroom suites are priced at $555 to $715. Weekend packages at special rates are also offered. Check on them.

The Westin has valet service and 24-hour room service, plus a health club and pool. Everyone at the concierge desk is bilingual, and among hotel employees, a total of 15 languages are spoken! Valet parking in the hotel's garage is available at a fee of $16 for 24 hours, with no extra in-and-out charges.

Three restaurants and three bars offer a variety of dining experiences: Ten Huntington is the hotel's bar and grill. Seafood is the specialty of Turner Fisheries, which has an oyster bar and greenhouse-style lounge. The Brasserie, an informal dining room by the waterfall, stays open from 6 a.m. to 11:30 p.m.

Boston Marriott Hotel/Copley Place, 110 Huntington Ave., Boston, MA 02116 (tel. 617/236-5800 or toll free 800/228-9290), shares the excitement of Copley Place, since its lobby opens directly into the complex. But the Marriott has its own sense of excitement that makes it an outstanding hostelry.

There are 1,147 guest rooms on 39 floors, including 77 suites and 36 rooms for the disabled; plus three restaurants, a lounge and bar, and an excellent indoor swimming pool with a double skylight and hydrotherapy whirlpool. A health club with sauna is available to guests. The lobby is strikingly attractive with a four-story–long chandelier of glittering little lights, Italian marble floors, full-size trees, and a waterfall. But the guest rooms are what really matter in a fine hotel, and the Marriott Copley Place excels in that area too.

The rooms are decorated in tones of pale green and rose, with mahogany furniture in Queen Anne style, armchairs or ottoman, and desk and table. There are full-length mirrors on the closet doors, individually controlled heat and air conditioning, phones, clock radio, and cable TV.

Rates are $160 single, $180 double; add $10 for the concierge rooms with their extra services. Suites go for $375 to $1,000—and you can choose one with individual whirlpool baths, or perhaps a grand piano. There are some good package deals too, including a honeymoon plan, family plan, military and corporate plans. Valet parking is available for overnight guests in the hotel's garage or in the Prudential Center garage.

A glass walkway with gazebo-style turrets connects the Marriott with the Prudential Center. No need to cross busy Huntington Avenue, near the Massachusetts Turnpike. But don't leave the hotel until you check out the restaurants. There's Gourmeli's Seafood, for seafood, naturally; Bello Mondo, for Italian entrees; and Champions, a sports bar where you can watch sporting events from any seat while you munch a burger or other light fare with your drink.

The **Boston Marriott Hotel/Long Wharf,** 296 State St., Boston, MA 02109 (tel. 617/227-0800, or toll free 800/228-9290), pointing out to sea like an ocean liner, is an exciting hotel on the waterfront. Located near Faneuil Hall Marketplace, the Aquarium, and Waterfront Park, and just across the harbor from Logan International Airport, the multitiered, 400-room brick hotel is something of a tourist attraction itself with a 50-foot-wide public walkway on the lower level.

At the entrance, an escalator, spotlighted in a pyramid-shaped glass-and-steel structure, leads to the second-floor lobby. To one side is the Palm Garden, a café and lounge in a serene Venetian-style atrium which is crowned with a magnificent 420-foot ceiling mural. On the other side is the busy, trendy Rachael's Lounge, and the Harbor Terrace restaurant with a 180° expanse of glass wall fronting the harbor.

Guest rooms, located on the second to seventh floors, include 20 rooms with special facilities for the handicapped. Most rooms have views of the wharfs—either Long Wharf and the Aquarium or Mercantile Wharf and Waterfront Park. Two luxury suites, one with grand piano and fireplace, face the harbor. The decor varies from room to room, but all are large with a choice of either king-size or double beds. Quilted spreads in soft floral prints add color accents, and a round table and chairs are arranged for viewing the waterfront scene below the windows. Each room has individual climate control, direct-dial telephone, radio, color TV, and in-room movies. An indoor swimming pool with an outdoor terrace for warm weather looks down on the harbor from the deck on the third level. Facilities also include an exercise room, saunas, whirlpools, and game room.

Rates range from $175 to $210. And if you like extra personalized services—fresh flowers in your room, complimentary continental breakfast, cocktails, and hors d'oeuvres served in a private lounge—the seventh-floor Concierge Level offers these amenities at $200 single and $220 double. Family Plan is $150 flat rate, subject to availability. There are also weekend "escape packages" for one or two nights with choice of breakfast, brunch, or dinner priced from $245 double. Valet parking is offered in the adjacent garage at an extra charge of $15 per day.

Note: A Rufus Porter harbor scene, one of the few remaining

original frescos painted by the 19th-century artist, dominates the lobby wall near the escalator. Although the locale is not identified, it is thought to be Boston Harbor in the early 1800s—well worth seeing, even if you're not a hotel guest.

The **Sheraton Boston Hotel & Towers,** Prudential Center, 39 Dalton St. (directly connected to the Hynes Convention Center), Boston, MA 02199 (tel. 617/236-2000 or toll free 800/325-3535), is one of the most exciting hotels in the city with its three top-rated restaurants and 1,250 attractive rooms including 85 suites. Newly remodeled both inside and out, it is actually two hotels in one—the original Sheraton and the luxurious Sheraton Towers, with private elevators to the top floors of the hotel.

The rooms are decorated with traditional furnishings in mahogany and cherrywood and accented with floral drapes and bedspreads. Each room has a phone and cable TV. Many of the suites have an extra phone in the bathroom, a wet bar, and a refrigerator. All doors lock automatically and are opened with individually coded, computerized cards. Special accommodations are available for the disabled.

The Sheraton Towers, on the 26th to 29th floors of the hotel, has a private registration area, an elegant decor accented by antiques, and a fantastic view from the lounge where Tower guests can enjoy complimentary breakfast and late-day hors d'oeuvres and beverages. Luxury touches in the Tower rooms include remote-control TV and clock radio, electric blankets, a "valet-hanger" for suits, shoe trees, phones in the bathrooms, an extension mirror with one side magnified, and even a wall-mounted TV in some bathrooms for those who like to soak and soap with the soap operas. And for the ultimate luxury, guests have their own personal butler to pamper them.

Single rooms in the main house range from $140 to $160, and doubles run $160 to $180 per night. Suites go for $255 to $495. In the Sheraton Towers, rates range from $195 single to $215 double, with suites at $305 to $455, and $900 for the lavish Presidential Suite. There is no charge for children under 17 in the same room with their parents. Students, faculty, and retired persons with IDs receive a 25% discount, depending on availability. The tropical domed pool pavilion with Jacuzzi, Universal, and other fitness equipment is open year round, and there is parking in the Prudential garage below the hotel.

In addition to 24-hour room service, the Sheraton has three restaurants: the Boylston Park Café, for breakfast, lunch, and Sunday brunch; the Mass. Bay Co., for lunch and dinner; and Kon-Tiki, for Oriental dinners. You can also get take-out food at the Edible Express in the upper lobby.

Back Bay Hilton, 40 Dalton St., Boston, MA 02115 (tel. 617/236-1100 or toll free 800/445-8667), is a 340-room triangular building near the Prudential Center, Hynes Convention Center, and the Christian Science complex. Architecturally designed so that each room has a wonderful view of Boston, it is a busy place with an indoor pool in a greenhouse setting, an executive fitness center, nightclub, and restaurant, Boodle's, which features meals from the grill.

Room rates are $135 to $165 for singles, $155 to $185 for doubles. One-bedroom suites start at $450; two-bedroom suites begin at $600. There is no charge for children regardless of age if they occupy the same room as their parents, and Back Bay Hilton is one of the few hotels in the city that makes accommodations for your pets.

DELUXE HOTELS
(DOUBLES, $100 TO $150)

Don't let the utilitarian Howard Johnson name fool you. The **57 Park Plaza Hotel–Howard Johnson,** 200 Stuart St. (at Park Square), Boston, MA 02116 (tel. 617/482-1800, or toll free 800/654-2000), may not sound glamorous, but its 350 rooms are on a par with those of luxury hotels. The hotel is centrally located downtown, within walking distance of theaters, shops, the Public Garden, and Boston Common; and it's about a 20-minute drive from Logan Airport (traffic permitting).

Now for those rooms. Each has its own private balcony with a commanding city view, one or two double beds, a sitting area, shower-bath combination, full-length mirror, attractive furniture, color TV, climate control, and a wakeup alarm and message center, plus a complete fire alarm system. The bedrooms are decorated in soft, comfortable tones. Also available are mini-suites with one king-sized bed and a parlor area with sofa, round table, and chairs.

You can swim year round in the seventh-floor pool or take a free sauna.

The hotel is part of a new complex that includes the renowned 57 Restaurant and two cinemas. Rates start at $105 for singles and $120 for doubles, the price increasing with the view. Mini-suite rates are $130 to $145. There's no charge for children under 18 with their parents, or for cribs, but there is a $10 tab for extra cots. And, joy of joys, there's free indoor parking with direct access to your floor in the hotel's 1,000-car garage. Excellent weekend specials are available.

The **Boston Park Plaza Hotel & Towers,** a 977-room hotel at 50 Park Plaza, Boston, MA 02116 (tel. 617/426-2000, or toll free 800/225-2008), is just a few giant steps away from the Public Garden, and within walking distance of Beacon Hill, Boston Common, the Esplanade, the theater district, and the shops on Boylston and Newbury Streets. Light, cheerful colors predominate in the guest rooms, which have air conditioning, direct-dial phones, color TV, AM/FM radio, and video check-out. Rates in the main hotel are $95 to $132 for singles and $115 to $152 for doubles. Children stay free in their parents' rooms.

If you're traveling in style and want luxury accommodations, the top-floor Towers offers extra services and a hospitality suite serving continental breakfast, evening hors d'oeuvres, and cocktails. Rates in the Towers are $127 to $160 for singles, $147 to $180 for doubles. Suites start at $300.

The hotel offers overnight garage parking and airport shuttle service. The excellent dining facilities include Legal Sea Foods Restaurant, and the four-star Fox and Hounds. There's a great cabaret-theater in the Terrace Room; and Swans, the lobby lounge, features a continental buffet breakfast, afternoon tea, and cocktails. (You can work off all the calories in the Health Club.)

Note: The Boston Park Plaza Hotel & Towers is within walking distance of the Greyhound Bus Station on St. James Avenue, and the Back Bay Amtrak Station, and just across Park Plaza from the Arlington Street MBTA station.

The **Lenox Hotel,** 710 Boylston St., Boston, MA 02116 (tel. 617/536-5300, or toll free 800/225-7676), is a lovely small hotel near Copley Place and the Prudential Center. Built in 1900, it has been beautifully restored with spacious, well-appointed rooms and suites furnished in either Early American, French, or Oriental style. The 220 rooms have high ceilings, separate sitting areas, color TV with in-room movies, alarm clock radios, and complimentary toiletries. And the large corner rooms have working fireplaces! Singles are $95 to $175; doubles, $100 to $195. Children under 18 are free in the same room with their parents (no charge for cribs), and additional adults in the room are $15. Suites go from $250 and corner rooms range from $175 to $195. There is valet parking service for the adjacent indoor garage; and if you're flying in, the hotel provides airport shuttle service for a fee of $5. The Lenox also has special corporate rates.

Delmonico's, the hotel's main restaurant, has a Victorian decor and an excellent menu. And for before- or after-dinner entertainment there's the very popular Diamond Jim's piano bar.

The star of Boston's Theater District is **Quality Inn,** or the "Q," 275 Tremont St., Boston, MA 02116 (tel. 617/426-1400 or toll free 800/228-5151). Located in the heart of the district, across from the Wang Center for the Performing Arts, it is one block from Boston Common and within walking distance of both Back Bay and Downtown Crossing.

Built in 1925, the 15-story, 288-room brick building was formerly the landmark Hotel Bradford. It has been completely renovated to preserve its classic art deco style while modern interiors and furnishings have been added. The original gold-leaf decorations and crafted ceilings in the lobby and ballrooms have been restored, the original marble walls and columns refurbished, and elegant, sparkling-new chandeliers installed.

The "Q" is geared to travelers on a modest budget, so prices for guest rooms are among the most affordable in town. Singles go from $85 to $105; doubles from $98 to $120; and suites from $135 to $175. There are three top-of-the-line units that feature kitchenettes with a range, sink, and refrigerator—great for families wanting to eat in. One floor of 42 rooms is reserved for nonsmokers, and there are 14 equal-access rooms.

The hotel has a wonderful "Quality Care" program for families of patients in any of Boston's hospitals or medical centers, charging only $65 per night for a maximum of four in a room plus a complimentary seventh night if needed. The New England Medical Center, the Floating Hospital, and Tufts University Medical and Dental Schools are directly across the street. A special shuttle service is provided at no charge to all other hospitals.

If you'd like an evening of dancing without leaving the hotel, try the beautiful Roxy nightclub, featuring swing, jazz, and big-band music from the '40s, Thursday, Friday, and Saturday nights; or the N.Y.C. Juke Box Club for the beat of the '80s, Monday through Saturday. And for breakfast, lunch, dinner, or late-evening snacks, the "Q" features a branch of New York's famous Stage Deli.

FIRST-CLASS HOTELS (DOUBLES, $85 TO $130)

The **Midtown Hotel,** 220 Huntington Ave., Boston, MA 02115 (tel. 617/262-1000), is located in the midst of Boston's cultural belt. Stay here and you'll be within easy walking distance of Symphony Hall, the Museum of Fine Arts, the Christian Science Center, and the Prudential Center. The rooms are modern and attractive, all 160 of them equipped with air conditioning and color TV. Rates go from $79 to $99 for singles, $85 to $105 for doubles, adjusted seasonally. Children under 18 are free with their parents, and an extra person in the room is $5 additional. Senior citizens may take 10% off the tab with an AARP card; and government employees are offered a discount, subject to availability. There is free covered parking. The Seyoken, featuring Japanese/French cuisine, open 7 a.m. to 9 p.m., and a heated outdoor pool are more plus features.

Nestled at the base of Beacon Hill, near the Charles River, and convenient to Massachusetts General Hosptial and Faneuil Hall Marketpalce, **Holiday Inn,** 5 Blossom St., Boston, MA 02114 (tel. 617/742-7630 or toll free 800/HOLIDAY), is an attractive modern hotel. Its 300 rooms are spread across 14 floors, with an attractive top-floor dining room and cocktail lounge. The hotel is part of a plaza complex that includes a movie theater and a garage with discount parking for hotel guests.

As you would expect, the rooms are streamlined in style, each with a picture-window view of the city, tubs as well as showers, and TV. Rates are $105 to $130. Children uner 18 are free in their parents' room; there is a charge of $16 for an extra person in the room. Senior citizens with AARP cards get a 10% discount; and in season an outdoor pool is open from 10 a.m. to 9 p.m. Weekend and corporate packages are available.

Practically on the Boston University campus, the **Howard Johnson Hotel,** 575 Commonwealth Ave., Boston, MA 02215 (tel. 617/267-3100), is a great choice, since it's just a few subway stops from downtown, near Kenmore Square and Fenway Park, and across the Charles River from the MIT campus. You can spot it easily by the glass-enclosed elevator which goes to the Starlight Roof Lounge and gives you a good view of the area.

Singles are $75 to $100 and doubles run $85 to $115. Children under 18 stay free with their parents, and an extra cot is $10.

The indoor swimming pool and skylighted sundeck on the roof are open year round from 11 a.m. to 9 p.m. And your car is garaged free.

MODERATE TO BUDGET HOTELS (DOUBLES, $75 TO $120)

Although it's an older, unpretentious hotel in an area of glamorous neighbors—the Prudential Center and Copley Place —the **Copley Square Hotel,** 47 Huntington Ave., Boston, MA 02116 (tel. 617/536-9000, or toll free 800/225-7062), near the entrance to the Massachusetts Turnpike, offers excellent values. The rooms are large with a traditional decor and all have recently undergone renovation. The unusual shape of the building gives a bonus of uniquely shaped guest rooms, including a series of hexagonal corner rooms with six windows to catch the sun and the view of the Prudential Center. Singles are $69 to $99; doubles and twins, $82 to $109. Family suites, at $145, have two bedrooms, and there is no charge for children under 18 sharing a room with their parents. And if you don't mind sharing a bathroom, you can get economy rates of $55 single and $60 double on rooms with running water. Rates include free coffee and color TV in your room.

Parking is available in the adjoining Prudential Center Garage. Pop's Place, an attractive restaurant in the lobby, is open for breakfast, lunch, and dinner seven days a week, including holidays. In the lower lobby is one of the finest restaurants in Boston, the Café Budapest.

Red Sox fans take note: There's no hotel in Boston closer to Fenway Park than the **Howard Johnson Lodge Fenway,** 1271 Boylston St. Boston, MA 02215 (tel. 617/267-8300 or toll free 800/654-200). Besides being adjacent to the park (you might even catch a home-run ball hit over the left-field wall), this 94-room hotel is also convenient to the Back Bay colleges and to the Museum of Fine Arts and the Gardner Museum. And it's a quick subway ride to downtown Boston, which makes it a big favorite with visiting business people. Room rates are $70 to $95 single and $80 to $105 double. Children under 18 can stay free with their parents; otherwise an extra person is $10 additional. After the game—or whatever—you can relax in the outdoor pool, open 9 a.m. to 7 p.m., or dine at Bumpers, a restaurant and lounge, open 7 a.m. to 2 a.m. Parking is free.

A quiet, residential hotel or an international inn? The **Eliot Hotel,** 370 Commonwealth Ave., Boston, MA 02215 (tel. 617/267-1607), near Kenmore Square, answers both descriptions. Since it rents suites with kitchens, it attracts visitors who prefer to prepare their own meals as well as permanent residents who like the cheerful, attractive rooms and its proximity to subway transportation, the Prudential Center, Symphony Hall, and the Charles River. Some international visitors have included 20 Russian art experts who were in Boston to supervise the exhibit at the Museum of Fine Arts and wanted a place where they could cook their own borscht, and Japanese marathon runners who found the beds too comfortable and slept on the floor.

Singles rent for $65 to $75; doubles $75 to $95. If you're staying in Boston for at least two weeks, consider renting one of the one- or two-bedroom kitchen suites, $300 to $700 a week. Studios are $275 to $330 a week. Nearby garages are available for parking. The Eliot Lounge is the favorite watering spot of Boston Marathon runners.

The Inn at Children's, 342 Longwood Ave., Boston, MA 02115, near the Brookline line (tel. 617/731-4700), is located in the heart of a large medical complex, including Beth Israel, Brigham and Women's, New England Deaconess, and Children's Hospitals (hence the name Children's), Dana Farber Cancer Institute, and Joslin Diabetes Center. But this attractive modern inn is also an excellent base for business travelers and tourists as it's near museums, colleges, and Fenway Park. With a bus stop at the door, downtown Boston is only minutes away.

The 153 guest rooms, which include 14 kitchenette suites, are pleasantly roomy with a livng area, color TV, air conditioning, bath, and shower. Rates range from $85 to $109, single; and $95 to $119, double. Children under 17 stay free with adults. The facilities include a restaurant, café, and lounge in the hotel. And since the Inn adjoins a business complex—the Longwood Galleria—there's access to a food court, retail stores, and a fitness center that hotel guests may use at a small fee.

Sometimes your best buys are just beyond the city out of the high-rent district. We've found some good spots just a few miles out of the center of Boston.

IN BROOKLINE: Just a few stops from Boston via subway (the Green Line), the **Holiday Inn,** 1200 Beacon St., Brookline, MA 02146 (tel. 617/277-1200 or toll free 800/HOLIDAY), is a sparkling 208-room hotel built around a colorful atrium with a garden lounge, putting green, sundeck, and a 40-foot swimming pool plus whirlpool.

On the site of the former Travel Lodge, it has been completely remodeled, redecorated, and landscaped. Pin lights entwined in the trees and shrubs in the atrium and along the front of the building are a welcoming signal in the evening.

Rooms are furnished in either pecan, walnut, or oak finish and have TV, telephone, and individual climate control. They are priced in three categories: Queens, $90 to $100; Double/ Doubles, $97 to $107; and King/Leisure (with couch and other extras), $110 to $120. Suites go from $185 to $195. Children stay for free with their parents, otherwise an extra person is $15. An entire floor is designated for nonsmokers, and ten rooms are equipped for disabled guests. Free parking in the hotel's underground garage is a special bonus.

Anthony's Town House, 1085 Beacon St., Brookline, MA 02146 (tel. 617/566-3972), is an authentic four-story brownstone town house located one mile from Kenmore Square in Boston and just 12 minutes to the center of town. Each of the floors has three rooms and a shared bath with enclosed shower. All are decorated with Queen Anne–and Victorian-style furnishings, and the large front rooms have bay windows and comfortable

A BUDGET DISCOVERY: When we first heard several years ago that there was a hotel offering luxury accommodations at bargain prices, we were sure somebody was joking. But off we went to the **Susse Chalet Motor Lodge,** ten minutes from downtown Boston at 800 Morrissey Blvd., Dorchester, MA 02122, off the Southeast Expressway (tel. 617/287-9100, or toll free 800/258-1980), to see for ourselves. And we found that it was absolutely true.

Now, some years later, owner Matthew J. Strazzula has enlarged the motor lodge and in addition built an attractive inn, the **Susse Chalet Inn,** at 900 Morrissey Blvd., Dorchester, MA 02122 (tel. 617/287-9200, or toll free 800/258-1980), while still keeping the standards up and the prices down.

The original chalet-style motor lodge with balconies has 177 rooms on three floors with free cable TV including HBO, FM stereo radio, direct-dial phone, electric heat, and air conditioning. The single-bedded room is the same size as the double and is a favorite with salespeople who use the free space as a work area. For all this largesse the charge is $39.70 single and $43.70 double.

The inn is a four-story building with 106 large guest rooms including nonsmoking rooms and rooms for the disabled. The amenities are the same as in the motor lodge, and in addition all the double-bedded rooms have a comfortable reclining chair. The fee at the inn is $49.05 single, $53.45 double. Our absolute favorite room is the suite on the second floor with three skylights, two windows, two double beds that can be folded into a wall niche, a sofa bed, wet bar, sink, and refrigerator. It can be used for receptions and conferences, but we think it's terrific for a large family of up to six people. And the current rate is only $94.70.

An outdoor swimming pool in a colorful courtyard is available in season to all guests at the motor lodge and inn. There are coin-operated washers and dryers and free parking in the outdoor lot. And just across the lot is Boston Bowl, a very popular recreational facility with ten pocket billiard tables, 20 candlepin lanes, 30 ten-pin lanes, and a video game room, open 24 hours. The adjoining Swiss House Restaurant is open for breakfast, lunch, and dinner from 6:30 a.m. to 10:30 p.m. with reasonable prices and good food. And be sure to visit the popular Phillips Candy House and watch the candy maker hand-dip the chocolates in the tradition of the old-world candy makers. You must take some home!

lounge chairs. Rates are $30 to $50 for doubles and $25 to $40 for singles. Special weekly rates are available.

IN BRIGHTON: Terrace Motor Lodge, 1650 Commonwealth Ave., Brighton, MA 02135 (tel. 617/566-6260), is a complex of motel units just off one of Boston's major boulevards (and trolley-bus lines). Most of the rooms (some with ceiling-to-floor picture windows) face a pleasant residential street in the rear crescent.

This is a nice place for families, since there are two-room suites available, from $85 up, and you can have the free use of a kitchenette (dishes and utensils not provided). Children under 16 can stay in their parents' rooms free, but an extra cot or crib costs $3. As for the other rooms, singles go for $49 to $57, doubles run $55 to $63, and twins cost $57 to $67.

A complimentary continental breakfast is served in the attractive reception lounge.

HOTELS IN CAMBRIDGE

We've listed the Cambridge hotels by two locations: near Harvard Square and along the Charles River. The Hyatt Regency, Royal Sonesta, and Howard Johnson's Hotel, Cambridge, are on the Cambridge side of the river. Guest Quarters Suite Hotel is near Harvard Business School and actually on the Boston side of the river. The Charles Hotel, Harvard Motor House, Sheraton Commander, and Quality Inn are near Harvard Square.

Let's start at Harvard Square, where most of the action is.

NEAR HARVARD SQUARE: The Charles Hotel at Harvard Square, 1 Bennett St., at Eliot Street, Cambridge, MA 02138 (tel. 617/864-1200, or toll free 800/882-1818), is actually in Charles Square, the new upscale shopping, dining, and office complex just a corner away from the halls of ivy. The hotel reflects the color and excitement of the area while creating a special niche of its own with an award-winning jazz bar, a European-style health spa, a gourmet four-star restaurant and informal café, and especially its 300 distinctive guest rooms, including 44 suites.

The updated-country style of the guest rooms is light and airy with custom-designed adaptations of early American Shaker pieces. The light wood tones of the armoires and apothecary chests, the four-poster beds and spindle headboards, are accented with homespun fabrics of blue and yellow and with down-filled comforters used as spreads on every bed. There are ten individual plans for the rooms but they all have luxurious amenities that include three phones (one by the bed, one on the armoire, and one in the bathroom), two TVs (a remote-control color TV in the bedroom and a small black-and-white TV on the long bathroom vanity), and a fully stocked refrigerated honor bar. There are also terry-cloth bathrobes, AM/FM clock radios, an amenities basket that includes a sewing kit, and scales to check your weight. All rooms have large windows that can be opened, and original commissioned prints of Cambridge locales. Some rooms are equipped with telephone modems for personal computer hookups, and there are facilities for teleconferencing.

Room service is available around the clock, there is twice-daily maid service, and the evening turndown includes a bottle of iced mineral water. And for security, the keys are coded to operate a preset combination in the door locks. Parking is available in the hotel's underground garage with valet service.

Room rates vary with the view and the season: $151 to $191 for singles and $171 to $211 for doubles. Suites go for $275 to $1,200. Children under 18 are free in their parents' rooms, and pets can be accommodated. One floor is set aside for nonsmokers, 13 rooms are for the disabled, and others are designed with special amenities for women travelers. Included in the daily rate is use of the glass-enclosed heated lap pool, Jacuzzi, sun terrace, and exercise room at Le Pli Health Spa. There are five great weekend packages, including a workout weekend for two with a full day of pampering at the spa for about $500. In addition there is a $1,000 spa weekend with spa and salon treatments and gourmet low-calorie meals.

There are excellent dining facilities in the hotel: the Bennett St. Café serves breakfast, lunch, dinner, and Sunday buffet brunch; and Rarities, the highly acclaimed gourmet restaurant, emphasizes creative American cuisine at dinner (see our recommendation in Chapter IV).

Note: The antique blue-and-white New England quilts that hang in the Charles's great oak staircase were handmade between 1865 and 1885. The entrance to each guest room floor also displays an antique quilt.

Practically in Harvard Square and convenient to everything, **Harvard Motor House,** 110 Mt. Auburn St., Cambridge, MA 02138 (tel. 617/864-5200), is a modern brick, six-floor motel, not in the least traditional, but a good base for Cambridge living. The rooms all have wide picture windows, and the furnishings are compact, comfortably Danish-inspired modern, with TV, radio, air conditioning, and combination tub-showers. Especially nice is the free continental breakfast (assorted doughnuts, coffee or tea) included in the price of your room. Singles cost $81 to $83; doubles, from $91 to $93. An additional person is $8. No restaurants or cocktail lounges downstairs, but they're hardly necessary with

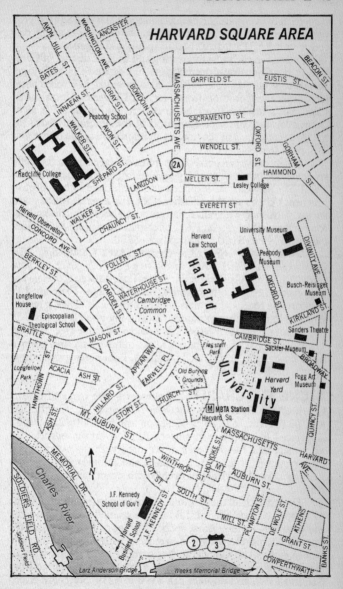

HARVARD SQUARE AREA

the wealth of eating and drinking facilities in Harvard Square. Free parking is available for hotel guests. Senior citizens get a 10% discount with AARP card except during July and August.

Located in the most interesting and historic district of Cambridge, the **Sheraton-Commander,** 16 Garden St., Cambridge, MA 02138 (tel. 617/547-4800), is a substantial, 173-room hotel just across the Common from Harvard University. It claims to stand only a few feet from the elm where, on July 3, 1775, Gen. George Washington took command of the American troops (in the front courtyard of the hotel is an impressive statue of the first U.S. president).

Traditionally patronized by parents of Harvard and Radcliffe students, the hotel successfully captures the spirit of old New England. The neocolonial decor begins in the lounge with its Boston Hitchcock chairs and grandfather clock, and extends to the guest rooms, furnished with tall, slim four-poster beds, pine desks, Boston rockers, oil lamps, and TV, of course. Singles are $139; doubles run $149 to $160. Suites go from $250.

Quality Inn, 1651 Massachusetts Ave., Cambridge, MA 02138 (tel. 617/491-1000, or toll free 800/321-2828), is situated on historic Cambridge Heritage Trail, adjacent to Harvard University, Lesley College, and Radcliffe College. There are 135 comfortable rooms and suites with cable TV and HBO, a restaurant and lounge, plus an outdoor swimming pool. Rates are $68 to $80 single and $76 to $98 double, and include free parking. There are special seasonal rates and discounts for groups, government employees, and AARP members. Public transportation is right at the front door.

ALONG THE CHARLES: Nicknamed "the pyramid on the Charles," the **Hyatt Regency,** 575 Memorial Dr., Cambridge, MA 02139 (tel. 617/492-1234, or toll free 800/228-9000), is terraced like a tower in ancient Babylon on the outside. Inside, there is a 14-story atrium accented with diamond-shaped glass elevators, fountains, balconies, and a junior Olympic-size swimming pool and full health club with steam, sauna, and whirlpool.

Underneath all the glamour is some sound practicality. Of its 471 rooms, 15 on the third floor are designed to accommodate the disabled—wide doors, special bathroom facilities. And the seventh floor is reserved for nonsmokers, with not a match or ashtray in sight! The Concierge Department helps guests with arrangements for dining, theater, and travel. Singles range from $160 to $190, and doubles run $190 to $210. Suites are priced from $325 to $500. There's a $15 charge for an extra person, but children under 12 are free on the family plan. Good deals are the weekend plans that include dining privileges.

Try breakfast, lunch, or Sunday brunch at Jonah's Seafood Café, a bright, airy restaurant, open to the atrium on one side and with a view of the river on the other. Hours are 7 a.m. to 11:30 p.m. and prices range from $7 to $15 at lunch and $10 to $22 at dinner. On the rooftop, the revolving, glass-enclosed Spinnaker Lounge serves lunch from 11:45 a.m. to 2 p.m. Monday through Friday, and dinner Sunday through Saturday from 6 to 9 p.m. Brunch is from 10 a.m. to 3 p.m. on Sunday. And drinks till 1 a.m. weekdays, 2 a.m. on Friday and Saturday.

Parking for guests is $9 a day, with no "in and out" charge. Nonguests pay $2/hour. The Hyatt Regency is convenient for college visiting since it's halfway between Harvard and MIT, and across the bridge from Boston University. There's no public transportation nearby, but a complimentary shuttle van takes guests to local points of interest, Monday through Saturday. And for arrivals and departures in high style, try the helicopter shuttle service to and from Logan Airport on weekdays.

Although it's technically in Cambridge, the 400-room **Royal Sonesta Hotel,** 5 Cambridge Parkway, Cambridge, MA 02142 (tel. 617/491-3600), is still very close to Boston; it's near Longfellow Bridge, MIT, and the Museum of Science. Each room is designed to provide a lovely view of the Charles River and the city. Everything is custom designed, with decorator furnishings, living-bedroom combinations, luxurious bathrooms, color TV, desks, and space for social get-togethers.

Singles are in the $135 to $165 range, and doubles run from $150 to $180. Suites go from $195 to $250 a day. Children under 18 are free in the same room with their parents. There's a health facility with a heated pool and free parking, plus courtesy van service to Cambridge and Boston. The hotel has seasonal promotions with special rates, giveaways for children, and fun events for adults.

On the second floor, facing the river, is the Riverfront Restaurant, one of the area's fine eating places.

Incidental intelligence for shoppers: Lechmere Sales, a huge bargain center for cameras, stereos, appliances, camping goods, whathave-you, is right nearby.

Well situated near the major Boston campuses—Harvard is to the right, MIT to the left, and Boston University across the bridge—**Howard Johnson Hotel Cambridge,** 777 Memorial Dr., Cambridge, MA 02139 (tel. 617/492-7777), on the banks of the Charles River, is just ten minutes by car to the heart of Boston and less to Harvard Square in Cambridge. It's an attractive, modern motel, with swimming pool and sundeck plus free parking.

Each of the bedrooms is equipped with a picture window (the better to enjoy the splendid views of the Boston skyline). Rooms are large, nicely furnished, and some have a private balcony. Rates range from $75 to $125 in a single, and from $85 to $135 doubles, the prices varying with the size of the room, the floor, and the view. It's $10 for each extra person, no charge for cribs; children under 18 stay free with their parents. Senior citizen discounts are available with the AARP card.

Also at the hotel is the Bisuteki Japanese Steak House, where dinners are prepared at your table in the hibachi style of "firebowl" cooking, daily from 5 to 10 p.m. Complete meals run $8.95 to $17.95, and there's a special children's menu.

We've always liked two-for-one deals, and **Guest Quarters Suite Hotel, Boston-Cambridge,** 400 Soldiers Field Rd., Boston, MA 02134 (tel. 617/783-0090, or toll free 800/424-2900), has one of the best deals in town—two-bedroom suites for the price many hotels charge for a single unit. In fact, all 310 rooms are suites with living room, bedroom, and bath. Some floors are reserved for nonsmoking guests, and there are suites on each floor for the disabled.

The suites are located around a 15-story sun-lit atrium and can be reached via glass elevators. The rooms are large and decorated in soft shades of pink, gray, and gold against a beige background. Floral-printed fabrics on the headboards accent the light wood of the furniture. All bedrooms have king-size beds, writing desk, AM/FM clock radio, and remote-controlled color TV. Living rooms feature full-size sofa beds, a dining table, plus another TV. The bathrooms have large vanities and an amenities package that includes lotions, cotton balls, Q-tips, and a sewing kit. A trio of push-button telephones in bedroom, living room, and bath are all computer adaptable. Each room has a fully stocked honor bar and refrigerator large enough to stash away food and drinks for breakfast and lunch—great for the family traveling with children (who can stay free in their parents' room if they're under 18). And for a big family there are some corner rooms available at an extra charge of $20. Use of the indoor swimming pool, whirlpool, and sauna are included in the daily fee.

Rates are $145 to $170 single and $165 to $190 double, and include a complimentary American breakfast with eggs cooked to order, fresh-squeezed juices, an assortment of fruits, pastries, and beverages, plus a two-hour private reception each evening. There is entertainment in the lounge, and breakfast, lunch, and dinner are served in **Scullers Grille.**

Several weekend packages are available for $118 to $138 per night, including a University Package for prospective students and their parents. (Guest Quarters Suite Hotel overlooks the Charles River which separates Boston and Cambridge.)

State-of-the-art safety and security features include electronically coded door locks and keys, and fire prevention devices above and beyond state requirements. The enclosed park-and-lock garage is serviced by a security patrol. Round-trip van service to Boston and Cambridge is also available.

RESORT HOTELS

If you've always wanted to visit Boston but your heart's set on a resort vacation, check this trio of resort hotels within a half-hour drive of the city, each offering complete vacation packages.

Just off I-95 in Wakefield, the **Colonial Hilton,** Wakefield, MA 01880 (tel. 617/245-9300), at the Colonial Country Club, offers a 200-acre luxury resort with an 18-hole championship golf course. The sports complex includes tennis and racquetball courts, jogging and walking paths, and an exercise room and gym. At the entrance to the inn is a glass-domed tropical pool. The peaceful hideaway, about 15 miles from Boston, is a quick drive north on Rte. 128 to Salem and Gloucester and south to Lexington and Concord.

Rooms are attractive, cloned in motel decor, with the fanciest in the 11-story 130-room tower, and good standard accommodations in the 170-room inn. Singles are priced from $80 to $105 and doubles are $90 to $115.

Vacation packages are available. And on a hilltop overlooking the golf course is the famous Colonial at Lynnfield Restaurant for dining and a lounge for drinks and dancing.

The Stouffer **Bedford Glen Hotel,** Bedford, MA 01730 (tel. 617/275-5500, or toll free 800/HOTELS-1), three miles north of I-95 on the Middlesex Turnpike and near Lexington's historical points, is in the midst of the headquarters area of many leading corporations, yet it looks like a country resort in its scenic pine-wooded setting. In a welcome change from the tower effect of many hotels, this is a two-level rambling structure of 286 rooms with a fitness center, indoor pool, whirlpool, sauna, and indoor and outdoor tennis courts. A fine restaurant and lounge is conveniently located in the hotel.

BE MY GUEST: With good budget hotels at a premium, we're always looking for a way to find inexpensive rooms for visitors to the Boston area. One alternative that offers an especially good value is the bed-and-breakfast concept, where a local family provides a room, breakfast, and hospitality for a reasonable fee, ranging from $30 to $100 depending on location and the number of guests. The tab includes breakfast, which may be anything from juice and danish to lox and bagels and eggs Benedict. With this type of accommodation, you get the feel of the community and even have the chance to commute like the locals, traffic jams and all!

To make a match between visitors and hosts, contact these bed-and-breakfast organizations:

Pineapple Hospitality, Inc., 47 North Second St., Suite 3A, New Bedford, MA 02744 (tel. 508/990-1696). They list pre-inspected private homes in Boston, Cambridge, Charlestown, and in many suburbs north and south of Boston, including Cape Cod. (How about a sailboat on the Cape?) They also have listings throughout New England. Write or call the above address.

New England Bed and Breakfast, 1045 Centre St., Newton, MA 02159 (tel. 617/244-2112), lists homes in the area that are a 10- to 20-minute drive to Boston or within walking distance to public transportation.

Bed and Breakfast Associates, P.O. Box 166, Babson Park Branch, Boston, MA 02157 (tel. 617/449-5302), has homes in the metropolitan Boston area and throughout eastern Massachusetts. They can also arrange long-term lodging.

A Cambridge House, P.O. Box 211, Massachusetts Ave., Cambridge, MA 02140 (tel. 617/491-6300), near Harvard Square and the MBTA's Red Line, is a lovely federal-style house with eight air-conditioned rooms and shared bath. A full home-made breakfast is served each morning, and parking is available.

If you're headed for the Cape, Nantucket, or Martha's Vineyard, **House Guests, Cape Cod** can find a private home for you. Write Richard E. Griffen, P.O. Box 1881, Orleans, MA 02653, or call 508/896-7053. There is a two-night minimum stay in July and August.

The guest rooms are decorated in soft tones of taupe, pink, and brown, and have individual temperature controls, AM/FM radio, color TV, complimentary in-room movies, digital clock with alarm, and direct-dial phone. There is a choice of king-size or twin beds in the single and double rooms which are priced from $130 to $150 single, and $140 to $160 double. There's no charge for children in the same room with their parents. Eleven rooms have special facilities for the disabled. There are also several suites with sofas and conference tables, and a Presidential Suite featuring a circular staircase, balcony, and canopied bed. Complimentary morning paper and coffee are brought to your room with your wakeup call. And if you want a swim before starting on the day's activities, the pool opens at 7 a.m. and stays open with lifeguard on duty until 10 p.m.

For the tourist, the weekend packages are an excellent deal, ranging from $59 to $249.

The **Sheraton Tara Hotel & Resort at Ferncroft**, Danvers, MA 01923 (tel. 508/777-2500, or toll free 800/325-3535), is the perfect spot for a golfing vacation. The 18-hole championship course hosts the LPGA tournament each July, and the 367 rooms located high above Rte. 1 North have a view of either the course or the surrounding countryside. Since it's only a half hour from Boston, about 20 minutes to Gloucester and Rockport, and even closer to Salem, it's the perfect anchor for sightseeing on the North Shore.

The hotel has been completely redecorated since it was purchased by the present owners and the facilities are on a par with fine hotels in Boston. Peach and green tones predominate and are accented with fabrics in floral patterns. All rooms have a sofa, desk, phone, clock radio, individual air-conditioning and heat controls, TV, and either double or king-size beds. Special amenities are an electric shoeshine buffer and a large vanity mirror with salon-style makeup lights in the bedroom. Room rates vary according to season: singles begin at $98, doubles start at $110, and executive kings run $115 and $135 during the golf season (May through November). Children under 18 stay free in their parent's room, and AARP members get a 20% senior citizen discount. A selection of rooms at the top of the Tara have additional amenities and are priced slightly higher. There is also a nonsmoking floor and 20 rooms for the disabled.

If golf isn't your game, other sports facilities are available, including tennis, racquetball, basketball, volleyball, horseshoes, an indoor game room, a beautiful large indoor pool, and a health and fitness center. Attractive weekend package deals include a lavish Sunday brunch.

TRAVEL TIPS: Write to the **Greater Boston Convention & Tourist Bureau,** Prudential Plaza, Box 490, Boston, MA 02199 (tel. 617/267-6446), for their booklet on Boston Weekend packages. It lists all the special package deals in the area, and could help you stay at some of the great places at substantial savings.

The **Massachusetts Office of Travel and Tourism,** 100 Cambridge St., Boston, MA 02202 (tel. 617/727-3203 or toll free 800/632-8038 for Massachusetts and 800/343-9072 for other Northeast states), publishes a *Bed-and-Breakfast Guide,* which lists guest houses across the state organized by region and town. Write to them at the above address for a copy and for other free publications about Massachusetts vacations.

CHAPTER IV

DINING OUT
IN BOSTON

□ □ □

To read some travel writers, one would assume that Bostonians lived on a steady diet of seafood and baked beans, with perhaps a New England boiled dinner or two thrown in for good measure. It's just not that way, at least not anymore.

True, Boston has been influenced by being a seaport. But that doesn't mean just fish. It means people from all over the world coming to Boston with distinctive tastes in food and many ideas for its preparation and presentation. From the sailing ships to the jets, visitors and settlers have brought vitality to the city and to its cuisine. There are a vast number of restaurants offering everything from regional New England to Tex-Mex-American to Cajun and European and Oriental foods. Boston has its share of fine French and continental restaurants, its hallowed seafood temples, and the shrines to beef and hearty eating. There is an outstanding selection of Italian, Chinese, Middle Eastern, Mexican, Japanese, Indian, Thai, and Vietnamese restaurants plus macrobiotic and natural food choices, and a bevy of spots for sumptuous brunches and relaxed outdoor dining.

And, of course, the seafood. Boston is the "seafood capital of the world," and no seafood lover in his right mind would dispute the excellence of the Ipswich clams, Atlantic lobsters, Wellfleet oysters, mussels, cod, haddock, and flounder that have won the city this acclaim. The waters off Massachusetts have abounded in these for centuries (at the Old State House, in fact, a wooden codfish commemorates the commercial importance of the fish to the people of the Commonwealth), and Bostonians have responded by creating and maintaining a superb culinary tradition. The old, cherished recipes for steamed clams in drawn butter, for finnan haddie (smoked haddock), and for that famed Boston scrod (not a separate species of fish but the name given to a small haddock or cod) are still yours to enjoy when you visit the city. The clam chowder, by the way, is made without the tomatoes added in other parts of the country, and in our opinion is far superior to any other. Major restaurants and hotels vie each year for the chowder-of-the-year award.

Baked beans, once practically synonymous with Boston, are more likely to turn up on supermarket shelves than in most Boston restaurants. Boston brownbread has been practically replaced by croissants and tacos, and the New England boiled dinner is also hard to find, since the reason for its original existence has faded. In olden days, every ingredient—corned beef, carrots, potato, cabbage, whatever—was cooked in one pot, since that was all that would conveniently hang on a crane over the open fire.

And if you watch your foods carefully and are concerned about calories, cholesterol, and salt, don't despair about dining out. Many of Boston's best restaurants have special "spa-type" menus that make counting calories a pleasure. We've noted them in our restaurant descriptions. In fact, most restaurants will honor your requests for special entrees. Just ask.

The choice is yours in Boston, and if you run out of interesting places to dine, you're just not trying.

FACTS AND FIGURES: To simplify your dining selections, we've placed the restaurants into categories based on their price range and the nature of their cuisine. "Haute Cuisine" includes those restaurants charging $20 to $39 per entree; "Upper Bracket" designates restaurants pricing entrees at $12 to $20; and "Moderate" covers eating places with a tab of $8 to $12 per entree. However, if you order wines, appetizers, soups, salad, dessert, and coffee, the prices in each category may rise substantially. In top places you can pay over $100 for two. As for the "Budget" category, it still exists if you can budget around $7 for a meal. Look in Cambridge with its vast population of money-conscious students and to the ethnic restaurants for the best values. And there are always the fast-food places and the "fancy" fast-food places in Faneuil Hall Market Place.

Now for some general rules. It's always wise to phone ahead and make reservations, particularly for dinner, and at the better restaurants, for lunch too. When you call, check on whether or not they accept the credit cards you're carrying; some places accept only their own house cards or cash. Also check on dress requirements; although Boston is not a "dressy" city, most of the better restaurants do require jacket (but not necessarily a tie) for men. For the ladies, pants (but pants, *not* jeans) are acceptable everywhere.

And when you make those reservations, specify smoking or nonsmoking section. Massachusetts has a Clean Indoor Air Act, which requires all restaurants with a seating capacity of 75 or more to set aside a nonsmoking area of at least 25 seats or 200 square feet. Some restaurants have banned smoking completely—as we go to press these restaurants include Fox and Hounds in the Boston Park Plaza Hotel, Pillar House in Newton, and Pentimento in Cambridge.

As for tipping, it's a standard 15% everywhere, more if you're especially pleased, or if there's a captain. There's a 5% meal tax added to all bills. And even in expensive restaurants it's perfectly okay to ask for a bag to take home leftovers.

If you have a car, it's wise to call ahead to see if there is valet or validated parking.

So then, let's begin.

HAUTE CUISINE
(ENTREES FOR $20 TO $39)

CONNOISSEUR'S CHOICES: Rarely is there agreement among gourmets in choosing the finest restaurant in town, especially in Boston where there are so many superb dining rooms. But there are a few that consistently appear on "The Best" lists of food critics and connoisseurs-about-town. Each one is tops in every detail, from food preparation to service to dining room ambience. At all, reservations are a must.

Here are some outstanding choices, from A to Z:

Aujourd'hui, the four-star restaurant in the Four Seasons Hotel, 200 Boylston St. (tel. 338-4400), has one of the best and most expensive dining rooms in Boston. You feel the luxury the minute you ascend the grand staircase to reach the quietly elegant room with floor-to-ceiling windows overlooking the Public Garden. The well-spaced tables are set with antique service plates and the food is served on Royal Dalton china designed for the Four Seasons. Embroidered tapestry banquettes and chairs and floral bouquets provide muted color against the rich oak paneling.

The menu choices are eclectic, contemporary, and simply delicious. Executive chef Mark Baker showcases regional products using the freshest ingredients available, and the wine list is one of the best in the city. Main courses might include veal chop with Vermont goat cheese; whole roasted native pheasant with honey and grilled dates; rack of lamb with a basil zucchini flan, or blue-fin tuna steak with Ossetra caviar fettuccine. Appetizers are as innovative as the entrees. Consider the creamed soup of Maine lobster with lentils; an appetizer such as terrine of grilled duck liver and three-color noodles; and a salad of field greens and grilled sweet-breads with onion marmalade. The dessert pastry cart overflows with cakes, pies, fresh fruits, and berries. Or you can order an individual soufflé for your grand finale.

If you're counting calories or watching cholesterol and sodium, you can order an elegant meal from the Alternative Menu, which has offerings as creative as those on the regular menu.

Prices at dinner are in the $23 to $36 range for main courses and in the $8 to $29 range for appetizers. Lunch goes from $13 to $19, with a three-course meal that includes appetizer, entree, dessert, and wine for $25. A three-course pre-theater dinner is served until 7 p.m. at the fixed price of $42.

Dinner hours are from 6 to 10:30 p.m., Sunday to Thursday; until 11 p.m. on Friday and Saturday. Lunch is served from 11:30 a.m. to 2:30 p.m., Monday through Friday; and Sunday brunch is from 11 a.m. to 2:30 p.m. Breakfast is offered daily. Afternoon tea is served in the Bristol Lounge every day from 3 to 4:30 p.m. Paid valet parking is available.

The **Café Plaza** is probably what you have in mind when you think of Plaza. This classic restaurant in the Copley Plaza Hotel, 138 St. James Ave. (tel. 267-5300), has Waterford crystal chandeliers, ornately sculpted vaulted ceilings, fresh flowers on each elegantly set table, and an elegant menu to match. Among the 15 or more daily entrees, the chef prepares a masterful roast breast of Indiana duckling with orange and pineapple compote, a Chateaubriand for two, and a fricassee of lobster with truffles. As starters, there are hot and chilled hors d'oeuvres, salads, soups, and seasonal offerings utilizing the best produce in the market. And if you want to try some of everything, try the Taster's Menu, which offers soup, hors d'oeuvres, salad, fish course, entree, cheese tray, and dessert for $48. At dessert time, there's a taster's plate of sherbets or ice creams, chocolate génoise mousse cake, fresh fruits, and soufflés. Entrees are priced from $24 to $33 ($55 for Chateaubriand), hors d'oeuvres are $5 to $18. The wine list is superior.

Dinner is served Monday through Saturday from 5:30 to 10:30 p.m.

The newest star in Boston's culinary scene is **The Colony,** 384 Boylston St. (tel. 536-8500), where owners David Kantrowitz and Bruce Frankel have gone back to early New England recipes to produce some of the best cooking in Boston today. They've researched old cookbooks, focused on local ingredients, and encouraged local purveyors to raise vegetables, cheeses, and meats just for The Colony. They prepare all these treasures with French techniques, such as thickening sauces by reduction rather than with flour, and frying their corn oysters in oil instead of the lard used in the original eighteenth-century recipe. As a result, they've eliminated the "quaint" from New England cooking and replaced it with a dynamic dimension.

The menu changes every month or two but usually includes their souffléd corn oysters (not really oysters but fritters) among the first courses, an aged rack of lamb, a Maine veal steak, or perhaps a lobster-and-vegetable pie for a main course. The desserts may include a frozen maple parfait, strawberry shortcake with real shortbread, or a chocolate bread-and-butter pudding with custard sauce and real whipped cream that rivals the best chocolate cakes. If you prefer something less sweet, there is a collection of New England farmstead cheeses with about 15 varieties to choose.

The New England sampling menu, at $48, includes a first course, soup or stew, main dish, cheese, dessert, and coffee. Entrees range from $27 to $30; first courses, $7 to $9; and desserts are $7.50. The excellent wine list includes selections from New England and Long Island.

The Colony is located in a second-story dining room, reached by private elevator and decorated to give the feeling of a Boston townhouse. The chairs are Chippendale; the walls, Georgian yellow; and the hand-wrought chandeliers are solid brass. There is ample space between the tables to allow for private conversation. Dinner is served Tuesday through Saturday from 6 to 10 p.m., and reservations are recommended.

Bostonians usually favor well-established restaurants that have earned their pedigrees over many years, so newcomers have to prove themselves for a long period of time before winning laurels. But **Restaurant Jasper,** 240 Commercial St., on the waterfront (tel. 523-1126), won acclaim from the beginning and has grown every year to become one of the top restaurants in Boston.

The young and talented chef/proprietor, Jasper White, makes full use of seasonal products, changing his menu about eight times a year. There are usually about six entrees plus daily specials with something for everyone's taste—fish, chicken, veal, lamb, and steak. We liked the red snapper with sesame seeds and scallions, a refreshing contrast of moist white fish and crunchy sesame. Rack of lamb with gratin of artichoke and white turnip, and charred rib-eye steak with blue cheese butter, are unusual renditions of old favorites. Appetizers may include choices as upbeat as johnny cakes with Ossetra caviar and chive crème fraîche, grilled Nantucket quail, or Cape Cod oysters with a sparkling ravigote sauce. A wonderful Seafood Tasting Menu is also offered for $45 per person. Entrees are priced from $20 to $35; appetizers $6 to $20. Desserts, which are presented with the same flair as other offerings, run about $5.

Jasper's seats about 70 in three dining areas with mirrored walls and exposed brick, dabbed with white and pink to a soft-toned finish. Japanese prints, floral paintings, and lavish flower arrangements help create a romantic mood. The extensive wine list emphasizes French choices in a varied price range.

The Restaurant Jasper is open Monday through Thursday from 6 to 10 p.m., and on Friday and Saturday until 11 p.m. Light meals are served in the bar from 6 to 10 or 11 p.m. On Thursday, Friday, and Saturday evenings a pianist presents jazz and classical music. Valet parking is available.

For the height of luxury, consider **Julien,** the elegant French dining room at the Hotel Meridien, 250 Franklin St. (tel. 451-1900). The Meridien is the former Federal Reserve Bank of Boston, and Julien was once the "Member's Court." There are two original murals by noted artist and illustrator N. C. Wyeth, plus gold-leaf edging on the vaulted ceiling, wingback Queen Anne chairs, and choice silver and china, all adding to the beauty of the room.

The seasonal menus in the French nouvelle style are prepared in consultation with top French chefs who come to Boston three or four times a year to share their expertise with the Julien staff. (The Meridien is a subsidiary of Air France.) They have combined a variety of unusual, flavorful ingredients to create an outstanding cuisine. The portions are good-sized and arranged on the dinner plate with an artful balance of colors and textures. For example, a combination of tenderloin of veal and sweetbreads with a dried plum sauce; and noisettes of venison with white grapes and chestnuts in an Armagnac sauce. The breast of duck is very special, completely de-fatted, sliced like roast beef, and served with duck foie gras, lemon, and maple syrup. The fish selection is very elaborate with fresh Dover sole served with Indian spices; rouget barbet from the Mediterranean Sea served with artichokes and chicken fumet; and John Dory served with shrimp. The desserts, which are served from a multitiered cart or in grand style by your waiter, include a warm passion fruit gratin and bittersweet chocolate bites with a grilled coffee sauce.

Entrees are priced from $25 to $34; appetizers from $7 to $15; and desserts are $7. But you do get a complimentary hors d'oeuvre before you order and petit fours and chocolates at the conclusion of your meal. The wines are carefully chosen from the best French, German, Italian, and American wineries and are priced from about $18 to $200 per bottle. (Alsatian wines are very good values.)

Julien is open for dinner daily from 6 to 10:30 p.m., and until

11 p.m. on weekends. A fixed-price lunch is served weekdays from noon to 2 p.m. for $23.

Note: The **Café Fleuri,** the atrium-style informal dining room in the Meridien, serves a most delicious buffet lunch at $14.50 (without dessert) from 11:30 a.m. to 2:30 p.m. weekdays. On Sunday a more sumptuous buffet is served at 11 a.m. and 1:30 p.m. and includes sparkling wine—$24, adults, and $12, children. Café Fleuri is open from 7 a.m. to late evening, serving breakfast, lunch, and dinner. Live entertainment nightly and dancing on Fridays and Saturdays.

To dine at **L'Espalier,** 30 Gloucester St. (tel. 262-3023), is to dine on superb cuisine in the elegance of a Beacon Hill town house. Chef Frank McClelland and Catherine McClelland are the husband-and-wife team who make the restaurant so exciting. Frank first learned about food from his great grandmother in the kitchen of the family's farm in New Hampshire, and over the years has studied with many talented international chefs. In college he majored in environmental affairs; his interest in the land has given him an expert's background in choosing fresh organic produce that he buys in season from small New England farmers. The breads, sorbets, ice creams, and desserts (many adapted from the family's heirloom cookbooks) are all made in L'Espalier's kitchen.

The prix-fixe menu at $52 features "starters"—a first course—main course, and dessert. There are six choices in each category, every one a presentation par excellence. The menu changes about once a week, but there is always a caviar selection, a hot or cold soup, fish, lamb, veal, beef, or venison. If they're on the menu, try the soup of Maine lobster and native salsify with watercress and vanilla butter as a first course, and then choose the sautéed veal medallions with grilled black-walnut polenta as an entree. Our favorite dessert is the violet-and-wildflower-honey ice cream in a chocolate walnut tuile.

If you can't make a decision, there is a dégustation menu available Monday through Friday, which includes two appetizers, two main courses, and a selection of desserts for $62. An elegant vegetarian menu is also available. And if you wish an à la carte cheese tray, the Grand Fromage, with 25 local cheeses to choose from, is presented. The wine cellar is extensive with 150 bottles, including local and California wines and some excellent Alsatian wines.

This is all presented in three dining rooms, which have intricate carvings on the walls, fireplaces, striking floral arrangements, and special lighting effects. They are reached by a spiral staircase typical of those in the 19th-century town houses. L'Espalier is open Monday through Saturday from 6 to 10 p.m.

Maison Robert, 45 School St. (tel. 227-3370), is one of the finest French restaurants anywhere. To be exact, two of the finest French restaurants—the elegantly formal Bonhomme Richard on the main floor, and the cozy Ben's Café on the ground floor. When the great chefs of France come to Boston, they dine with Lucien Robert, a restaurateur of uncompromising standards.

Decorated in French Second Empire style, the Bonhomme Richard is a gracious dining room with ornate molding and butternut window panelings, crystal chandeliers, potted palms, and fresh flowers. Lunch (noon to 2:30 p.m.) and dinner (6 to 10 p.m.) are served in the classical French tradition, with entrees starting at $15 and going up and up. You'll feast on the likes of mignon de veau, homard au whiskey (lobster with whisky sauce), and poulet Bonhomme Richard (roast chicken with Calvados and cream). We can also vouch for the properly done roast rack of lamb and the light Dover sole. The service is as superb as the food, and there is a wine list of vintage bordeaux and burgundies.

Dinner entrees run from about $20 to $35; lunch is less expensive. Maison Robert is open from 11:30 a.m. to 9:30 p.m. Menus change seasonally.

Ben's Café has a less formal environment and meals are not as expensive, though they are thoroughly French in style and prepared with superb care. Entrees are $15 to $32; appetizers, $7 to $13; and desserts $4 to $6. Dinner at Ben's Café is served Wednesday through Friday, from 5:30 to 9:30 p.m.; Saturday from 6 to 10:30 p.m. Paid valet parking is available for both restaurants.

If you're here in summer, get a table on the outdoor terrace next to the statue of Benjamin Franklin (he's the Ben of Ben's Café). This was the first outdoor statue in Puritan New England.

Le Marquis de Lafayette in the Lafayette Hotel, 1 Avenue de Lafayette (tel. 451-2800), is Boston's world-class restaurant with top ratings from local, national, and international food critics. The impressive French cuisine, adapted to modern tastes, is supervised by Louis Outhier, one of the eight top-rated chefs in Europe and owner of La Napoule, a Michelin-rated three-star restaurant in the south of France. He visits Le Marquis on a regular basis for consultations with the executive chef, whom he trained at La Napoule.

This is a splendid restaurant where the quality of the food is matched by impeccable service and tasteful decor. Silk wall fabrics and wood paneling in soft gray are the background for rose-patterned armchairs and padded banquettes. Crystal chandeliers and wall sconces provide soft light in the dining room. Bone-china place settings with the coat-of-arms of the Lafayette family, sterling-silver flatware, and crystal goblets sparkle on the tables. Original prints depicting hunting scenes are on the walls.

Although the menu changes seasonally, some items are so popular that they will always be there, especially the hors d'oeuvre, l'oeuf au caviar—a shirred egg served in its own shell with vodka, whipped cream, and beluga caviar; and the brie aux truffes. There are always excellent veal, beef, poultry, and fish selections and a choice of soups. One of our favorites is the duckling with lime and maple syrup sauce. Desserts are an absolute must. La Caravane des Desserts Maison is a multilevel extravaganza of pastries that may include ouefs à la neige (snow eggs—meringues shaped like eggs), chocolate orange cake with orange liqueur, and delicious fruit tarts. A complimentary hors d'oeuvre is always served and there is a mid-meal sorbet plus petit fours to sweeten the check.

Two fixed-price menus are available. The very unusual Menu de Caviar, five courses of caviar and seafood, must be ordered by at least two people and costs $69 per person.

Le Marquis is expensive, with the average dinner check around $50 per person. And when you add wine from an impressive ten-category wine list, the tab can reach $200 for a party of two. If these prices are too much to digest, try the excellent lunch for around $25, a wonderful way to savor Le Marquis without breaking the bank.

Le Marquis is open for lunch Monday through Friday from noon to 2:30 p.m.; and for dinner Monday through Saturday from 6 to 10:30 p.m. Reservations are requested. (Hotel guests often reserve tables when booking their rooms.) There are special parking rates with validations after 5:30 p.m.

Rarities, in the Charles Hotel at Harvard Square, 1 Bennett St., Cambridge (tel. 864-1200), belongs to that rare class of dining room that has everything—a stunning setting, perfect service, and superlative food.

The dining room is decorated in a monochromatic scheme of gray, black, and white with sprays of purple dendrobium orchids on the tables for a splash of color. Soft lights, deep carpets, and white Royal Dalton china rimmed with silver add to the feeling of luxury. A nonsmoking section is available.

The menu at Rarities features the new American cuisine with emphasis on regional specialties, local fresh ingredients, and generous portions. The talented chef, Walter Zuromski, prepares innovative combinations of meat, fish, and game using wine-based sauces and unusual vegetables and spices, yet everything blends together perfectly and tastefully. We loved the young duckling grilled with dates, clementines, and madeirized potatoes; and the salmon filet served with black truffles and leeks. A rack of lamb roasted with flavorful spices was also delicious. Among the appetizers we highly recommend the sea scallop and hominy chowder and the Norwegian smoked salmon mousse with caviar.

The menu is seasonal (changes four times a year) but there are always some constants, such as a complimentary plate of three different hors d'oeuvres, the presentation of a sorbet between the appetizer and the entree, and Fiuggi mineral water from Italy. Croissants, herb-flavored breadsticks, and dinner rolls are baked in the hotel, and are so delicious we had to be careful not to fill up on them. Perrier is served before dessert to clear the palate for some of the most delicious chocolate cakes, walnut pies, and apple dumplings in town. And we must mention the "four-napkin" service. Anytime you leave the table, your large, starched napkin is replaced with a fresh one by the time you return.

Rarities manager and maître d', Thomas Sweetland, has compiled an extensive wine list ranging from moderately priced California white to the not-so-moderate Château Lafite Rothschild ($1,300). And he's also stocked the largest selection of wines in half bottles in town—a great idea for those of us who would like more than one type of wine at a meal.

Entree prices are about $23 up to $32, and appetizers and salads in the $5 to $10 range. Desserts are $4.50. You should figure $110 to $120 for two, depending on your choice of wines. The chocolate truffles and sweets presented with the check are complimentary.

Open for dinner only from 6 to 10 p.m. seven days a week. Reservations required.

The **Ritz-Carlton Dining Room,** 15 Arlington St. (tel. 536-5700). A unique fame attends the magnificent second-floor restaurant of this elegant hotel overlooking the Boston Public Garden. Whether it's dinner under the soft lights of the crystal chandeliers with soft piano music, French menu, and gracious service, or Sunday brunch by the blue-and-white-draped windows, a meal here is a memorable experience. The captain carves the lamb or flames the steak tableside and then transfers the hot food to your warm plates; the waiters watch discreetly nearby to anticipate your every need; and the buspersons keep your cobalt-blue water glasses filled.

The restaurant concentrates mostly on the classics that have been its mainstay for years, such as a superb rack of lamb served on a platter festive with flowers and frills, flamed sirloin steak with cognac and peppercorns, and the Maine lobster "au whiskey." But it has also added innovative entrees and a "Fitness Cuisine" of light, low-calorie dishes, noted on the menu. These might include filet of scrod, medallions of venison, sea bass, or veal cutlet. Nearly 30 in all, the superb appetizers range from beluga caviar to French snails in garlic butter and baked clams with curry cream. There's a wonderful selection of desserts, including chocolate and Grand Marnier soufflés ($12), and a baked Alaska ($17) from which dreams are made.

The average price for entrees is $37.50, while hors d'oeuvres run from $7 to $15. Lunch costs $27.50 on the average. Dinner is served from 6 to 10 p.m. Sunday through Thursday, and until 11 p.m. on Friday and Saturday. Lunch is offered noon to 2:30 p.m. Monday through Saturday. The Ritz also has a wonderful Sunday buffet brunch from 11 a.m. to 3 p.m. at $34 for adults and $17.50 for children.

SAMPLING THE GRAND HOTELS: From mid-January through mid-April, the Ritz-Carlton Hotel, 15 Arlington St., presents an **International Cultural Festival** that includes music, lectures, art exhibits, and week-long visits of chefs from the grand hotels around the world. The chefs and their culinary teams incorporate their specialties into the menus served in the hotel's dining room (Sunday brunch included), café, bar, and lounge. It's a great way to dine on superb food from Europe, Africa, Asia, and the Middle East in the luxurious atmosphere of the Ritz. For information on the schedule, call the Ritz-Carlton Hotel (tel. 536-5700).

Some restaurants trade off a great view for ordinary food, drink, and service; but **Seasons** in the Bostonian Hotel, at North and Blackstone Streets (tel. 523-3600), has it all—superlative food, service, and setting. On the fourth floor of the hotel, it is reached by its own glass elevator, and looks out on the panorama of Faneuil Hall Marketplace from its windowed walls and glass-vaulted ceiling. Floral arrangements of orchids on the tables, comfortable Louis XV–style chairs, and a subdued color scheme of grays and greens create a luxurious setting for the 125-seat room.

Seasons features regional New England food specialties prepared with a flair that has won raves from restaurant critics. Most of the meat, seafood, and produce comes from local markets, but suppliers all over the country provide herbs, spices, rare cheeses, and fresh game. The menu changes four times a year to feature seasonal food; and depending on when you come you might find fresh salmon, Dover sole with champagne sauce and fresh black truffles, quail, or venison. One of our favorites, served all year, is duckling with ginger and scallions; and there is usually prime sirloin steak, lamb, and veal.

For an appetizer, try the lobster and oyster stew or varied pâtés. For dessert, everything is irresistible, but our personal favorites are the chocolate fantasies and the fresh fruit sorbets.

American wines are featured and include 50 different chardonnays, 65 cabernet sauvignons, and some rare selections from the country's top wine makers. Service is impeccable, with attention given to all the little details that add up to greatness.

Prices for entrees range from $25 to $35 at dinner, and $12 to $19 at lunch. Appetizers are $7 to $14. Seasons is open for breakfast from 7 to 10:30 a.m., for lunch from 11:30 a.m. to 2:30 p.m., and for dinner from 6 to 10 p.m. Sunday through Thursday, till 11 p.m. on Friday and Saturday. Valet parking is $6.

Zachary's, 120 Huntington Ave. (tel. 424-7000), is a splendid dining room in the Colonnade Hotel, decorated in tones of taupe and amber, accented with chrome mirrors and crystal. And although it seats 130, it has a feeling of intimacy and warmth.

Entrees in a price range of $21.50 to $29.50 include rack of lamb (for two), chateaubriand (for two), duck with Curaçao, roast loin of veal with prosciutto, and Dover sole. Most of the appetizers are on the exotic side: chilled oysters with sturgeon caviar, thin-sliced smoked goose with yogurt and horseradish, and snails in red wine with garlic are not exactly your everyday hors d'oeuvres, but they're really worth trying. As for soups, you can have a basic New England clam chowder, a vegetable purée, or a chilled fruit soup. Zachary's also provides complete nutritional information for the entire menu plus special items for diners concerned with nutrient composition. And when it comes to dessert, there's marinated fresh fruit for the diet-conscious plus indulgences that include the extraordinary gâteau Colonnade, a dense, rich chocolate mint cake.

Zachary's composite wine list (about 600) has won international awards and is one of the best in town. And the tea service wins our award. It's all freshly brewed tea—no teabags. Zachary's is open Monday through Saturday from 5:30 to 10:30 p.m.

PROPER BOSTONIANS: Back in the time of Emerson and Longfellow, the Omni Parker House, 60 School St. (tel. 227-8600), was *the* place in town—home to Boston's literati and an elegant dining spot. **Parker's,** the hotel's main dining room, is still a bastion of haute cuisine. Tables are set with Rosenthal china and sterling-silver flatware. The original walnut-paneled walls are still there, providing an elegant backdrop to the brown and beige decor. This is one of the most comfortable dining rooms any-where, and the polished service is in keeping with the grand offer-ings on the menu.

Medallions of veal with pink grapefruit sauce and roast rack of lamb with garlic and rosemary share honors with Dover sole belle meunière prepared tableside and served with classic Caesar salad. All entrees include vegetables and potatoes, and of course, the fa-mous Parker House rolls. Prices range from $20 to $32.

The weekday luncheon menu is equally delicious and features salads, omelets, several fish choices including clam chowder, and pasta. It is served from 11:30 a.m. to 2:30 p.m. Dinner hours are 5:30 to 10 p.m. Monday through Friday, to 10:30 p.m. on Satur-day. An excellent Sunday brunch is served at 11:30 a.m. and 1:30 p.m. Reservations for brunch are advisable. Free valet parking at dinner and brunch.

Locke-Ober, 3 Winter Pl. (tel. 542-1340), one of Boston's oldest traditional restaurants, is something of a legend in this town. The huge classic menu offers selections that have been favor-ites of Bostonians for several generations. The plates are stacked high and so are the prices. Part of the attraction of this famous res-taurant is the setting—the carved paneling, silver-plated service pieces, mammoth German silver buffet covers on the long, mir-rored (1880 vintage) downstairs bar. And the peach-complexioned nude painting over the bar! While this room is the most favored by tourists, the upstairs dining room with crystal chandeliers, heraldic stained-glass windows, and leather chairs is the choice of those who prefer a club-like atmosphere—Harvard club, perhaps.

You'll want to sample the famous lobster stew, of course. Other popular dishes include roast leg of lamb, finnan haddie, and the greatest dish on the menu, lobster Savannah, Locke-Ober's star for decades. Entrees are priced from $13 to $50. You might have a problem choosing from among the 30 desserts on the menu. We offer to help by suggesting you try either the Indian pudding or the zabaglione.

Dinner is served Monday through Saturday from 3 to 10 p.m., on Sunday from 5 to 10 p.m.; and lunch, from 11:30 a.m. to 3 p.m.

UPPER-BRACKET RESTAURANTS
(ENTREES FOR $12 TO $20)

FOR SEAFOOD: Boston, by virtue of its geographic location, is naturally a seafood town. Natives and tourists alike expect to be served the very best in fresh fish in the area's restaurants. And they're not disappointed. Each restaurant has buyers at the piers at daybreak, bidding for the top of the catch (the finest fish of the day). And the best restaurants in town settle for nothing less. Some of our choices have built their reputations over many years; others are newcomers. All are worth a visit. Just choose—plain or fancy, expensive or reasonable in price. We're starting with the best known in town, but you'll find many more in our moderate and budget price sections.

One of the most outstanding restaurants in New England, winner of the Business Executive's Dining Award as America's most popular restaurant for many years, is **Anthony's Pier 4**, 140 Northern Ave. (tel. 423-6363). Dramatically situated at the end of a pier, its waterfront walls are made of glass, allowing clear views of incoming liners, fishing boats, tugs, and yachts.

There is often a long wait for a table since there are no reservations taken, but once seated you're served hot popovers, marinated mushrooms, and relishes. Among the featured dishes are Dover sole from the English Channel (flown over especially for Anthony's), bouillabaisse, roast beef, and if you're in the mood to splurge, lobster Savannah with mushrooms, peppers, spices, wines, and mornay sauce. The price range for entrees is $10 to $20. Leave a little room for the Grand Marnier soufflé or the baked Alaska on the dessert menu.

Pier 4 is open every day but Christmas, serving lunch Monday to Saturday from 11:30 a.m. to 3:45 p.m., and dinner from 3:45 to 11 p.m. On Sunday, dinner is 12:30 to 10:30 p.m. Free parking on the wharf. Jackets are requested for men.

Jimmy's Harbor Side Restaurant, 242 Northern Ave. (tel. 423-1000), is a Boston landmark with a fine view of the harbor and Logan Airport from both the main downstairs dining room and the sunny Merchant's Club on the upper level. The overall feeling in both rooms is warm and friendly. As for the food, we wish you could try everything. But if you only come once, take one of the shore dinners, perhaps broiled scallops à la Jimmy or colossal Alaskan king crab legs. Dinners include appetizer (order the creamy fish chowder with generous chunks of white fish), cut-up sea scallops, salad, potato, dessert, and beverage. (A bowl of fish à la carte makes a fine lunch.) Occasionally there are specialties not listed on the menu that only the regular diners ask for, such as gray sole. Check to see if it's available—excellent and not too expensive. The à la carte menu includes prime ribs of beef, shrimp Charles, and the famous finnan haddie, a specialty of the house. The price range is $9 to $25. Special dinners are available for children. Lunch is served from 11:30 a.m. to 3 p.m., dinner from 3 to 9:30 p.m., Monday to Saturday. Closed on Sunday. Limited reservations.

While you're waiting to be seated, you can enjoy delicious complimentary hors d'oeuvres in the lounge—and you don't necessarily have to have a drink!

Legal Sea Foods, in the Boston Park Plaza Hotel, 50 Park Plaza (tel. 426-4444), is head and scales above most of the seafood restaurants in the city. In the years that it has grown from a small family fishmarket in Cambridge, Legal has earned an international reputation for serving only top-quality fish—broiled, baked, grilled, fried, steamed, and in casserole. For dinner and lunch there is a vast "school" to select from: scrod, haddock, bluefish, trout, salmon, or more esoteric selections such as monk fish, tile fish, butterfish, and mako shark. Dinner prices are in the $9.50 to $22.95 range, and lunch is a good catch at $5 to $9. Try one of Legal's homemade ice creams for dessert.

The dining room skips the nautical effects and has mirrored walls and cushioned wicker chairs in soft neutral tones. The ceilings have an unusual baffle effect that adds nicely to the comfortable ambience. Hours are Monday through Saturday from 11 a.m. to 10 p.m. Open Sunday from noon to 10 p.m. Legal is also in Cambridge, Chestnut Hill, Burlington, and Worcester.

The very upscale Copley Place shopping mall, with its fine shops and boutiques, is the perfect location for an upscale seafood restaurant. And **Arne's Fine Seafood,** at Copley Place, 100 Huntington Ave. (tel. 267-4900), fits in beautifully: very contemporary, very attractive with blond wood and blue tile, and with a very fine product—good, fresh fish. The restaurant can seat 200 but it is cleverly designed in tiers so there are four dining areas to give an overall intimate effect.

Owner and manager Arne Soreide has put together a tremendous menu with about 25 hot and cold appetizers and salads, 17 basic seafood selections, plus over 20 chef's special preparations, fried seafoods, and lobster choices, and still has been able to maintain high standards of food and service. Although you can have your fish broiled, sautéed, or baked, the most popular is mesquite grilled. And it's nothing like your home barbecue grill. Try the mesquite-grilled red snapper, tuna, king salmon, or the swordfish, which comes off the grill with a flavor close to steak. Arne's has an excellent bouillabaisse, brimming with fish and shellfish in a saffron broth, and a San Francisco cioppino, a tomato-based fish stew topped with half a lobster. Order gravlax for an appetizer—fresh Norwegian salmon marinated in beer and served with dill mustard sauce, chopped red onion, and capers—or try the escargot ravioli served hot in butter sauce. Arne also serves mesquite-grilled steaks, and range chicken.

Dinner prices go from $10 to $18 for entrees and $5 to $9 for appetizers. Lobsters are $25 and up, according to size. Prices are less at lunch, ranging from $5.50 to $9.50, with an excellent broiled scrod for $5.50.

Arne's is open seven days a week with lunch served from 11:30 a.m. to 3 p.m. and dinner from 5:30 to 11 p.m. Sunday brunch is served from noon until 4 p.m. The oyster bar in a flower-decked gazebo in front of the restaurant is open from 11 a.m. to midnight, serving salads, sandwiches, and some hot seafood dishes, plus specialties from the raw bar.

The **Mass. Bay Co.,** a ship-shape restaurant on the first level of the Sheraton Boston Hotel, 39 Dalton St. (tel. 236-2600), offers New England seafood at its best. They specialize in grilling over mesquite charcoal, a technique that subtly enhances the flavor of the fish whether it be flounder, swordfish, salmon, or shrimp. You can also order your seafood broiled, fried, poached, or steamed. But whatever you order, get some of the great clam chowder. The restaurant also excels in combining pasta dishes with seafood such as mussels or shrimp. The raw bar in the Mass. Bay Lounge is an attractive and popular spot for shellfish and drinks.

The Mass. Bay Co. is open for lunch on weekdays only from 11:30 a.m. to 2:30 p.m., and for dinner daily from 5:30 until 10:30 p.m. Prices at dinner run $11 to $19, and at lunch, $7 to $11.

Turner Fisheries in the Westin Hotel, 10 Huntington Ave., Copley Place (tel. 424-7425), is perhaps best known for winning the Boston Harborfest Chowderfest for three years in a row and being elevated to the Chowderfest Hall of Fame. But the chefs know that there's more to seafood than chowder and they serve some of the freshest fish in town, with the menu changing daily to feature each catch of the day. You might find everything from lemon sole to mahi-mahi, trout to mako shark, lobster to bass; and you can request your choice pan-fried, broiled, grilled, or blackened. All are served with vegetable medley and red-skinned potato. There are comfortable booths if you like privacy, and tables spaced beneath ceiling paddle fans if you like a breeze.

Turner's is open daily from 11 a.m. to 11:30 p.m., except Sunday, when it opens at 10:30 a.m. for brunch (served till 2:30 p.m.). Reservations are recommended. Turner's also serves up live jazz for listening and dancing every night until 1 a.m. in the bar.

FOR BEEF: It's back to the basics again in many of the restaurants in Boston, and the day of the meat-and-potatoes man (or woman) has returned. But it's returned with a style and flair that not only showcases the traditional roast beef and broiled steak but includes some fancy grill work with woodchips that imparts a unique flavor to the food. Try these upper-bracket choices and others that we've listed in the moderate and less expensive sections.

Morton's of Chicago, One Exeter Place (tel. 266-5858), evidently believes that bigger is better. Big cuts of beef, big salads, big potatoes, big bowls of soup, and a really big steak knife for slicing through two inches of beef are all offered. And to make sure you see how big is big, the waiters wheel a rolling cart laden with raw samples of porterhouse steak, double filet mignon, New York sirloin, veal, lamb chops, and swordfish steak to your table. You make your choices, the white-tocqued chefs at the grills prepare them to your taste, and everything turns out tender and extremely flavorful. There are also other items such as whole lemon-oregano chicken, lobster, and fish. And do try the big bowl of black bean soup or the big Gulf shrimp for your appetizer.

Prices are not that big considering the size and quality of the selections. Dinner entrees are $11.95 to $22.95 (vegetable side dishes are à la carte); and lunches run from $6.95 to $16.95. Morton's dining room is tasteful with a blend of brick-and-white colors along with tan leather banquettes and white tablecloths. It is below street level in a new office building at the corner of Boylston and Exeter Streets, and is reached either by the sidewalk stairway or elevators in the building. Dinner is served Monday through Saturday from 5:30 to 11 p.m.; and lunch runs from 11:30 a.m. to 2:30 p.m. Monday through Friday.

The **57 Restaurant,** 200 Stuart St. at Park Plaza (tel. 423-5000), still features the roast beef that made it famous when it was located at 57 Carver St. and was a landmark Boston restaurant. Now located in an elegant rust-and-beige dining room next to the 57 Park Plaza Hotel, it continues to serve succulent ribs and steaks, including an excellent peppercorn sirloin and filet mignon. But there's more than steak on the menu, including our favorite Athenian-shore–style shrimp—a Greek-inspired classic with large gulf shrimp sautéed with whole tomatoes and feta cheese. And the chef has a recipe for actually making liver taste good! All entrees are served with potato, vegetable, and salad. Desserts are worth resigning from Weight Watchers for, especially the grasshopper pie, a crème de menthe chiffon concoction. Figure on $14 to $28 for entrees. Dinner is served from 3 to 11 p.m., Monday through Saturday; and noon to 10 p.m. on Sunday. Lunch hours are 11:30 a.m. to 3 p.m. Reservations are accepted, and there is two-hour validated parking in the adjacent "57" Garage.

There's more than scotch and sirloin at the **Scotch 'n Sirloin,** 77 N. Washington St. (tel. 723-3677). There's an excellent steak-house menu with 17 entrees, unusual decor, and an all-points view of Boston from huge window walls.

Occupying the eighth floor of a former trade building near the Boston Garden sports arena, the restaurant uses the old industrial fittings as focal points. Fire doors have been sprayed bright colors and are now backdrops for the three well-stocked salad bars, structural pipes are exposed, and a drill press and a printing press are reminders of the building's former occupants. Early-1900s photographs and plants and hanging baskets of greenery accent the red-brick walls.

Menus are stenciled on black lunchboxes with prices ranging from $10.95 to $25.95. Portions are large and well prepared. The teriyaki sirloin is excellent, as is the prime rib. Ale-battered fried shrimp, broiled scrod, and swordfish are other good choices. Mushroom caps sautéed in butter are just about the best we've had, and the cheesecake is delicious.

Dinner hours are 5:30 to 10:30 p.m. Sunday to Thursday, till 11:30 p.m. on Friday and Saturday. Reservations are accepted, and there is valet parking but no dress code.

The cocktail lounge features entertainment and dancing Tuesday through Sunday from 9 p.m. to 1:30 a.m. No admission charge for dining room guests.

If you ever thought that cooking over a grill meant lighting a few coals and tossing on the meat, you'll be amazed at what the chefs at **Boodle's** do. Boodles, a British-style hunt club restaurant at the Back Bay Hilton Hotel, 40 Dalton St. (tel. BOODLES), specializes in grilling aged steak, poultry, and fish over the coals. They use mesquite, hickory, sassafras, or applewood on their two grills, and even have a woodchip of the day! (Only mesquite is used at lunch.) The menu is extensive, ranging from grilled duckling to grilled prime rib, from lobster brochette to swordfish. There is also a good selection of appetizers, salads, and soups (not everything is grilled). Two vegetables are included with the main course plus a choice of sauces, butters, and savory condiments. And at dinner you can get a crock of real Boston baked beans.

Entrees at dinner are priced from $9.50 to $26.50, and $7.50 to $16.50 at lunch. Burgers grilled on mesquite are offered at lunch for $8.50.

Boodle's is open seven days a week from 11:30 a.m. to 2:30 p.m. for lunch, and from 5 to 11:30 p.m. for dinner.

THE TOWERS: For the sheer height of luxury we can think of nothing finer than dining in a glass-walled restaurant high above the city. Boston has two towers that rank with the best in the country for the view and the food: the Bay Tower Room and the Top of the Hub.

The **Bay Tower Room,** 60 State St. (tel. 723-1666), is a beautiful glass-walled room overlooking the spectacular panorama of Faneuil Hall Marketplace, the harbor, and the airport. Located on the 33rd floor, it is on eye level with the clock in the Custom House Tower. Tables are arranged in ascending tiers so that every diner shares the view, and candlelight casts a romantic glow on the brass rails and crimson chairs reminiscent of a cruise ship.

The "Creative American Cuisine" is based on traditional ingredients prepared with a new approach. Loin of veal in peppercorn crust has a maple demi-glacé, a combination of sweetness and spice; the roasted rack of lamb comes with a gorgonzola herb crust; and salmon and sole are braided and topped with a ginger sauce. There is one special each evening for diners on a limited diet, and a seasonal vegetable plate with a lemon butter or cheese sauce is also available. All entrees may be ordered broiled, poached, or baked, where possible, and may be requested without sauces. Appetizers include vegetable strudel with peach chutney and smoked salmon cheesecake with caviar. And if you order Caesar salad, your waiter will prepare it tableside as you watch. The menu changes seasonally. Entrees are priced from $19 (for the vegetable plate) to $39.

Dinner is served from 5:30 to 10 p.m., and there's dancing in the Custom House Lounge from 8:30 p.m. Discounted parking is available in the 60 State St. garage under the building after 5 p.m.

For high-style dining—52 stories high—the **Top of the Hub** (tel. 536-1775), at the Prudential Center, is a top choice. The view is spectacular: on a clear day you can see all of Boston below you from the three glass-walled sides of the restaurant and lounge. And at night, the twinkling lights from the city and the airport, plus the starlight, create a special magic. We suggest coming before sunset and lingering over your meal till dark—this way you get the best of both worlds.

The accent is on fresh seafood from the Boston fishing fleet. Sample the grilled swordfish, the shrimp tempura, or the fisherman's platter. The house specialty is a bouillabaisse flavored with saffron and herbs. You can order steak or roast beef if you prefer something other than fish. Entrees are priced from $13 to $18 at dinner, and $5 to $11 at lunch. The lunch menu includes sandwiches, salads, and pastas, along with the seafood entrees. The adjoining lounge, the Hub Cap, has dancing nightly.

Hours are 11:30 a.m. to 2:30 p.m. for lunch Monday through Friday and noon to 3 p.m. on Saturday; and 5:30 to 10 p.m. for dinner Sunday through Thursday, until 11 p.m. on Friday and Saturday. A Sunday buffet brunch is tops from 10:30 a.m. to 2 p.m. Reduced parking rates are available in the Prudential garage after 4 p.m. weekdays and all day on Saturday and Sunday.

MODERATE RESTAURANTS (ENTREES FOR $8 TO $12)

OLD BOSTON: One of the unwritten laws of Boston seems to be that you must not leave town without visiting **Durgin-Park,** 30 N. Market St. (tel. 227-2038), and judging from the mobs of people (approximately 2,000 a day) always waiting in line to get into this restaurant in the Faneuil Hall Market, it's a law that's pretty well obeyed. Durgin-Park has been here forever, and it's now part of the chic new market area (which was built around it), though there's still nothing chic about Durgin-Park: the place is noisy, crowded, and you must share a long table with about ten other patrons. But if you don't expect gracious service, are in a convivial mood, and think that exposed heating pipes are period pieces, then join the long lines of kings and commoners (you'll brush elbows with politicians and business people and market butchers and Back Bay society matrons here) and wait your turn (no reservations) for good, old-fashioned New England food. The food is still of the highest quality, the portions are very large—and after all, food is what you do go to a restaurant for.

If you can, go for dinner (old Boston-ese for the noontime meal), served from 11:30 a.m. to 2:30 p.m., when hearty meals begin at $3. Order Poor Man's roast beef or Yankee pot roast. At supper (served 4 to 9 p.m.) prices range from $5 to $14 à la carte. Try a tremendous slab of prime rib of beef with vegetable. All steaks and chops are broiled on an open fireplace over real wood charcoal. Seafood is received twice daily and fish dinners are broiled to order. Be sure to try Boston baked beans, which must have been invented here. (Buy some to take home at the Beanery in the Marketplace.) Homemade cornbread comes with every meal. For dessert, we staunchly recommend that venerable New England specialty, baked Indian pudding (a molasses and cornmeal concoction, slow baked for hours and hours), luscious with ice cream; or the strawberry shortcake with fresh berries and real whipped cream!

Durgin-Park is open from 11:30 a.m. to 10 p.m. Monday through Saturday, and from noon to 9 p.m. on Sunday. If you're going for "dinner," beat the crowd by getting there before 11:30 a.m. Otherwise, the long line may drive you to drink; happily, a stop at the Gaslight Pub downstairs permits you to wait in a shorter line before being seated in quarters upstairs.

And on Sunday when every other restaurant is serving a brunch of eggs and quiche, you can feast on full-course Durgin-Park dinners at their midday rates until 2:30 p.m. No credit cards accepted.

Note: There is a second and more modern Durgin-Park at Copley Place.

Union Oyster House, 41 Union St., between Faneuil Hall and City Hall (tel. 227-2750), the oldest restaurant in Boston, started serving oysters in 1826 and they're still the best value in town. At the crescent-shaped bar on the lower level, "where Daniel Webster drank many a toddy in his day," you can enjoy the Oyster House sampler, a mixed appetizer of about a dozen pieces of oysters, clams, and scampi, for $11.95 for two (Webster probably paid about 15¢ a dozen). The stalls and oyster bar are still "in their original positions."

From the windows of the upstairs dining room you can look down on City Hall Plaza. Although the view is modern, the food is traditional New England. An oyster stew doused in fresh milk and country butter makes a good beginning. Follow that with a broiled or fried dish such as scrod or salmon, or perhaps shrimp curry or a seafood platter. A complete shore dinner with chowder, steamers, broiled live lobster, salad, corn, and dessert is definitely something to write home about. For dessert, try traditional Boston gingerbread with whipped cream. Prices on entrees are $10, up to $27.95 for the shore dinner. Daily luncheon specials run from $6.25.

Hours are 11 a.m. to 9:30 p.m. Sunday through Thursday, until 10 p.m. on Friday and Saturday. Lunch is served daily to 5 p.m., until 6 p.m. on Saturday.

Jacob Wirth Company has been serving Bostonians for almost 120 years, and is still going strong at 33-37 Stuart St. (tel. 338-8585), near the theater district and the New England Medical Center. The hearty German meals are all reasonably priced and at dinner include Vienna schnitzel, Hungarian goulash, pig's knuckles, and bratwurst and knockwurst along with fish and prime ribs. There are daily specials on the luncheon menu and a large selection of sandwiches and hot meals. Price range for dinner is $8.95 to $11.95 for entrees, with salad included. Sandwiches are $5 to $7.

Open Monday through Saturday, 11:30 a.m. to 10:30 p.m., and Sunday from noon to 10:30 p.m.

Paul and Maria Freddura, owners of the **Daily Catch** in Boston's North End, created such a successful restaurant on Hanover Street that they have opened two branches to meet the demand for Sicilian-style seafood. So now there are three locations: 323 Hanover St. (tel. 523-8567); 261 Northern Ave. (tel. 338-3093), on the Fish Pier; and One Kendall Square, Cambridge (tel. 225-2300). Prices at all branches go from $4 to $12 for appetizers and $10 to $16 for entrees.

Try the North End if you like to "sop-up" atmosphere along with your garlic-flavored mussel sauce and freshly shucked clams. The stove stands in the middle of the small dining room area, and much of the food is served in the skillet in which it was cooked. But the lines form outdoors (no room indoors) for Sicilian-style calamari (squid), clams, mussels, and both broiled and fried fish. For those who love calamari, you can find it served eight different ways here. And if you've never tasted it before, try the fried version or order it with linguini for a good introduction.

The Daily Catch on Northern Avenue, near Jimmy's Harborside, has a stainless-steel kitchen to replace the middle-of-the-room stove (to allow room for more customers) and parking. The food is basically the same as the original restaurant.

The Kendall Square location is the fanciest with a full bar, but the same basic good food and relaxed atmosphere prevail. And though the address is One Kendall Square, it is actually at Hampshire Street and Cardinal Medeiros Avenue.

Hours in the North End are 5 to 10:30 p.m., Monday and Tuesday, and 11:30 a.m. to 10:30 p.m., Wednesday through Sunday. On the Fish Pier, Daily Catch is open from 11:30 a.m. to 10:30 p.m., Sunday through Saturday. At the Kendall Square location, it's open from 11:30 a.m. to 10:30 p.m., Monday through Saturday, and 5 p.m. to 10:30 p.m. on Sunday.

Dini's Sea Grill, One Beacon St. (tel. 227-0380), has been part of the Boston scene for so long that most natives tend to take it for granted. But that's a mistake. We "rediscovered" it recently in its new location (it had been on Tremont Street for eons and eons) and were very impressed with the sparkling new dining room and the extensive array of seafood cocktails, soups, chowders, steaks, chops, and lobster—all six varieties of it. There's an excellent broiled salmon, baked stuffed shrimp, and a seafood platter with lobster, clams, shrimp, and scallops. A seasonal special is fresh shad roe and bacon. Order à la carte or get a complete dinner. Prices range from $7 to $12. Dini's is open weekdays for lunch and dinner from 11 a.m. to 9 p.m.; closed on Sunday.

LE BISTRO, BOSTON STYLE: A bistro is defined as a small, unpretentious café or restaurant in the European style. While many establishments fit that description, some are especially worth noting for their style and excellent food. Here, then, some of the most popular Boston bistros.

One of our favorite places, whatever the season, is the very charming **Another Season,** 97 Mt. Vernon St. (tel. 367-0880), a continental bistro near Charles Street on Beacon Hill. A few steps below street level, it's a romantic hideaway with murals of Gay '90s Paris, flowers, and mirrored walls. Odette Bery, chef and owner, chooses seasonal produce and seafood from nearby markets and creates a menu that may contain Mexican, Italian, or Oriental recipes which she translates with a French nouvelle cuisine accent.

The menu changes monthly, and if you're lucky you might be able to order the salmon citron, poached with lemon, mint, and cream sauce; or the chicken with brie in a sauce of brie, thyme, and cream. The chicken Mexican style with coriander and chilies, and the saddle of lamb with zinfandel and shiitake mushrooms are also excellent. There is always a vegetarian selection, such as eggplant noisette or mushrooms provençale. All entrees are served with vegetables, dinner salad, and home-baked whole-wheat bread. Desserts are among the best in town. There's always something deliciously chocolate—a cake, mousse, or torte—or a fruit dessert, fresh fruit sorbet, and cheeses.

A nice feature of Another Season is that with advance notice the chef will prepare a special meal for those on restricted diets. The restaurant is open for lunch Tuesday through Friday from noon to 2 p.m. with main dishes in the $8 range; and for dinner, Monday through Saturday from 6 to 10 p.m., with entrees priced from $12 to $20.

Rebecca's is one of the "in" spots on Beacon Hill that made its mark a few years back and continues to be one of the most popular bistros in the area. Located at 21 Charles St. (tel. 742-9747), near the Public Garden, it features a menu based on seasonal ingredients, fresh vegetables, and light sauces. Rebecca Caras, owner/chef, puts them all together into delicious entrees, appetizers, and desserts that change daily. The pleasant, brick-walled dining room, highlighted with light wood panels, is open Monday through Saturday from 7:30 a.m. to midnight for breakfast, lunch, and dinner. Sunday, brunch is served from 11 a.m. to 4 p.m., and dinner from 5:30 p.m. to midnight. Entrees range in price from $15 to $19. Lunch is $7 to $8.50.

Also under the Rebecca aegis is **St. Cloud,** 557 Tremont St. (tel. 353-0202), a chic new restaurant with an expensive menu that mixes Mexican, Thai, Mediterranean, and New England cuisines—all very popular with the Yuppie crowd in this South End neighborhood. The decor is a trendy mix of purple and lavender with black latticed ceilings. Entrees are around $25, hors d'oeuvres $4 to $9, and desserts, $5. St. Cloud is open Tuesday through Saturday from 11:30 a.m. to midnight, and until 10 p.m. on Sunday.

Hammersley's Bistro, 578 Tremont St. (tel. 267-6068) in the South End, is a new restaurant that has quickly established itself as one of the outstanding places to eat in town. Created by a husband-and-wife team, Gordon and Fiona Hammersley, Hammersley's has a small dining room with white walls, shiny black seating, and an open kitchen with chefs in bright red baseball caps.

A limited number of entrees are on the menu, but each one is prepared with an emphasis on taste and texture that transforms an everyday dish into a memorable one. For example, the roast chicken that has become a standard on the menu is crispy on the outside, moist inside, enhanced in a marinade of garlic, lemon, and parsley, and served with roast potato, roast onions, and whole cloves of baked garlic that become sweet when cooked. The grilled mushroom and garlic sandwich on country bread features shiitake mushrooms brushed with olive oil, grilled, and heaped on thick slices of bread spread with roasted garlic. Served with tomato garnish or celeriac salad, it makes a wonderful appetizer or light supper entree. There are several seafood dishes, bouillabaisse, an excellent rack of lamb, and occasionally veal and steak served with homemade mashed potatoes. The menu changes seasonally. Some excellent and expensive vintages are featured on the wine list, and wines by the glass are also available.

Prices range from $15.50 to $22 for entrees and $4.50 to $8.50 for appetizers, salads, and soups. Desserts are $4.50 to $5.50.

Hammersley's Bistro is open Monday through Saturday from 6 to 10:30 p.m.; and from 5 to 9:30 p.m. on Sunday. Valet parking is available on Thursday, Friday, and Saturday.

Cornucopia, 15 West St. (tel. 338-4600), near Lafayette Place and the theater district, is one of the status places in town. Good food, classy decor, regular wine tastings, and art show openings attract the diner looking for a special ambience along with the meal.

There are three dining levels in contrasting styles: the informal café floor, the sunny mezzanine spanned by a huge skylight, and the formal top level with working fireplace. The building, once a center for feminists, transcendental thinkers, and poets when it was the home of the Peabody family from 1840 to 1854, has been redesigned by architect Tom Piatt and his wife, Kris, who manages the restaurant.

Cornucopia's colorful menu features "New American Cookery," which translates as light on sauces and flours and strong on fresh ingredients. There are also Italian and French influences in some of the selections and an inspired use of fresh herbs. The menu changes monthly to utilize the best offerings of the marketplace, but there is always a fish, chicken, beef, and vegetarian item, grilled steak, two homemade soups, and a homemade pâté. A nice touch is the listing of a recommended wine with each entree, and the option of "tastes"—two-ounce glasses from the dispenser so you can have a variety of wines with your meal.

Desserts include homey American fare such as strawberry apple pie and rhubarb "fool," plus a continental-style pastry tray. Entrees at dinner are priced from $15 to $25, and at lunch from $8 to $10.

A great deal in the afternoon or evening is the special cafe menu of light fare served from 2 p.m. until closing Tuesday through Saturday. Entrees are about $6.

Cornucopia is open Monday through Saturday from 11:30 a.m. to midnight. Lunch is served Monday through Friday from 11:30 a.m. to 2 p.m.; dinner, Tuesday through Thursday from 6 to 10:15 p.m., until 11 p.m. on Friday and Saturday. The bar is open until midnight.

IN THE THEATER DISTRICT: A cluster of new restaurants has blossomed in the Theater District bringing excitement to the newly revitalized area dominated by the State Transportation Building. Located on Stuart Street and South Charles Street near the Boston Common and Public Garden, they give a new impetus to dining in Boston.

Rocco's, 5 Charles St., South (tel. 723-6800), is a fun place, a slick restaurant that owner Patrick Bowe calls "High Café." However, it is different from other fun places in that it's serious about its food and gives customers an eclectic, whimsical menu prepared from the finest choices in the marketplace. The entrees change monthly and may include anything from a "really great hamburger" to roasted rack of lamb, Jamaican goat stew, a fancy risotto, a hot-and-sour soup with sliced Thai squid, or a simple green salad. There is an excellent selection of wines by the bottle and glass, and the beer list is outstanding too.

The dinning room is lavishly decorated in rococco style (hence the name, Rocco's) with a hand-painted ceiling mural depicting bacchanalian scenes including cherubs and satyrs. Paintings and sculptures (which are for sale) adorn the blue-and-white faux-marble walls, and two massive brass chandeliers hang from the 20-foot ceiling. The ambience is comfortable and unpretentious with a background beat of rock- and pop-music tapes, people in both jeans and formal wear, and everyone, as the owners hope, having a good time.

Dinner entrees are priced from $12.50 to $26; appetizers, salads, and soups, $4 to $8; desserts, $4.25 to $5.50. Luncheon entrees are $6.50 to $9.00. Rocco's is open from 5:30 to 11:30 p.m. every evening, and for lunch and brunch daily from 11:30 a.m. to 3 p.m.

Bnu, 123 Stuart St. (tel. 367-8405), is a wonderful place to go either before or after the theater, or anytime when you want really good food without spending too much money. Everything is fresh—nothing is frozen, microwaved, or left under heating lamps. The kitchen is tiny but so well organized that the chefs prepare terrific entrees, salads, pastas, gourmet pizzas, and desserts with flair. Consider roasted chicken with black peppercorns and crushed chili pepper pods, or fettuccine with grilled shrimp for an evening entree. If you want something lighter try the spinach, mushroom, and cheddar pizza accompanied by panzanella, a popular vegetable salad. At lunch Bnu offers sandwiches, salads, and pastas as well as hot entrees and pizzas. The cannoli is just about the best in town, with ricotta as light as whipped cream piped into a perfect pastry shell.

The dining room is modeled to represent an outdoor café of a 16th-century Italian piazza, with an oil painting of a church in Orvieto painted in faux techniques on one wall. The room is octagonal in shape with two small trellised garden areas by the front windows, and the ceiling is painted blue with small spot lights for stars.

Prices at dinner go from $8 to $16 for entrees, $3.50 to $6.25 for salads and appetizers, and $7.50 to $12 for pizza. The price range at lunch is $5.75 to $8.50 for entrees, $3.50 to $6.50 for appetizers, and $6.50 to $10 for pizza.

Dinner is served seven nights a week: from 5 to 9:30 p.m. on Monday, Tuesday, and Wednesday; until 11:30 p.m. on Thursday, Friday, and Saturday; and until 9 p.m. on Sunday. Lunch is offered from 11:30 a.m. to 2:30 p.m., Monday through Friday, and a light lunch is served 2:30 to 5 p.m. Limited reservations are accepted for pre-theater dining.

Note: Don't look for Bnu in your Italian dictionary. It's the nickname of owner Linda Criniti.

Bennigan's, Stuart and Charles Streets (tel. 227-3754),

dishes up big sandwiches, salads, and hot entrees in a very attractive dining room at City Place in the Transportation Building. For less than $6.95 you can get sweet-and-sour chicken, shrimp Creole, or pasta primavera. And if you're in a hurry, try the Express Lunch, 11 a.m. to 3 p.m.—Bennigan's promises to serve you within 15 minutes or give you lunch free.

Joyce Chen, the celebrated TV cook and Cambridge restaurateur, has opened a second restaurant at 115 Stuart St. at City Place in the Transportation Building (tel. 720-1331). (See our listing under Chinese restaurants.)

SUPER-SAVERS: We're happy to pass along the word that you can dine elegantly—and not too expensively—at some of the finest restaurants in town. All you have to do is make reservations for the early dinner specials usually served between 5 and 7 p.m. on weeknights. Some of the hotels, including the **Marriott Hotel, Long Wharf,** 296 State St., Boston (tel. 227-0800), and the **Westin Hotel,** 10 Huntington Ave., Boston (tel. 424-7425), offer early-bird specials, as do other restaurants in Boston and along the North Shore and the Cape. Since these arrangements are sometimes temporary, we can't list them for you, but we suggest you ask what's available when you call for reservations.

BUDGET RESTAURANTS (ENTREES AROUND $7)

At first you don't know if you're in a restaurant or a toy store at Christmastime. The crowd is elbow to elbow. The model trains circle endlessly overhead on tracks suspended from the ceiling, and they set the mood. **Jimbo's Fish Shanty** is a fun place. "Jimbo" is supposedly a retired hobo who converted an old grotto at 245 Northern Ave. (tel. 542-5600) to a hobo shanty with a line of switchyard food. (Actually, this informal restaurant is run by Charlie Doulos, owner of Jimmy's Harborside across the street.) Bindlestiff (hobo) or not, you'll enjoy the stick food (skewers) threaded with fish or beef, and the fish stew similar to that served across the way at Jimmy's. Favorite dessert is amaretto pie (a mocha ice cream, amaretto liqueur, and chocolate mousse concoction). Prices range from $4 to $10.

You might not expect a budget restaurant in the financial district, but bankers know how to make every penny count. **Brandy Pete's,** at 267 Franklin St. (tel. 439-4165), serves everything in large portions: huge sandwiches, big bowls of soup, and martinis in water glasses (no water, just martini). Also, generous portions of fish, chops, chicken, and steak, priced from $5.95 to $12.50. It serves only "real" food—no freezer, no microwave, everything made fresh and from scratch, except when it's labeled "yesterday's fish chowder" or "yesterday's beef stew." Brandy Pete's serves about 400 people a day from a menu of over 40 entrees.

The martini crowd at lunchtime stands around four deep at the bar. If you like to eavesdrop on financial conversations, get a table near the bar; but if you want to hear your own conversation, ask for seating upstairs.

Open Monday through Friday from 11:30 a.m. to 9 p.m.; closed weekends.

DELICATESSENS: Boston has two delis on a par with the best in New York. One, **Mavens,** is home-grown in Cambridge, and the other, the **Stage Deli,** is a New York import.

Mavens, 95 Winthrop St., Cambridge (tel. 492-DELI), is the creation of two Harvard Law School professors, Alan Dershowitz and Marcus Weiss, who researched the Greater Boston area for years for the perfect Kosher delicatessen. When they couldn't find what they wanted closer than New York City, they opened their own place and stocked it with New York–style Kosher pastrami, corned beef, tongue, frankfurters, and salami. Also on the menu are several East European specialties, smoked fish, roast brisket, stuffed cabbage, noodle kugel, and chicken soup with matzoh balls. Many dishes are named for lawyers and judges and after legal issues—for example, Split Decisions is the name of a soup and half-sandwich special. The decor is nostalgic deli with pictures of famous delicatessens on the wall. Since Mavens is strictly Kosher, no dairy products are allowed, and substitutes for cream and butter are served. Smoking is not allowed either.

Prices for single sandwiches are $5 and up; combination "fresser" sandwiches are $7 to $12; and fish platters are $7.45 to $12.95. Breakfasts are priced from $3 to $7.45. Mavens' hours are 7 a.m. to 1 a.m., Monday through Thursday and on Sunday. On Friday, they close two hours before sundown in observance of the Jewish sabbath, and are closed until one hour after sundown on Saturday.

The **Stage Delicatessen of New York,** a gathering spot for New York celebrities for over 50 years, has brought its authentic deli food (and New York prices) to Boston's theater district. Located in the Quality Inn, 275 Tremont St. (tel. 426-1400), it serves top deli products with specially selected breads, pickles, and relishes. Various sandwiches are named after local celebs, and the menu is great fun to read. Stage Deli serves breakfast, lunch, dinner, and late-evening snacks for theater-goers.

SALAD BARS: There are only a few good salad bars left in town, and they're no longer strictly soup and salad. They're diversified, offering a good deal for bargain hunters, since they now serve sandwiches, quiche, and pasta at low prices. **Souper Salad,** with three locations in Boston and six in the suburbs, is one of the best spots if you want to eat well, but cheaply. All of their restaurants have unlimited salad bar with up to 40 items for $3.95, plus homemade soups, burgers, quiche, meat and vegetarian entrees, sandwiches, and desserts. Beer and wine are available. Boston locations are at 119 Newbury St., 524 Commonwealth Ave. (at Kenmore Square), and 102 Water St. Most are open seven days a week from 11 a.m. to 11 p.m. In Cambridge, Souper Salad is in the Garage at Harvard Square.

The Great Buffet, 71 Bromfield St. (tel. 338-9170), and 82 Broad St. (tel. 357-5696), claims to have Boston's largest salad bar —over 100 items. It also features hot dishes and soups rotated on a regular schedule—five hot entrees, one vegetable, and two soups available each day in addition to the salad bar. Most of the food is priced by weight at 24 cents per ounce, except fruit cups and soups, which are $1 for a cup and $1.65 for a bowl. If you choose carefully, you can get a good meal for under $5. Eat at one of the small tables in the restaurant or have the food packed for take-out.

The Great Buffet is open Monday through Friday from 11 a.m. to 3 p.m.

Many full-service restaurants have good salad bars too, including the **Last Hurrah** in the Omni Parker House, 60 School St., and the **33 Dunster St.** restaurant in Cambridge. **Wendy's,** the fast-food chain, has a good multichoice salad bar.

KOSHER FOODS: Right in the heart of Boston's financial district is the city's only Kosher dairy restaurant. The **Milk Street Café,** 50 Milk St. (tel. 542-2433), on the ground floor of an office building, is large, modern, bright, and busy from 7 a.m. to 3 p.m. Monday through Friday. The menu doesn't mention Kosher, but the sandwiches, soups, croissants, and pastry all have the rabbinical seal of approval. The cheese for quiche, pizza, and sandwiches is even imported from New York, where it is made according to dietary standards. Prices are reasonable, and you can get an entree with soup or salad for under $7. There's a branch in Cambridge at 101 Main St. (tel. 491-8286).

There are two Kosher restaurants in the area serving meat

products: **Rubins,** 500 Harvard St., Brookline (tel. 731-8787), and **Mavens,** 95 Winthrop St., Cambridge (tel. 492-DELI). Rubin's, which has been in business for almost 60 years, serves à la carte or complete dinners (no dairy foods) from 9 a.m. to 8 p.m. except Saturday, and from 8 a.m. until sunset on Friday. Expect your tab to be between $5 and $10.

For detailed information on Mavens, the new kid in town, see our previous section on delis. They are also strictly Kosher and observe the sabbath.

On the North Shore, you can stop at **Lynn Kosher Meat Market & Deli,** 224 Lewis St., Lynn (tel. 599-7220), and they will prepare and pack broiled chicken, chopped liver, hamburgers, and sandwiches, or other Kosher foods for you to eat picnic style as you travel to the beach areas.

NATURAL FOODS: **Country Life Restaurant,** 112 Broad St. (tel. 350-8846), is a vegetarian restaurant with no meat, chicken, fish, or dairy products. But what a great selection of grains, vegetables, fruits, and nuts! A hot entree and a soup is featured each day along with two tremendous salad bars—one with fresh vegetables, tabbouli, and tofu, and one with fresh fruits and nuts. The hot entree and the soup change every day and you can call ahead (tel. 350-8625) to see what they're serving—perhaps oatburgers with home fries, Hawaiian barbecue, spinach quiche, corn chowder, minestrone soup, or some other delicious hot dish. There are always two or three varieties of whole grain breads, herbal tea, grain coffee, and spring water. Diners can make unlimited trips to the buffet tables for the bargain price of $4.99. The fruit bar on its own is only $2.95 a person. Desserts are extra.

Country Life Restaurant is open Monday through Friday from 11:30 a.m. to 3 p.m. The restaurant just added a dinner buffet, Wednesday and Thursday only, 5 to 8 p.m. for $6.95 per person.

Open Sesame, 48 Boylston St., Brookline (tel. 277-9241), a short distance from Huntington Avenue on Rte. 9, is an excellent macrobiotic restaurant. Some of the entrees and sea vegetables are in the Japanese tradition and are worth trying just for the flavor and interesting presentation, even if you're not macrobiotic or vegetarian. Prices are in the moderate range.

Open daily for breakfast from 8 to 11 a.m., and from 11:30 a.m. to 11 p.m. for lunch and dinner. Sunday hours are 4 to 11 p.m.

Note: **Erewhon,** one of the leading purveyors of natural foods, is at 342 Newbury St., and sells sandwiches and a few other take-out items.

TWO OTHER BUDGET BETS: **The Black Rose,** 160 State St. (tel. 742-2286), near Faneuil Hall Marketplace, serves good Irish food, including Mother Sweeney's Sunday buffet brunch from 10 a.m. to 2:30 p.m. for $6.95.

Legal Sea Foods has an **Oyster Bar Café** with oyster bar, take-out counter, and café-style seating area in the Statler office building adjoining its main room in the Park Plaza Hotel. Prices are lower than in the main restaurant.

INTERNATIONAL FAVORITES

You can find food from just about anyplace in the world in Boston, if you look hard enough. And to enable you to spend time eating, rather than looking, we've compiled an international sampling covering all the price brackets.

HUNGARIAN: Café Budapest, 90 Exeter St. (tel. 734-3388), is in the lower level of the Copley Square Hotel, with its own mirrored entrance on Exeter Street. It's a beautiful restaurant with three dining rooms: the elegant Pink Room; the peasant-style Blue Room; and the wood-paneled main dining room, accented with stained glass, ruby goblets, and red leather chairs.

The Hungarian cuisine is among the best in town. If you're splurging, order a full-course dinner for two consisting of a mixed grill of filet mignon, wienerschnitzel, pork chops, and other delights, topped off by a rich pastry and coffee. Well recommended on the à la carte menu are beef Stroganoff, veal gulyas, veal cutlet supreme—or just about any veal dish. Entrees range from about $17 to $30. Whatever else you have, be sure to start with soup. We've heard that the country-style soups are delicious, but we've never been able to pass up the iced, tart cherry soup with Hungarian burgundy wine. For dessert you must have Dobostorte (or strudel) and Viennese coffee.

Dinner is served from 5:30 to 11 p.m. Monday through Thursday, to midnight on Friday and Saturday, and from 1 to 11 p.m. on Sunday. A complete lunch including entree, soup, salad, dessert, tea or coffee is served from noon to 3 p.m. À la carte entrees are also available.

ITALIAN RESTAURANTS: Italian restaurants come in all styles in Boston—the cool, gourmet, northern Italian; the top-class traditional Italian; and the little family restaurants with mama, papa, and all the cousins cooking and serving.

The North End is Boston's "Little Italy," and there on the crowded narrow streets are the restaurants that give it its flavor. The most famous of the lot is **Felicia's,** 145A Richmond St. (tel. 523-9885).

Felicia's food, with entrees going for $8 to $13, is excellent. One of the specialties is chicken Verdicchio, boneless breast of chicken cooked with lemon, mushrooms, artichoke hearts, sautéed in Verdicchio white wine and served with spaghetti or salad. There's a complete dinner that includes the chicken or a veal scaloppine, plus shrimp marinara, fettuccine, salad, dessert, and coffee. Homemade cannelloni is another favorite, especially when filled with scallops and crabmeat and served with a sauce of melted cheese. The upstairs dining room has dark wooden booths, tables with red cloths, and candles that drip into colored patterns over a bottle.

Open daily, 5 to 10 p.m., on Sunday from 2 to 9:30 p.m. There's a fine selection of Italian wines.

When a restaurant is booked to capacity on a Monday evening, which is usually a slow time in Boston, you can be sure it has something special going for it: a top-notch kitchen, dedicated staff, pleasing atmosphere—or a combination of all, as in **Davio's,** the upscale northern Italian restaurant at 269 Newbury St. (tel. 262-4810). Look for the globe light in front.

The enthusiastic, young owner-chef, Steve DiFillipo, has created a continental menu with Italian heritage. Instead of the expected pasta with red meat sauce, you might find veal loin sautéed with balsamic vinegar, sirloin steak with basil/sun-dried-tomato butter, or filet of sole with fresh crabmeat, fontina cheese, and white wine butter sauce. There are usually three special entrees daily, plus a house pâté, homemade pasta, and a ravioli creation. There's also a soup of the day in addition to the always-available superb minestrone. Dessert choices include a white-chocolate cheesecake, an excellent mixed-fruit tart, cake, and gelati. Davio's has a fine selection of fine Italian, French, and California wines, including some rare and expensive old Italian vintages. Half bottles are also available.

Davio's main restaurant is in a downstairs location on Newbury Street, with brick walls, burgundy velvet drapes, and brass fixtures. There are white linens and flowers on the tables and soft music in the background. Prices for dinner entrees range from $15 to $23. Soups are $3.95. Luncheon prices are $9 to $11. Davio's also has an upstairs café with an outside dining terrace in good weather.

Dinner is served nightly from 5 to 10 p.m., until 11 p.m. on Friday and Saturday. Luncheon hours are 11:30 a.m. to 3 p.m. Monday through Saturday. Café hours are 11:30 a.m. to 3 p.m. and 5 to 11 p.m. Valet parking is available.

The owners of **Ristorante Toscano,** 41 Charles St. (tel. 723-4090), call it a neighborhood restaurant, although it's not what we would consider a typical neighborhood eating place. But then the upscale Beacon Hill section of Boston where it is located is not a typical neighborhood, either. Toscano (named after Tuscany) is a warm, friendly place where the Florentine chef prepares a varied Italian menu, including two excellent veal dishes—scaloppine Toscano and lombata alla griglia—an excellent tortellini with ham, cheese, and cream, and a pasta with wild mushroom sauce. In addition to the printed menu, which has chicken, steak, and seafood dishes, there are daily specials recited by the waiters. If you opt for dessert try tiramisu, a lavish concoction of sponge cake with four kinds of cream, mascarpone cheese, espresso, and cognac.

Prices for entrees range from $13.25 to $19; appetizers and pastas, $5.75 to $11.50. At lunch, pastas and entrees are $6 to $10. Dinner is served from 5 to 10:30 p.m. nightly, and lunch is available Monday through Saturday, 11:30 a.m. to 2:30 p.m. Valet parking is available.

And for those little family restaurants we mentioned, it's back to the North End, where you get extremely good values plus food that's on a par with that in many elegant dining rooms.

Sabatino's, 14 Parmenter St. (tel. 367-1504), has southern Italian cooking the way Americans like it—with lots of garlicky tomato sauce and big chunks of Italian bread to mop it up. Entrees run $6 to $12; pastas, $3 to $5. Open Tuesday through Saturday from 11 a.m. till 10 p.m.

The Pushcart, 61 Endicott St. (tel. 523-9616), is in the heart of the Haymarket pushcart district. It's a tiny, friendly place and offers home-style southern Italian cooking, lots of cacciatore and lasagne, but also shrimp, clams, veal, and steak. Prices range from $5.75 to $13.75. Open Tuesday through Saturday from 5 to 10:30 p.m. for dinner.

The **European,** 218 Hanover St. (tel. 523-5694), has reasonably priced complete dinners, a vast menu (you can concentrate on pizzas too), and fast service. It claims to be Boston's oldest Italian restaurant (since 1917). Open seven days from 11 a.m. to 12:15 a.m.

CHINESE RESTAURANTS:
Chinese restaurants in Boston are quite specialized now. You can go for Cantonese-style cooking (eggrolls, spareribs, butterfly shrimp, and sweet-and-sour pork); Szechuan (hot-and-spicy moo shi and yu hsiang); and Mandarin (beef with oyster sauce, moo shu pork, Peking duck), and more subtle flavors of northern Chinese cooking.

And you can go for dim sum which is a star attraction in many restaurants. Basically, it's a traditional midday meal featuring dozens of subtly seasoned, artfully presented dumplings, filled with meats and vegetables, steamed rolls, shrimp balls, spareribs, and items like thousand-layer cake which isn't really cake but a stack of steamed crêpes with a dab of fruit. The waiter wheels a cart laden with tempting bits and pieces up to your table, and you order by pointing (unless you know Chinese). Each piece ranges from about 75¢ to $1.50. As he comes back several times and everything looks so good, however, you can run up a high tab without even trying. When you're finished, the waiter figures the bill by counting the empty serving plates. Three excellent spots for dim sum are **Imperial Teahouse**, 70 Beach St.; **China Pavilion**, 14 Hudson St.; and **Golden Palace**, 14-20 Tyler St. (See descriptions of these restaurants below.)

Although there are Chinese restaurants almost everywhere, Chinatown itself is only a few densely crowded blocks around Beach Street and Harrison Avenue near the Southeast Expressway. Park in Chinatown's garage off the expressway, or at the Lafayette Place shopping center. From there walk down Chauncy Street to Beach Street to Chinatown.

Most Chinese restaurants are open every day, begin serving around 9 a.m., and stay open till 3 a.m. or later. The menus are geared to American palates, but sometimes there's a second menu for Chinese patrons. Ask for it, or tell your waiter you want your meal Chinese style.

Herewith some of our favorite places in and out of Chinatown:

Imperial Teahouse, 70 Beach St. (tel. 426-8439), is our choice for good Cantonese food. Start with the imperial eggroll, stuffed with crabmeat, mushrooms, ham, scallions, chicken, and bamboo shoots, or the eight delights soup, a light broth filled with seafood. Among the restaurant's most popular entrees are braised duck and char siu ding, an enormous production with pork cubes, straw mushrooms, vegetables, and cashews. We could become addicted to the shrimp, baked in shells and served with green peppers and scallions. Prices are moderate. Open from 9 a.m. to 2 a.m. daily. Dim sum is served till 3 p.m.

Golden Palace Restaurant and Teahouse, 14-20 Tyler St. (tel. 423-4565), is an ornate establishment, serving Hong Kong cuisine. The food isn't the usual American-Chinese fare, since this is home base for many of the local Chinese. Good bets are the fried pork chop Peking style, and the shrimp dinners. The dim sum, served daily from 9 a.m. to 3 p.m., is wonderful. Golden Palace is open from 9 a.m. to 11:30 p.m., and the prices range from about $5 to $15. The lunch menu offers some good, inexpensive items.

China Pavilion, 14 Hudson St. (tel. 542-1177), is where we were introduced to dim sum and the intricacies of choosing the plumpest dumplings, the sweetest shrimp bits, and the best noodles by Chinese cookbook author and teacher Nina Simonds. This unpretentious and very busy Cantonese restaurant is also a good choice for lunch or dinner, with specialties like lemon chicken and clams in black bean sauce. Entrees are reasonable at $6 and up. Open Monday to Saturday from 9 a.m. to 3 a.m., to midnight on Sunday.

For Chinese food away from Chinatown we recommend a little hideaway right on Boylston Street in Boston, across from the Prudential Center. **Chiu's Garden,** a Mandarin restaurant with Hunan and Szechuan cuisine, is down a flight of stairs at 757 Boylston St. (tel. 262-8978). Prices are low and the food is excellent. Luncheon specials (Monday to Friday) even include free soup. Chiu's opens at 11:30 a.m. on weekdays and at 2:30 p.m. on Saturday and Sunday. Closing time is 10 p.m. weekdays, 11 p.m. on Saturday.

Joyce Chen, the celebrated TV cook and cookbook author, offers authentic cuisine from China's different regions including Peking-Mandarin, Szechuan-Hunan, Shanghai, and Canton in her two local restaurants—390 Ringe Ave., Cambridge (tel. 492-7373), and in the theater district at 115 Stuart St., Boston (tel. 720-1331).

We've enjoyed dinners there with such exotic dishes as sizzling Peking five willow fish smothered in carrots, red onions, bamboo shoots, black mushrooms, and ginger; and Lake Dongting shrimp with a sauce made from puréed chicken and egg whites. The wonton soup is delicious. So is the octopus, Hunan style (cold). Figure $7.50 to $12 for entrees.

Both restaurants have all-you-can-eat luncheon buffets daily, and Cambridge has a dinner buffet every Tuesday and Wednesday from 6 to 8:30 p.m. A special vegetarian buffet is offered on Mondays. Joyce Chen restaurants are open from noon to 10:30 p.m., Sunday through Thursday, and from noon to 1:30 a.m. Friday and Saturday.

If you associate Chinese food with take-out in a paper box, turn in your chopsticks and eggroll and try the glamorous new restaurant, **Mr. Leung,** 434 Boylston St. (tel. 236-4040). Here in a contemporary room with hundreds of tiny spotlights in the ceiling, shiny black walls, and black plates on white cloths, tuxedoed waiters serve elegant Chinese food with practiced professionalism.

The menu is based on several styles of Chinese cooking and lists such standards as honey barbecued spareribs and pan fried raviolis plus esoteric tea-smoked duck, Peking duck, lamb with fresh ginger root, and "grape cluster" sea bass. And if everything on the menu sounds so appealing that you just can't pick and choose, do as we did and order a tasting dinner where you are served four appetizers, a soup, five entrees, a dessert, and tea or coffee for $32 per person (minimum of two). Of course these are sampling portions, but combined they make a good size meal. Or try the Boston seafood dinner with nine selections including lobster for the same price. À la carte entrees are $15 to $18; appetizers, $4.50 to $8.

The same gracious service is available at lunch when entrees are priced from $7.50 to $9.50; and a luncheon special combination including entree, hot-and-sour soup, spring roll, and fried rice is only $6.95.

Mr. Leung serves dinner Sunday through Thursday from 6 to 10 p.m., and Saturday from 6 to 11 p.m. It is open for lunch Monday through Friday from noon to 3 p.m. Sunday brunch is served from noon to 4 p.m. The dining room is down a flight of stairs from the sidewalk level, but may also be reached by elevator from an adjacent building. (The valet in charge of parking will show you the way.)

JAPANESE RESTAURANTS: Japanese restaurants are now rivaling or even surpassing Chinese restaurants in popularity. And the sushi bar is closing ranks with the traditional raw bar in claiming devoted followers. Sushi and sashimi are presentations of raw fish served either in artfully arranged slices or rolled over rice that has been marinated in vinegar. Sashimi is usually cut into quarter- or half-inch slices or perhaps shaped to look like a flower, served with hot green horseradish and soy sauce, and eaten with chopsticks. The bite-size cakes of sushi are created by highly trained specialty chefs who roll fish, shellfish, or vegetables over rice or nori seaweed into low-cal finger food served with garnishes of Japanese white radish, shiso (a delicate herb), grated fresh ginger, or other spicy condiments. They look beautiful on the platter, and taste good too. Sushi/sashimi can be served as a first course at your table or at the sushi bar in many restaurants.

Restaurant Suntory, 212 Stuart St. (tel. 338-2111), is the first restaurant on the American mainland owned by Suntory, Ltd., Japan's largest liquor company, and joins a chain of distinguished restaurants in such cities as Singapore, London, and São Paulo. Four and a half million dollars was poured into this showplace, which boasts three floors with totally different dining presentations, beautifully appointed rooms with Japanese art of gallery quality, and a sophisticated Japanese cuisine.

The sushi bar and cocktail lounge are on the first level, with picture-perfect sushi presentations. The shabu-shabu room on the second floor is the most elegant, with dark wood tables trimmed in copper and a built-in electric burner in the center of the table. If you order shabu-shabu, the waitress places a large pot of broth on the burner in which you cook vegetables and seafoods, and then enjoy the flavored broth. We chose the ishiyaki, which involves cooking beef and seafood on a super-hot rock. It's a do-it-yourself dish where you place the food on the rock, wait for it to sizzle, dip it in sauce and enjoy while you cook another fine morsel. The third floor is the teppanyaki room, where guests sit around a grill as meat and seafood are sautéed in seconds by Japanese grill chefs.

Diners can order from the full menu or choose multi-course shabu-shabu and teppanyaki dinners priced from $37 to $40. Entrees are $12.75 to $22. Appetizers are $6 to $10 and sushi and sashimi plates are $14 to $21 (or order by the piece). Full lunches are $10 to $18.

Dinner is served Monday through Thursday from 6 to 10 p.m., Friday and Saturday from 6 to 10:30 p.m., and Sunday from 5:30 to 9:30 p.m. Lunch, Monday through Friday, is from 11:30 a.m. to 2 p.m.

Agatha, 142 Berkeley St. (tel. 262-9700), has built an excellent reputation with both grilled and skewered selections and regular entrees. In the popular Japanese robatayaki style, meat, poultry, seafood and vegetables are tastefully arranged on skewers, grilled over hot Japanese charcoal and served as an entree or à la carte.

A skewer entree served with rice, miso soup, and salad might contain chicken, salmon, shrimp, swordfish, scallion and mushrooms, or could be an all-vegetable combination. Standard entrees include tempura, teriyaki and katsu dishes, and sashimi. We found the "Lunch Box," a presentation of skewers and tempura on a beautiful lacquered tray a visual and tasteful delight. It is served with miso soup, rice, salad, fruit, and pickles.

Dinner prices for entrees range from $9.75 to $14.75. Skewers at dinner are $10.75 to $15.95. Lunch boxes are priced from $5.25 to $7.75, and other luncheon selections run from $5 to $8.25.

Agatha is an attractive restaurant decorated in an understated Japanese style with lovely bowls, vases, and pottery. It is open Monday through Saturday from 5 to 10:30 p.m. for dinner; and Monday through Friday from noon to 2:30 p.m. for lunch. Valet parking is available from 6 p.m. to closing. (Agatha is named after the British mystery writer, Agatha Christie, and is appropriately located next to the Central Boston Police Headquarters in the Pledge of Allegiance Building.)

Another fine Japanese restaurant is **Tatsukichi,** 189 State St.

(tel. 720-2468), just one street over from the mélange of fast-food places at Faneuil Hall Marketplace. It's a favorite with the area's Japanese community and specializes in sushi, sashimi, and pot-cooked dinners. Entrees range from $8 to $15. Dinner hours are 5 to 10 p.m. Monday through Saturday.

Sakura-Bana means cherry blossom in Japanese. But **Sakura-Bana,** the little restaurant at 57 Broad St. (tel. 542-4311) in Boston's financial district, is not a demure little cherry blossom. It's a lively, casual place with good food, Japanese beer, and sake. There are Japanese hot dishes on the menu, and the expected teriyaki, yakitori, and tempura; but the main attraction is the sushi bar. It's open for dinner from 5 to 10 p.m. Sunday through Thursday, to 11 p.m. on Friday and Saturday. Also open for lunch Monday through Friday from 11:30 a.m. to 2:30 p.m. Prices range from $5 to $15.

ORIENTAL: We've always loved the ambience at **Kon Tiki,** in the Sheraton Boston Hotel & Towers, 39 Dalton St. (tel. 236-2000), with the small bridge, waterfall, and tropical fish at the entrance leading to a red-and-gold dining room. The new Oriental cuisine matches the elegance of the room. The specialties on Kon Tiki's menu include Szechuan, Cantonese, and Mandarin delicacies, and Madras and Bombay curries. Start with a sampler platter of appetizers that includes honey barbecued ribs, Shanghai eggrolls, and puffed shrimp. Then on to an entree such as Paradise Plate (shrimp, lobster, and scallops with cilantro sauce) or moo goo gai pan chicken and vegetables. And don't forget the frothy tropical drinks.

Kon Tiki is open for dinner only, Monday through Saturday from 5 until 11:30 p.m. Prices range from $13 to $20.

GREEK: The **Paramount Steak House** is a small cafeteria at 44 Charles St. (tel. 523-8832) that rates big in the good Greek food department. A heaping souvlaki platter of barbecued lamb, rice pilaf, Greek salad, and bread runs about $5, and there are good chicken and beef dishes, spinach pie, and sandwiches. Paramount is a friendly place that attracts many of the Beacon Hill natives and politicians from the nearby State House. Hours are 7 a.m. to 10 p.m. seven days a week.

MEXICAN: Mexican food is hot stuff in Boston these days, and taco places are almost as numerous as pizza parlors. However, you can also enjoy more sophisticated Mexican dining at places like:
Casa Romero, 30 Gloucester St., Back Bay (tel. 536-4341),

with the entrance in the adjoining alley, has authentic Mexican cuisine, with some dishes on the spicy-hot side for the true aficionado, and other regional dishes that are somewhat milder for those not yet initiated into south-of-the-border cooking. Señor Romero or one of the waiters will be happy to describe the ingredients used in preparation. The specialties include a very good mole poblano (chicken in a chocolate sauce), camarones Veracruz (giant shrimp sautéed in a spicy tomato sauce), and puerco adobado (pork tenderloin marinated in oranges, tamarind, and smoked peppers). A wonderful dessert is bananas flambé prepared tableside. Price range for entrees is $8 to $16.

The atmosphere at Casa Romero is handsome colonial Mexico: high-backed leather chairs, charming pottery, artwork everywhere, inlaid tiles, and flowers. Dinner is served from 5 to 10 p.m. Sunday through Thursday, till 11 p.m. on Friday and Saturday.

Some of the best foods are found in little basement restaurants (the rents are lower and more money can be used to stock the kitchen). One example is **Sol Azteca**, 914A Beacon St., at the Boston-Brookline line (tel. 262-0909). The three dining rooms in this below-ground-level Mexican restaurant have white stucco walls, orange chairs, and some beautiful Mexican articles for decoration. But the focus is primarily on the food. There are the traditional dishes—tacos, tostadas, and enchiladas—which may be enjoyed in a combination of two if you'd like to try a bit of everything, and there are the chef's specialties which make Sol Azteca worth writing about. For example, shrimp in coriander sauce, and Puerco en Adobo, a pork tenderloin dish marinated in orange juice and chipotle peppers. All entrees include rice, refried beans, and marinated red cabbage. And to cool the flames of the spicy dishes, there's a superb red sangría. Entrees are in the $10 to $16 range.

Sol Azteca is open for dinner only, Monday through Thursday from 6 to 10:30 p.m., on Friday and Saturday from 5:30 to 11 p.m., and on Sunday from 5 to 10 p.m.

We recommend **Acapulco**, 266 Newbury St. (tel. 247-9126), for inexpensive Mexican food superior to that at the fast-food joints. This is a no-frills place with spicy but not torrid food, and good Mexican beer. Two sidewalk patios for outdoor dining are open in warm weather. Open Monday through Saturday from 10:30 a.m. to 9:30 p.m. and Sunday from 1 to 6 p.m. Dinners cost from $6 to $10. Olé!

THAI AND BURMESE: The cooking of Thailand may be considered a cross between Chinese and Indian cuisine, mixed with hot peppers, garlic, coriander, and lemon grass, and then stirred in its own melting pot with coconut milk to produce an individual style. It is usually spicy hot, unless you ask for the entree to be "cooled down" a bit. If you order a curry dish, it is marked to indicate the degree of hotness. Our favorite restaurants had lots of rice and spices and everything nice.

Some like it hot, and head for **Thai Cuisine,** 14A Westland Ave. (tel. 262-1485), a small restaurant near Symphony Hall. Even though we prefer our food on the "cooler" side, we've been tempted by many of their dishes. For instance, tom ka kai is a creamy, refreshing chicken soup which has been raised to gastronomic heights. The boned half duck in a hot, red curry sauce is the specialty of the house. It is served with a garnish of eggplant, peppers, and green peas. The beef saté is another favorite—chunks of beef and cucumber on a skewer served with a spicy peanut sauce.

Thai Cuisine serves dinner from 5 to 10 p.m. Monday through Friday and Sunday, and until 10:30 p.m. on Saturday. Monday through Friday lunch is served from 11:30 a.m. to 3 p.m. Prices range from $2 for soups and appetizers and from $5 to $10 for entrees.

Bangkok Cuisine, 177A Massachusetts Ave. (tel. 262-5377), was Boston's first Thai restaurant, and it is still first choice for many devotees of this Southeast Asian cuisine. But unless you've built up a tolerance for incendiary dishes, start with something milder such as sweet-and-sour chicken. If you're more daring, try the red shrimp curry. The dining room with its stained-glass skylight only seats 50, and no reservations are taken. Entrees range from $6 to $12. Lunch is served from 11:30 a.m. to 3 p.m. and dinner hours are Monday through Friday from 5 to 10 p.m., on Saturday and Sunday to 10:30 p.m.

You can now take two roads to Mandalay, Boston's first Burmese restaurant. The original **Mandalay,** 329 Huntington Ave. (tel. 247-2111), near Northeastern University and Symphony Hall, is an unpretentious place below street level. The new Mandalay, 143 First St., Cambridge (tel. 876-2111), near Lechmere Sales, is much larger with four dining areas that can seat 150. But both offer the wonderful Burmese food that has won Mandalay a host of loyal patrons.

The cuisine is a little bit Indian, a little bit Chinese, a little bit Thai, and every bit delicious. Start with the chicken soup, a combination of chicken, coconut, coriander, and noodles; taste "sar moo sar," which are beef turnovers with curried onions; and enjoy roast lamb, marinated in lemon juice and served on a bed of onions. The chef's curry powder used with beef and chicken dishes is a blend of 17 herbs and spices. The menu in Cambridge is more extensive than in Boston, and the prices are slightly higher but still in the inexpensive to moderate range. Prices in Cambridge are $5.50 to $15.50; in Boston, $5.50 to $9.25.

Hours are 11:30 a.m. to 10 p.m., until 11 p.m. on Friday and Saturday. Both restaurants serve dinner only on Saturday and Sunday starting at 5 p.m.

INDIAN: Indian cuisine is rich and varied, with many adaptations according to region. Southern India is predominantly Hindu and basically vegetarian; northern and central India have a cuisine based on meat with vegetables served as accompaniments.

The Tandoor at Lafayette Place, Downtown Crossing (tel. 542-5572), is a very attractive restaurant in the courtyard of Lafayette Place decorated in tones of peach and soft green. And it specializes, as its name implies, in the tandoori style of Indian cooking, in which meat and poultry are prepared in a charcoal tandoor oven. Many other basic Indian dishes are on the good-sized menu, including lamb, shrimp, and chicken with the appropriate spices and flavorings.

The Tandoor is open from 11:30 a.m. to 2:30 p.m. for lunch and 5:30 to 8 p.m. for dinner. Prices range from $5.25 to $12.

Consider these excellent Cambridge restaurants, too; the decor might not be fancy, but they're all rated highly by the locals. **Ashoka,** 991 Massachusetts Ave. (tel. 661-9001), **India Restaurant,** 1780 Massachusetts Ave. (tel. 576-2111); **Oh Calcutta!,** 468 Massachusetts Ave. (tel. 576-2111); **Gandhi Restaurant,** 704 Massachusetts Ave. (tel. 491-1104); and **Passage to India,** 1900 Massachusetts Ave. (tel. 497-6113).

BOSTON CAFÉS

OUTDOOR CAFÉS: If you, like us, love the outdoor cafés with the bright umbrellas along the sidewalk and the continental feeling, check this list of where to have a snack, a glass of wine, or a cup of cappuccino. The best place to do your dining and people-watching is Newbury Street in the Back Bay, where the sidewalk cafés blossom in every block.

Magic Pan, 47 Newbury St., is one of the most attractive cafes with umbrellas and plantings setting off the terrace area. Lunch, dinner, and cocktails are served until late evening.

Café Florian, 85 Newbury St., the oldest and most authentic sidewalk café in Boston, is perfect for leisurely sipping of European coffees and exotic teas, wine, or beer, and for dining on light meals and continental entrees. Opens at 8:30 a.m. for breakfast and serves until 11 or noon; dinner is served until 10 p.m.

NOTHING COULD BE FINAH (THAN DINNER IN A DINER): Nostalgia leads us many places—even to the diner of the 1940s and '50s, with its neon sign, blueplate specials, and jukeboxes. We've tried several diners and come up with a favorite: The Blue Diner in Boston.

The Blue Diner, 215 South St. (tel. 338-4639), near South Station at the corner of Kneeland St., goes back to 1947. The booths and counters have been recently restored and fresh blue paint applied, but it is still the traditional diner with vintage rock and jazz on the jukebox and a music selector at each booth. There are blueplate specials daily, including good old diner macaroni and cheese, meatloaf, and franks and beans. You can opt for a burger with perfect French fries, grilled fish, or barbecue plate, or even go fancy with sirloin steak. Eggs, bagels, omelets, and muffins are standard for breakfast. We liked the huge French Arcadian buckwheat and wheat-flour griddle cakes called Ployes, preceded, of course, by freshly squeezed orange juice.

Entree prices for dinner go from $5.95 to $12.95; luncheon sandwiches and blueplate specials run $2 to $5, and you can get a hearty breakfast for about $3. Hours are 6 a.m. to 10 p.m., Monday through Thursday, and until midnight on Friday. The staff sleeps late on Saturday and Sunday, so the diner opens at 8 a.m. and 10 a.m. respectively. A Sunday brunch is served from 10 a.m. to 4 p.m.

Travis Restaurant, 135 Newbury St., is a "take-out" place. You can take out your hamburgers and sandwiches to the tables and chairs out front. Informal and inexpensive.

DuBarry, 159 Newbury St., a charming French restaurant, has a hideaway courtyard surrounded by a high wall. A very romantic place for dinner.

At the **Harvard Bookstore Café,** 190 Newbury St., a café in a bookstore, you eat surrounded by books. When the weather turns warm, the café expands out to the street; the books stay indoors unless you want to buy one to read at your table. They serve hot entrees, soups, sandwiches, cheeses, pâté, and dessert. And they're open from 8 a.m. to 11 p.m.

Davio's, the popular Italian restaurant at 269 Newbury St., also has an upstairs café with an outside dining terrace, where they serve gourmet pizzas, antipasto, calzone, spaghetti, and light entrees.

If you're sightseeing along the Freedom Trail, try the terrace café at **Maison Robert,** 45 School St. Named Ben's Café for the statue of Ben Franklin there, it is open for lunch, afternoon snacks, cocktails, and dinner.

The waterfront is a perfect spot for outdoor dining, and you'll find tables and chairs alongside many of the restaurants. We like **The Winery** on Lewis Wharf, which has a view of the ocean from its brick terrace, and musicians to serenade you on some enchanted evenings. One of the busiest waterfront cafés, both indoor and out, is **Tia's Seafood** next to the Marriott Hotel. Get an outdoor table under a colorful umbrella and enjoy the ocean breezes and the fascinating assemblage of people strolling along. The food is good too. **Rachel's Terrace** at the Marriott has a spectacular harbor view, and serves light, casual meals.

And of course the outdoor cafés at Faneuil Hall Marketplace are just the best people-watching spots in Boston with their view of the shopping areas, the busy plaza, and the flower markets. **Cricket's** in the South Market Building has a glassed-in palm court filled with greenery. A delightful place to eat large salads, sandwiches, desserts, and complete meals. In the evening and during the weekend brunch there's good piano music. Come warm weather and a patio is opened onto the marketplace. The **Café at Lily's,** styled in the manner of a Parisian café, serves light meals from early morning until late at night, including soup, quiche, salad, seafood, and beef. Try some of the dessert coffees and pastries too. Enjoy your meal in the market building or on the outdoor terrace. The **Bar at Lily's** is a very popular singles spot looking out on the North Market. Listen to the piano while you sip your cocktails.

AFTERNOON TEA: A spot of tea served mid-afternoon in a small café or lounge is a lovely way to relax. And in Boston it's done in style in some of the nicest hotels. You can choose the elaborate full tea, English set tea, or high tea (frankly we've never been able to find out the difference), the less formal light tea, tea with scones or pastry or just a cup o' tea. They all consist of brewed tea, and the price differential is in what you choose to go with the tea. When served properly, there is an extra pot of hot water to lighten the tea if it gets too strong.

Afternoon tea at the **Ritz-Carlton Hotel,** 15 Arlington St. (tel. 536-5700), is a long-established Boston tradition. This is a full tea with thinly sliced finger sandwiches, scones, preserves, and selections from the hotel's delicious pastry tray. It is served daily in the beautiful Ritz Lounge from 3 to 5:30 p.m. A harpist provides background music from 4 to 5:30 p.m. Price is $12.50 for full tea, or you can order à la carte.

The Bristol Lounge at the **Four Seasons Hotel,** 200 Boylston St. (tel. 338-4400), has full tea with finger sandwiches, scones with double Devon cream and homemade preserves, a fruit tartlett, and English tea breads for $8. Light tea at $6 comes with French pastry, fruit tartlett, and tea bread; and for $5 you can have tea with Scottish scones, Devon cream, and preserves. Served daily from 3 to 4:30 p.m.

The **Harbor View Lounge** at the Boston Harbor Hotel, 70 Rowes Wharf (tel. 439-7000), serves a delightful afternoon tea not far from the site of the historic Boston Tea Party. Two services are offered: the complete tea, with assorted tea sandwiches, petit French pastries and tea cakes, scones, Devonshire cream, and fruit preserves is $15; the light tea, served without the sandwiches, is $11. Both are offered from 2:30 to 4:30 p.m. daily with a pianist or harpist providing background music.

The Copley Tea Court in the **Copley Plaza Hotel,** 138 St. James Ave. (tel. 267-5300), serves English set tea for $7.25. It includes finger sandwiches, scones with whipped cream, and preserves, and perhaps some fresh fruit, such as strawberries.

The **Colonnade Hotel,** 120 Huntington Ave. (tel. 424-7000), has a Tea at the Café menu from which you can order tea and desserts à la carte in mid-afternoon. There are English scones, tea cakes, and French pastries, and the most delicious whipped cream ever! Tea is $1.50 and other dessert items are $3.50 to $5.

In the West Wing of the Museum of Fine Arts, 465 Huntington Ave., the **Galleria Café** (tel. 267-9300) is part of the plan to make the museum a social place as well as an art center. Little tables are set by the ficus trees near the gift shop, where you can sip tea, coffee, or wine and have arty little pastries and snacks on your way to or from the galleries.

THE BREAKFAST MENU

There's a lot to choose from when you breakfast in Boston, everything from the "power breakfast" in the lovely hotel dining room to the grab-it-and-run take-out. Some of the more interesting possibilities include:

Oca Nera, 21 Beacon St. (tel. 720-4500), is a friendly little restaurant next to the State House. You can have a muffin and coffee, or an Italian style breakfast, with caffè latte or cappuccino, croissant, brioche, and panettone with citron and raisins. And you can add scrambled eggs with sausage or bacon, fontina, and prosciutto. Breakfast hours are Monday through Friday from 8 to 10:30 a.m.

The **Milk Street Café,** 50 Milk St. (tel. 542-2433), opens for breakfast at 7 a.m. and serves a delicious all-dairy menu. Also open in Cambridge at 101 Main St. (tel. 491-8286).

For a hearty cafeteria-style breakfast, try **Ann's Cafeteria,** 250 Huntington Ave. (tel. 266-1980), near Symphony Hall. They serve an excellent feta cheese omelet with home fries and toast, and good French toast and griddle cakes at reasonable prices. Open from 6:30 a.m. to 7 p.m. The breakfast menu is available all day.

Stocks and Bonds, 53 State St. in the Exchange Building (723-8508), serves breakfast from 6 to 8 a.m. to a clientele of lawyers, bankers, and brokers who demand both good quality and service. Here you can watch the latest Wall Street trading figures flashed along the wall. Open until 11 p.m., Monday through Saturday.

In the North End, take coffee at one of the cafés, perhaps **Café Paradisio,** 29 Hanover St.; **Caffè Pompeii,** 280 Hanover St.; or **Modern Pastry,** 257 Hanover St. And in Chinatown you can have a dim sum breakfast at many of the big or little restaurants in the area.

You can find the **Steaming Kettle,** 65 Court St., by looking for the large gold-leafed solid copper kettle suspended over the entrance. A Boston symbol since 1875, the constantly steaming kettle holds 227 gallons of water. The restaurant is a popular spot for breakfast (and lunch).

The **Harvard Bookstore Café,** 190 Newbury St., opens for continental breakfast at 8 a.m. It's a good place to have that croissant and coffee.

Il Dolce Momento, 30 Charles St., best known for ice cream, opens at 8 a.m. for fancy coffees and continental breakfast. Try Dutch breakfast with ham, cheese, and smoked fish; the sfogliatelle and ventaglia; or some European sugared puff pastries.

Now for that "power breakfast." You can breakfast in high style in some of the best hotel dining rooms, where Boston's entrepreneurs often cook-up deals while the chef cooks-up their eggs. Naturally it's expensive, and you might have to take your other meals at McDonald's, but go ahead and splurge.

Aujourd'hui, at the Four Seasons Hotel, 200 Boylston St., serves weekday breakfast from 7 to 11 a.m., and offers, in addition to the regular omelets, cereals, and breakfast meats, an "alternative-cuisine breakfast" for diet-conscious patrons. **Café Fleuri** in the Meridien Hotel, 250 Franklin St., serves breakfast from 7 to 11 a.m. in a skylit, bright, and pretty room, with a selection that includes eggs Benedict, layered eggs with a fondue of vegetables, and omelets with smoked salmon and sour cream. The **Ritz Café** in the Ritz-Carlton Hotel, 15 Arlington St., is an intimate breakfast room serving from 6:30 to 10:30 a.m. You can expect the traditional Ritz service and the feel of luxury that goes with this fine hotel.

THE BOSTON BUFFET BRUNCH

Breakfast, lunch, afternoon tea, with a Bloody Mary or champagne thrown in for kicks—that's Boston's Sunday buffet-brunch picture. It's a good value too, for that one meal can last you through the day. We're listing some of the most popular for you:

The most magnificent brunch of all is served at the **Ritz-Carlton Hotel,** 15 Arlington St. (tel. 536-5700), every Sunday in the beautiful main dining room where a large ice sculpture of the Ritz lion surrounded by flowers highlights the center table. Before you make your selections from the myriad of hot and cold offerings arranged in several serving areas, your waiter pours French champagne and serves caviar. Then you can choose delicacies such as oysters on the half shell, gravlax, seafood mousse, sturgeon, assorted pâtés, soup, roast beef carved to order, lamb, chicken curry, pastas, crêpes, omelets to order, quiche, salads, and hot and cold vegetables. Later, it's on to the dessert table for pastries, fruit tarts, cakes, cheese, and fruit. Selections vary from week to week, and though it's a self-service buffet, there's a waiter to help you, a busboy to keep the table immaculate and fine chamber music in the background. Reservations are necessary and are taken for 11 a.m. to 3 p.m. Brunch is priced at $34 for adults and $17.50 for children.

The Sunday brunch at **Aujourd'hui** in the Four Seasons Hotel, 200 Boylston St. (tel. 338-4400), is a bountiful New England –style buffet served in a gracious dining room with a view of the Public Garden. Beautifully decorated serving tables are piled high with pâtés, salads, smoked and steamed fish, roast sirloin, chicken, lobster, egg dishes, waffles, and a fabulous assortment of desserts. Many of the items change on a weekly basis, but they're always terrific. Sunday brunch is available from 11 a.m. to 2:30 p.m., and costs $30 for adults and $17 for children. Reservations are recommended.

Located on Boston's historic waterfront, the **Rowes Wharf Restaurant** at the Boston Harbor Hotel, 70 Rowes Wharf (tel. 439-7000), offers a traditional American brunch buffet of both fresh and smoked seafood, carved prime rib and rack of lamb, seasonal garden salad, soused shrimp, and regional specialty items. Also featured are omelets made-to-order, Belgian waffles, freshly baked pastries, breakfast breads, and desserts. Served Sunday from 10 a.m. to 3 p.m., the brunch costs $24 for adults and $12 for children. When you make reservations, be sure to ask for a table over-looking the harbor.

The brunch at **Harbor Terrace** (tel. 227-0800), in the Marri-ott Hotel at Long Wharf, is like a gala buffet on board a cruise ship, for you have an ocean view along with more than 70 hot and cold items and a glass of champagne. Children under 12 are half price. Brunch hours are 10 a.m. to 2:30 p.m.

An elegant brunch is served at **Parker's**, 60 School St. (tel. 227-8600), with two reserved seatings at 11 a.m. and 1:30 p.m. It's a lavish meal, with finnan haddie, quiche, bacon, eggs, melons, cheeses, and delicious mousses for dessert. The tables are set beau-tifully, and there's soft background music. Adults pay $21.50, children pay $10.75.

One of the most delightful places for Sunday brunch is the **Café Fleuri** at the Hotel Meridien, 250 Franklin St. (tel. 451-1900). The setting is an elegant garden court, light and airy, with lots of greenery. The food is just as elegant, with a hot and cold buffet befitting the Meridien's French background. We've known people, though, who have been tempted to indulge exclu-sively at the sweets table. There are two seatings, at 11 a.m. and 1:30 p.m., at a charge of $20.50 with a complimentary mimosa. Reservations accepted.

One of the top choices (and not only because it's a 52 stories over Boston on top of the Prudential Tower) is the **Top of the Hub** (tel. 536-1775). You don't have to choose, so take a little of everything—eggs, sausage, chicken, vegetable, fruits, salad, cheese, and steamship-round. There's a hot chafing dish selection, and an array of desserts and pastries. Served between 10 a.m. and 2:30 p.m., the cost is $13.95 for adults and $5.95 for children un-der 10.

The tables at the Sunday buffet brunch at the **Bennett St. Café,** 1 Bennett St., Cambridge, in the Charles Hotel (tel. 864-1200), stretch through two dining areas with a seemingly endless display of food. And what variety! Salads, pâtés, sashimi, shrimp, cheeses, bagels and lox, hot entrees, roast beef, and an om-elet bar where you select your fillings and watch the chef deftly flip the omelet pan. The dessert table with cakes, pies, eclairs, mousse, and fruit is irresistible. And in the midst of all the food is a hand-carved ice sculpture.

Bennett St. Café is a large cheerful room with sliding glass doors that look out on the terrace, where meals are served in warm weather. Brunch is $22.75 ($12.75 for children) and is served from 11 a.m. to 2:30 p.m. Please make reservations.

The lines are long for the buffet brunch at **Jonah's Seafood**

Café, in the Cambridge Hyatt-Regency, 575 Memorial Dr. (tel. 492-1234), so come early if you want to heap your plates with eggs, sausages, roast beef, salads, cheeses, desserts, pastries, as well as a choice of hot dishes. The serving tables are decorated with flowers and an ice sculpture, and your own table overlooks either the river or the garden atrium. The price is $23.95 for adults, $10.95 for children under 12. Brunch is served from 10 a.m. to 3 p.m. (but be in line by 1 p.m. at the latest).

If you're in town for a month of Sundays, you might try some of the other buffet brunches, such as the one in the **Café Rouge** at the Park Plaza Hotel, 50 Park Plaza (tel. 426-2000), served from 9:30 a.m. to 2 p.m. for $16.95. Children under 12 are half price. The **Boylston Park Café,** in the Sheraton Boston Hotel & Towers (tel. 236-2000), has prime rib, stuffed lobster, and all the shrimp you can eat as part of its lavish buffet. Served from 11:30 a.m. to 2:30 p.m., it's $25 for adults, with children under 10 free. And in Cambridge at the **Brandywine Restaurant** in the Sheraton Commander Hotel, 16 Garden St. (tel. 547-4800), there's an elaborate brunch at $17.95 for adults, $8.95 for children, offered from 10 a.m. to 2:30 p.m.

Café Suisse in the Lafayette Hotel, 1 Avenue de Lafayette (tel. 451-2600), has a Sunday brunch blending Swiss and New England cuisines. Served from 11:30 a.m. to 3 p.m., the price is $19.95 adults, $12.95 children. There is also a theme buffet on Saturday night that features foods from around the world at the same price of $19.95.

DINING AROUND THE CLOCK

After the restaurants have closed for the evening, and the bars have shut down at 2 a.m., and you're hungry, what do you do? Here are some suggestions.

Try Chinatown. **Kim Toy,** 2 Tyler St., at the corner of Beach, threw away the keys, and it's open 24 hours. **Lucky Dragon,** 45 Beach St.; **Moon Villa,** 23 Edinborough St.; and **King Wah,** 29 Beach St.—all dish out the food until 3 a.m.

Also in Chinatown, the **Imperial Tea House** is open until 3 a.m. **The Chinatown Mall,** 44 Beach St., on the second floor, is open seven days a week until 3 a.m. There are five Chinese restaurants and a Thai dining spot there.

Try the North End. **Joe Tecce's Café** at 53 N. Washington St., in an unmarked blue-tiled building, has Italian snacks and pastries until 1 a.m., while **Caffè Pompeii** brews espresso, cappuccino, and caffè latte until 3 a.m. every morning.

For pastry extravaganzas there's **Montilio's,** at Copley Square, open 7 a.m. until 3 a.m. **Yellow Submarine** on 307 Cambridge Street, near the Massachusetts General Hospital, also fixes some of the best subs in the Boston area until 2 a.m. Also on Cambridge St., is **Buzzy's Roast Beef,** 327 Cambridge St., near Massachusetts General Hospital, serving until 5 a.m.

In Cambridge, **Elsie's,** at 71A Mt. Auburn St., keeps the roast beef hot until 1 a.m. In the Quincy Market and in the Waterfront areas, the watering places are open until 2 a.m.

DINING IN CAMBRIDGE

Even if you're not staying in Cambridge, you'll certainly be visiting there, and it's pleasant to combine a meal with your sightseeing excursions. And Cambridge is so close to Boston—most of the restaurants listed here can be reached on foot from the Harvard Square subway stop, just across the Charles River from the center of Boston—that it's no more difficult to dine here than any other place in Boston. Many of your fellow diners will include members of the huge academic community that makes Cambridge one of the most exciting cultural centers in the country.

THE TOP CHOICES: You may never be asked to join the "Pudding," Harvard's famed theatrical group, but you can go **Upstairs at the Pudding,** 10 Holyoke St. (tel. 864-1933), for a showpiece dinner. Located above the Hasty Pudding Playhouse in an attractive room with forest-green walls, brass chandeliers, and tables set with pink cloths and flowers, the restaurant has won bravos for its northern Italian cuisine. The menu changes daily to reflect the fresh purchases owner/chef Michael Silver has made that day. There may be polenta with grilled quail for the first course, or an incredibly delicious pasta, followed by duck, saltimbocca, or grilled lamb, and a dessert of Sicilian lemon pie. It's a prix-fixe menu, with three courses at $39.50, and a number of choices available for each course.

Upstairs at the Pudding is open Monday through Saturday from 6 to 10 p.m. Take some time to enjoy the gallery of theatrical posters in the halls and dining room.

The **Harvest,** 44 Brattle St. (tel. 492-1115), is a gathering place near Harvard Square for celebrities and literati, Harvard professors and young professionals. The chefs pride themselves on the creativity and color which constitute the menu; it is composed of only the freshest seasonal produce, and changes daily. A sample luncheon may start with a terrine du jour or Wellfleet oysters for appetizers, homemade pasta with red clam sauce or honey lime chicken as entrees. There are "light lunches" as well, such as grapefruit and avocado salad with poppy-seed dressing, or a marinated lamb and lentil salad. Dinner is more formal yet equally creative;

we sampled artichoke stuffed with Cape scallops and asparagus mousse as an appetizer, and shrimp Florentine with curry mousseline for the main course. Dinner entree prices range from $18 to $25; at lunch, $7 to $12. The desserts, especially the pastries and the fruit ices, are luscious.

The decor inside and on the outdoor terrace is light and airy, with Marimekko prints and tasteful antiques. In the evening the trees on the terrace are lit with delicately sparkling green and white lights.

Michela's, a charming Italian restaurant in Cambridge's hi-tech district at One Athenaeum St. (tel. 225-3366), is one of the great new restaurants in the area. The dynamic young owner, Michela Larsen, and her chef have created a highly original menu of homemade pastas, soups, and northern Italian entrees that are truly inspired. Consider grilled lamb chops with ham, and goat cheese "in carrozza" with an egg and lemon sauce; or a sautéed sea bass with green olive sauce and grilled oysters wrapped in pancetta. Chicken dishes are made from free-range chickens for extra tenderness and flavor. The pasta selections include carrot linguine with clam, oregano, garlic, and pancetta sauce; squid-ink pasta filled with sea bass; and cannelloni filled with lobster. Selections change about every three months depending on which ingredients are seasonal, but you can usually find the basic steak, fish, and chicken in an intriguing preparation.

The lunch menu includes some of the evening selections, but also more salads, and a pizza of the day made with a light, fluffy crust and fillings such as eggplant and goat cheese, or prosciutto topped with rosemary.

The price range at dinner is $15 to $21 for entrees, $7 to $12 for pastas, and $5 to $8 for appetizers. Lunch is priced from $5.50 for an Italian sandwich to $6.75 for scrod and $10.50 for steak. Soup is $3.50 and pizza is $8. Excellent desserts can be ordered for $4.25 to $6.50.

Michela's is open for dinner from 6 to 10 p.m. Monday through Friday, until 10:30 p.m. on Saturday. Lunch is served Monday through Friday from noon to 2:30 p.m. Parking is available in the indoor garage behind the restaurant, free in the evening and discounted at lunch.

When there's a great restaurant in town, people find it, even if it's hidden away in an unpretentious storefront. Local food critics and New York reviewers found **Panache** at 798 Main St., in Cambridge near MIT and Central Square (tel. 492-9500), and gave its young, self-taught chef, Bruce Frankel, rave reviews. Frankel is trying to create his ideal restaurant, and is always ready to try something new, different, and contemporary, yet always in balance and good taste. The menu changes frequently. You might find grilled salmon or swordfish, accented with the delicate licorice flavor of fresh fennel; sautéed duck might be served with fresh berries; and roast sirloin of veal with a truffle or perhaps pesto sauce. Prices range from $14 to $20 and vegetables are served à la carte.

The small dining room seats 38 people. Multi-colored plates, white tablecloths, and flowers provide contrast to the dark walls. A delightful touch are the seasonal images cast on the walls by a pattern projector. Panache is open for dinner Tuesday through Saturday from 6 to 10 p.m. There is a parking lot nearby.

THE MIDDLE BRACKET: The Peacock, 5 Craigie Circle (tel.
661-4073), is a study in simplicity. But it's a simplicity that is akin to elegance. The portions are modest and only lightly seasoned, presented to appeal to the eye as well as the palate. The menu changes in order to take advantage of the best offerings in the market; it might include sole suchet, venison, and fresh Massachusetts poussin. Among the desserts the vacherin—a meringue with apricots and hazelnuts—is so good that it is almost always on the menu. Entree prices range from $10 to $14, and you can get an excellent dinner with wine for about $20.

Located on the lower level of an apartment building near Harvard Square, The Peacock is open for dinner Tuesday through Thursday from 5:30 to 9:30 p.m. and to 10:30 p.m. on weekends.

With its stucco archways, chianti bottles, and waiters conversing animatedly in Italian, **La Groceria,** 853 Main St. (tel. 547-9258), off Central Square, could easily be off a main square in Bologna. For lunch, start out with an abundant antipasto (tuna, eggs, vegetables, meat, cheese, and fruit) or cheese ravioli. The daytime specials are also noteworthy, with prices ranging from $4.95 to $8.95. Dinner is more elaborate, with many varieties of pasta, fish, veal, and chicken to choose from. Our favorite is the chicken Verdicchio, with mushrooms and artichokes. Entrees range from $8.95 to $14.95. If you have room, finish off with homemade cannoli (filled to order) and a freshly ground cappuccino. Bellissimo! Open for lunch from 11:30 a.m. to 4:30 p.m.; for dinner, from 5 to 10 p.m., to 11 p.m. on weekends; on Sunday from 1 to 10 p.m.

Note: Check out the pasta machine at the entrance to La Groceria. The noodles you see may be rushed upstairs to be part of your dinner.

You must try the **East Coast Grill**—that is, if you can get in. This little restaurant at 1271 Cambridge St. (tel. 491-6568) is so popular that the locals line up early as no reservations are taken. It's a laid-back, friendly place with country and rock music and a grilling station in full view. Specialties are seafood, hearty soups, and southern barbecue. You have a choice of three barbecues: Texas beef, Missouri spareribs, and North Carolina pork. Barbecue platters come with baked beans, cornbread, and a slice of watermelon. And the vegetarians in the crowd can have a great time with grilled vegetables and fruits. The price range for entrees at dinner is $8.50 to $13.50. Open daily from 5:30 to 10:30 p.m.

The **Cajun Yankee,** 1193 Cambridge St., Cambridge (tel. 576-1971), serves Cajun cooking at its best. The owner/chef, John Silberman, worked a three-year apprenticeship with Paul Prudhomme in New Orleans, and although his restaurant is in a modest storefront in plebeian Inman Square, the food is definitely upper class. The menu is on a blackboard and is limited to four or five appetizers and entrees. Outstanding is the blackened redfish coated with three kinds of ground peppers and garlic, and fried in a white-hot iron skillet to create a thick, black crust over a moist interior. A bit milder to the taste is scrod pecan, a filet topped with roasted pecans and served with butter and Worcestershire sauce. A favorite appetizer is Cajun "popcorn"—crayfish tails or crabmeat fried in cornmeal batter. And if you have the shrimp rémoulade (shrimp-salad cocktail with spicy sauce), keep your water glass handy. For dessert try the pecan sweet-potato pie or Cajun bread pudding with raisins, nuts, lemon sauce, chantilly, and whipped cream.

Price range is $9.95 to $16.95 for entrees. Dinner is served Tuesday through Saturday from 6 to 10 p.m., and reservations are a must.

Lai Lai means "welcome" in Chinese, and friendliness is one of the reasons **Lai Lai,** 700 Massachusetts Ave., Cambridge (tel. 876-7000), is such a popular restaurant. The most important reason, though, is the quality and variety of the food served by Danny Woo and his staff. A full range of Chinese cuisine is presented, but seafood is the specialty—an important part of the Chinese diet. The menu features well over 100 items, and if you can't decide what to order, try the Tasting Menu, a seven-course mini-banquet with appetizers, soup, entree, and dessert. Prices range from $7.25 to $15.50 for entrees; from $5.25 to $6.95 for bean curd, noodles, and fried rice dishes; and $1.25 to $5 for appetizers and soups.

Also featured is the Firepot, an Oriental fondue. On a gas burner at your table, you cook slices of beef, chicken and fish in a sizzling chicken and garlic and onion and noodle and bean-curd broth, then dip the pieces in an assortment of five sauces. The soup base is $12.95, and the addition of shrimp, scallops, chicken, beef, pork, lamb, etc., go from $3.95 to $5.75.

Lai Lai is open daily from noon to 10:30 p.m., with lunch served from noon to 5 p.m.

THE BUDGET RANGE: One of the best buys in town is the daily luncheon buffet at **33 Dunster St.** (tel. 354-0636), which features soup, bountiful salad bar, hot entrees, homemade breads, pastries, and coffee. There's also a regular menu with burgers, quiche, lasagne, and sandwiches, and a full dinner menu. Lunch is served from 11:30 a.m. to 2 p.m.; dinner, 5 p.m. to 12:30 a.m. (till 1:30 a.m. on Thursday, Friday and Saturday). Choose from 150 items as you load up your brunch dishes from 10 a.m. to 3 p.m. on Sunday for $9.95.

The famous **Wursthaus,** directly on Harvard Square (tel. 491-7110), is very German and very crowded. It's open from 8 a.m. till midnight, and the bar with an attached eating counter is always jammed with a mixed bag of students, politicians, passersby, and the occasional businesspeople. The Wursthaus claims to feature the world's largest selection of foreign beers, and specializes in such items as bratwurst, knockwurst, sauerbraten, and imported wieners. Most main courses are in the $6 to $12 range, and over 30 varieties of sandwiches are also available. Lunch is available from 11 a.m. to 3 p.m. Monday through Friday. Dinner is served till midnight Sunday through Thursday, and until 1 a.m. on Friday and Saturday.

"Tapas" is Spanish for appetizers and hors d'oeuvres, usually served as bar food. The very popular tapas-style restaurants in this country have taken that concept and built a full restaurant operation around it. **Tapas,** 2067 Massachusetts Ave. (tel. 576-2240), offers about two dozen appetizers, hors d'oeuvres, and desserts, and you can order one or many. The price range is $1.95 to $9, so this is a budget deal or an expensive meal depending on how you resist temptation. That can be difficult as there are great items, including pastas, duck salad, vegetable curry, and carpaccio. In the inexpensive range are seafood chowders and soups, pasta, and sausage. Tapas is open Monday through Friday from 11:30 a.m. to 11 p.m., on Saturday and Sunday from noon to 11 p.m.

Colorful paintings and posters decorate the underground walls of the **Pâtisserie Française,** 54 John F. Kennedy St. (tel. 354-9850), a charming little coffeehouse with a French flavor and authentic croissants. With your delicious espresso or regular coffee, you can have a sandwich or choose one of the French specialties: pâté, quiche Lorraine, meat pies, or omelets at à la carte prices of 50¢ to $3.50. They also serve a moderately priced dinner with country French entrees. Open Monday through Saturday from 8 a.m. to 9:30 p.m., on Sunday from 9 a.m. to 5 p.m.

If you're planning on spending the morning in Cambridge, start with breakfast at the **Coffee Connection** in **The Garage,** with a choice of 20 varieties of freshly roasted coffee, homemade granola, and just-squeezed orange juice. Try **Pâtisserie Française,** 54 John F. Kennedy St., for French coffee and French pastry. **Vie de France,** 1100 Massachusetts Ave., makes the famous French bread and rolls that other restaurants buy, plus croissants and other goodies. Very popular for Sunday-morning brunch. Or try **Mavens,** the delicatessen-restaurant at 95 Winthrop St., which opens at 7 a.m. (except Saturday when it is closed all day) for hearty Kosher breakfasts, including lox, fried kippers, and French toast made from challah.

THE CHOCOLATE CONNECTION

Bostonians have a history of being chocoholics even though historians claim they subsisted on baked beans and New England boiled dinners. The first chocolate mill in the United States was opened in Milton Lower Mills in 1735 and became the Walter Baker Chocolate Company in 1780. Throughout the years many famous candy companies have flourished in the Boston area, and today you can still get locally made chocolates in some small candy houses and watch them being made in a few select shops.

Philips Candy House, 818 Morrissey Blvd., Dorchester (tel. 282-2090), just two miles from the original Baker chocolate mill, provides tours for individuals and small groups by appointment. These prize-winning chocolates, which do not contain any preservatives and additives, are handmade daily in small batches over open fire kettles. A guide will explain every step to you from the mixing of the syrup to the dipping and swirling that identifies the chocolate filling. Reservations for tours may be made by calling Mary Ann Nagle at 282-2090.

Salem is the home of the extraordinary **Harbor Sweets,** 85 Leavitt St. (tel. 745-7648), said to be the most expensive candy in the country—gift boxes selling for $16 to $44. Only six types of candy are offered, with sweet sloops, sand dollars, and Marblehead mints among the favorites. There are no formal tours, but there is a gift shop; and you just might get to meet their creator, Ben Strohecker.

And if you're ready for a chocolate binge, **The Chocolate Bar** at the Café Fleuri in the Hotel Meridien, 250 Franklin St., Boston (tel. 451-1900), has an all-you-can-eat chocolate buffet, Saturday and Sunday from 4 to 6 p.m., for $8.50. There are 20 or more chocolate treats—desserts, cookies, brownies, and other confections. The table centerpieces are carved out of chocolate—you'll find a chocolate baby-grand piano filled with truffles and a basket woven of chocolate and filled with berries for dipping. Incredibly delicious!

And don't miss a Bailey's hot fudge sundae at any of the **Bailey's** ice-cream parlors in Boston and Cambridge, or chocolate ice cream made with real chocolate at **Toscanini's,** 899 Main St., Cambridge.

CHAPTER V

SIGHTS IN BOSTON

□ □ □

Boston is an eminently pleasant town for leisurely sightseeing and strolling. You can see the city by sightseeing bus, guided walking tour, or even sightseeing boat (more about which later), but you can also walk around on your own, poking your way into odd little corners as you go; and since Boston is not a large city (geographically), for us that's the most rewarding way to see it. You can see most of the major sights in two or three days. Take the subway or a cab to the major areas you want to see, then explore in depth the best way of all: by walking. For an overall view of the city, start at one of its dazzling observation towers: the **Prudential** or **John Hancock**. See details in Chapter II, "Finding Your Way Around Boston."

VISITOR INFORMATION

Now, before you start your walk around town, stop by one of Boston's Visitor Information Centers for free maps, folders, weekly listings of special exhibits, and a list of visiting hours and fees at the historic shrines.

The **National Park Service Visitor Center**, at 15 State St. (tel. 242-5642), right next to the Old State House and the State Street "T" station, is a good place to start your tour of historic Boston. The audio-visual show, *The Freedom Trail*, gives you basic information on those 16 historic sites and the knowledgeable uniformed park rangers are eager to help. In the warm weather they give free guided tours of the Freedom Trail and Boston's parks and gardens. There are special ramps for the disabled, comfortable chairs for relaxing, and rest rooms. (Their map of Boston even designates public rest rooms.) Open daily from 9 a.m. to 5 p.m. except Thanksgiving, Christmas, and New Year's Days.

The **City Hall Visitor Information Center** is open Monday to Friday from 9 a.m. to 5 p.m. Get brochures there plus a free print-out of happenings in Boston from the Info Boston computer. City Hall is located across the street from Faneuil Hall Marketplace on City Hall Plaza. (You can bypass the steps at City Hall by walking up State Street toward Government Center, past the "Steaming Kettle" restaurant, to the Plaza.)

The **Freedom Trail Information Center** is on the Tremont Street side of the Common, open daily from 9 a.m. to 5 p.m., and there you can get maps and brochures. To guide you, there's a red-brick line in the sidewalks from the Common to the end of the trail.

In the Back Bay area of Boston, the visitor information center is in the **John Hancock Observatory** ticket office at Copley Square, corner St. James Avenue and Trinity Place (tel. 249-1977), open Monday to Saturday from 9 a.m. to 11 p.m. and on Sunday from noon to 11 p.m., with the exception of Thanksgiving and Christmas.

And the **Greater Boston Convention and Visitors Bureau,** at Prudential Plaza, has a live number (tel. 536-4100), open from 9 a.m. to 5 p.m. Monday through Friday, giving the latest information on goings-on about town. Call 267-6446 for recorded information anytime. There is a multilingual staff for foreign visitors.

MAPS

At one time you could always tell tourists from natives by the maps they carried, but there has been so much reconstruction in the "New Boston" that the locals find maps helpful too. Free maps of downtown Boston and the rapid transit lines are available at the visitor information centers. The Prudential Life Insurance Company, 800 Boylston St. (tel. 236-3318), has a neighborhood map of Boston which it distributes at its Skywalk viewing platform, open Monday through Saturday, 10 a.m. to 10 p.m.; Sunday from noon to 10 p.m. It's very helpful for walking trips of Beacon Hill, North End, Chinatown, South End, Charlestown, and Harvard Square.

The **Metropolitan District Commission (MDC)** has an excellent map of the reservations, parks, and recreation areas in Greater Boston. It tells where to find salt- and freshwater beaches, swimming and wading pools, picnic areas, foot trails and bridge paths, playgrounds, tennis and golf courses, freshwater and saltwater fishing, bicycle paths, and outdoor ice-skating rinks. Write to the MDC, 20 Somerset St., Boston, MA 02108 (c/o Public Information Office), for a copy.

A "House Guide" listing 23 historical houses and museums in New England is available from the **Society for the Preserva-**

tion of New England Antiquities, 141 Cambridge St., Boston, MA 02114. The **Massachusetts Association of Campground Owners (MACO)** has a directory listing private campgrounds in the state. Write to MACO, P.O. Box 28, Boston, MA 02122.

THE FREEDOM TRAIL

The one walking tour that everyone must make, of course, is the **Freedom Trail,** which consists of 16 numbered historical sights spread out over an area of three or four square miles in the downtown section and Charlestown. In two to three hours, depending on how long you spend at each site, you'll cover 2½ centuries of America's most important history. "A visit to Boston is a must for every American," say the historians, "for without Boston there would have been no free American life."

And to show how free-spirited Bostonians are, the Freedom Trail has been expanded and rerouted in the last few years. There are now two loops—one through downtown Boston and the other through the North End—making the trail easier to follow. Although the new "official" start is at the City Hall Visitor Center, we like to stick to tradition and begin the tour at the **Boston Common.** Either way, there are trailblazer signs and a red sidewalk line to mark the trail.

To reach the Boston Common, take the subway to Park Street, or drive and park in the Common's 1,500-car underground garage (entrance on Arlington Street). From there a free bus takes you to the Information Booth on the Common. The Common is an integral part of Boston's past and present. It is the oldest public park in the country (1634), a place where cows once grazed, soldiers drilled, witches were hanged, and "common scolds" were dunked in the Frog Pond (now used for wading and ice skating). Today you'll find band concerts, rock concerts, sidewalk musicians, soapbox orators, demonstrations for or against almost anything, a free playground for the young, park benches for the elderly, Bostonians brown-bagging their lunch, flowers and ancient trees, and pigeons—and street people—begging for handouts.

Now that you've got your bearings, proceed to the "new" **State House,** with its great gold dome, one of the masterpieces of the career of Charles Bulfinch (to the original Bulfinch building have been added new wings, none as handsome). Although the building is called "new," it was actually built in 1795 to replace the smaller "old" State House (which you'll see later on your tour). Samuel Adams laid the cornerstone, and the original dome, now gold-leafed, was done in copper purchased from Paul Revere. The building is replete with flags, paintings, and such specialties as "the sacred codfish," a pine wood fish which hangs opposite the Speaker's desk.

Heading down one side of five-sided Boston Common, from which the British troops set off for Concord in 1775, the trail next pauses at the **Park Street Church,** at the corner of Park and Tremont Streets, built in 1809 and once described by Henry James as "the most interesting mass of bricks and mortar in America," with its white steeple and original exterior designed by Englishman Peter Banner. The church is rich in its associations: William Lloyd Garrison gave his first antislavery address here on July 4, 1829. Incidentally, the site on which the church stands has long been known as "Brimstone Corner," since gunpowder was stored in the church's basement during the War of 1812. During July and August, the church is open from 9:30 a.m. to 4 p.m. Tuesday through Saturday. Services (Congregational) are on Sunday at 10:30 a.m. and 6 p.m., on Friday at 7 p.m.

Just to the left of the church on Tremont Street is the **Granary Burying Ground,** once part of the Common and later the site of a public granary. Pause for a moment and pay tribute to some illustrious Americans who are buried here: John Hancock, Samuel Adams, Paul Revere, Benjamin Franklin's parents, the victims of the Boston Massacre (five colonists shot in a fracas with British troops on March 5, 1770), and the wife of Isaac Goose, otherwise known as "Mother Goose" from the nursery rhymes of the same name. But don't try any gravestone rubbing. Once a popular pastime, it has been prohibited in Boston's historic cemeteries as the rubbing process was beginning to wear off the engraving on the tombstones. Open daily from 8 a.m. to 4 p.m.

King's Chapel is next on your tour: built in 1754 and worshipped in by the royal governors, it was the first Episcopal church in Boston. George III sent gifts, as did Queen Anne and William and Mary, who presented the communion table and chancel tablets (still in use today) before the church was constructed. The Crown's religion was never too popular with the colonists, and after the Revolution it became the first Unitarian church in America. Unitarian/Universalist services are now conducted here. Open Tuesday through Saturday from 10 a.m. to 4 p.m.

Now follow the red-brick line to School Street, where you'll find two stops on the trail: the **Site of the First Public School,** Boston Latin School, where Adams, Franklin, and Cotton Mather were students (Boston Latin is now in the Fenway area); and the **statue of Benjamin Franklin,** the first portrait statue erected in Boston. If you look closely you'll see that one side of the statue is smiling, the other serious. (Old Ben is probably wondering how to react to the fact that the location of his old school is now Maison

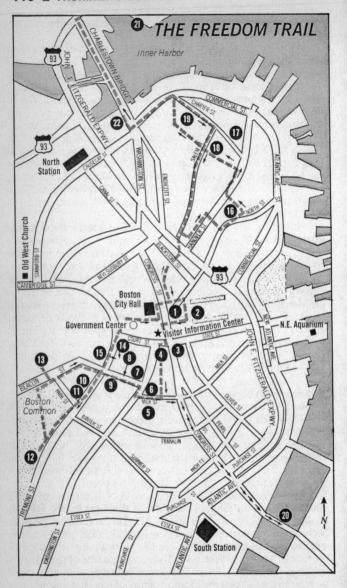

THE FREEDOM TRAIL

KEY TO THE NUMBERED REFERENCES ON OUR MAP OF THE FREEDOM TRAIL: 1—Faneuil Hall; 2—Faneuil Hall Market; 3—Boston Massacre Site; 4—Old State House; 5—Site of Benjamin Franklin Birthplace; 6—Old South Meetinghouse; 7—Old Corner Bookstore; 8—Statue of Benjamin Franklin erected 1856; 9—Site of the First Public School, 1635; 10—Granary Burying Ground; 11—Park Street Church; 12—Boston Common; 13—State House and Archives Museum; 14—King's Chapel; 15—King's Chapel Burying Ground; 16—Paul Revere House; 17—Paul Revere Mall; 18—Old North Church; 19—Copp's Hill Burying Ground; 20—Boston Tea Party Ship and Museum; 21—Bunker Hill Monument; 22—U.S.S. *Constitution ("Old Ironsides")*.

Robert, a chic French restaurant. It was Boston City Hall until the new building was erected.) Next on the trail is the building that once housed the **Old Corner Bookstore,** and the publishing house of Ticknor & Fields. This was the literary center of America, where such Boston literati as Longfellow, Lowell, Thoreau, Emerson, Hawthorne, and Harriet Beecher Stowe used to meet and chat. It is now a bookstore and is somewhat restored to what it was in the old days.

The **Old South Meetinghouse,** 310 Washington St. at the corner of Washington and Milk Streets (tel. 482-6439), next on your walk, was used by the early colonists for both religious and political meetings, overflowing from nearby Faneuil Hall. It was here, in 1770, that an angry crowd met to wait for Governor Hutchinson's promise to withdraw British troops after the Boston Massacre. And it was also here, on December 16, 1773, that several thousand citizens sent messengers to the governor that the newly arrived tea be removed from the harbor and sent back to England. At last they were informed by Samuel Adams of the governor's refusal; a whoop went up from the citizens disguised as Indians who then rushed to the docks to begin the famous Boston Tea Party. Today the Meetinghouse is a fascinating museum of revolutionary history, with its pews still on the ground floor; a centuries-old clock ticking away; and a multimedia exhibit, "In Prayer and Protest: Old South Meeting House Remembers," that highlights Old South's history. Look for the sign that reads "The Boston Tea Party started here December 16, 1773," and the vial of tea, washed up on the shore of the harbor the morning after, that's there to prove it. Open daily 9:30 a.m. to 5 p.m., April through

October; and 10 a.m. to 4 p.m., Monday through Friday (until 5 p.m. on weekends from November through March). Admission is $1.25; seniors pay 75¢; children 6 to 18 pay only 50¢. Old South also offers special activities and events that help bring American history to life. Call for schedules and times.

Now plan to spend a little time poring over the priceless collection of colonial and revolutionary memorabilia at the **Old State House,** Washington and State Streets (tel. 242-5655), which dates back to 1713. It was the seat of the colonial government of Massachusetts before the Revolution, and the state's capitol afterward. It was from its balcony that the Declaration of Independence was first read to the citizens of Boston in 1776. In 1789 George Washington, as president, reviewed a parade from the building. The Old State House is an impressive building with a magnificent spiral staircase, and as you roam around, you'll see rooms filled with old furniture and paintings, and a varied collection of early Boston memorabilia: ship models, uniforms, guns, policemen's hats, and a few leaves that survived the Boston Tea Party. November 1 to March 31 it is open from 10 a.m. to 4 p.m. Monday through Friday, from 9:30 a.m. to 5 p.m. on Saturday, and from 11 a.m. to 5 p.m. on Sunday. Hours from April 1 to October 31 are 9:30 a.m. to 5 p.m. daily. Admission is $1.25 for adults; senior citizens, and students, 75¢; children 6 to 12, 50¢; under 6, free.

Outside the Old State House, a ring of cobblestones marks the site of the **Boston Massacre,** March 5, 1770, an event which helped consolidate the spirit of rebellion in the colonies. Colonists, angered at the presence of British troops in Boston, stoned a group of redcoats who panicked and fired into the crowd, killing five men.

Faneuil Hall, at Dock Square, is the next important stop on the Freedom Trail. Built in 1742 and given to the city of Boston by merchant Peter Faneuil, it became known as the "Cradle of Liberty" because of the frequent protest meetings that took place here, while orators such as Samuel Adams exhorted the crowd against the British. The upstairs is still a meeting hall for state and local civic and political groups and the new breed of political protesters, the downstairs still a produce market, all according to Faneuil's will. On the top floor the military-minded can examine the weapons collection of the Ancient and Honorable Artillery Company of Massachusetts, open weekdays from 10 a.m. to 4 p.m. Faneuil Hall is open seven days a week from 9 a.m. to 5 p.m. with hourly talks by the National Park Service. Free.

The North End Loop of the Freedom Trail starts at the Paul Revere House, but before going on you might want to stop here and visit the Faneuil Hall Marketplace, which is next to Faneuil Hall (we'll describe it fully later in this chapter).

To reach the Paul Revere House, follow the red-brick path that takes you under the expressway to the North End.

The **Paul Revere House,** (tel. 523-2338) was about 90 years old when Revere bought it in 1770 and is still standing today, at 19 North Square. The two-story wooden structure, the oldest in Boston, is filled with 17th- and 18th-century furnishings and artifacts, and is one of the major landmarks along the Freedom Trail. Revere, a brilliant silversmith as well as a patriot, had good training for his famous ride of April 18, 1775; he had been hired on several occasions by the selectmen to carry news of their deliberations to other parts of the colonies. In 1774, for example, he bore dispatches to Philadelphia and New York calling for a congress; the year before, he had spread the news of (after taking part in) the Boston Tea Party to New York. You can even gaze at Revere's saddlebags. Hours are 9:30 a.m. to 4:15 p.m. from November 1 to April 14, 9:30 a.m. to 5:15 p.m. from April 15 to October 31. Admission charged.

The area around Paul Revere's House is pleasantly unspoiled in some ways, although the architectural styles are mixed. You may want to note, too, at the beginning of the little cobbled street on which Revere's house stands, the **Moses–Pierce Hitchborn House,** another venerable one for Boston, built around 1680. A few blocks up, at James Rego Square, is a little park with a statue of Paul Revere on horseback. Here you'll also see **St. Stephen's Church,** a beautiful edifice created by Bulfinch in 1802. Walk into the park, pausing at the fountain in the square, and emerge at the **Old North Church,** Salem Street at Paul Revere Mall. It's a thoroughly beautiful structure which dates back to 1723, and is modeled in the style of Sir Christopher Wren's buildings, with its red-brick façade and tall steeple. It was from this steeple, of course, that Revere had arranged for Robert Newman to hang two lanterns ("One if by land, two if by sea"), the signal that the British were on their way to Lexington and Concord. The Revere family attended this church (you can still see their plaque on Pew 54), and other famous visitors who have attended services at Old North have included Presidents James Monroe, Theodore Roosevelt, and F.D.R. And, more recently, Gerald R. Ford and Her Majesty Queen Elizabeth II. Have a look at the interior of the church, noting the pulpit shaped like a wine glass, the ancient chandeliers, and organ. Then stop at the museum shop next door, also in an old building, where you can buy maps of Paul Revere's ride, pewter, and silver, as well as less historic-type items like maple sugar candy. Proceeds go to support the church. Old North Church is open daily from 9 a.m. to 5 p.m. And you can attend Sunday services (Episcopal) at 9:30 and 11 a.m.

On your way to the last two stops on the Freedom Trail, pause for a while at the **Copps Hill Burial Ground,** just up the hill from Old North Church. Used by the colonists as early as 1659, this is where Cotton Mather and his brother are buried along with other early Bostonians. On this ground, once the site of a windmill, were planted the British batteries which destroyed the village of Charlestown during the Battle of Bunker Hill, June 17, 1775. Open daily from 9 a.m. to 4 p.m. From the heights of Copps Hill you can see across the river to Charlestown, spotting the masts of the U.S.S. *Constitution.* The *Constitution*— *"Old Ironsides"* of War of 1812 fame—was built at a cost of $302,718 (that was back in 1797), and since she never lost a battle, this must have been one of the biggest naval bargains in history. First used to help drive the French privateers from West Indian waters, the *Constitution* won a succession of famous victories over the British fleet in the War of 1812. Participating in 40 engagements, she captured 20 vessels without ever being beaten. The ship is now preserved—"not only as a monument to its glorious past, but as a symbol of the spirit which established our nation." Open from 9:30 a.m. to 3:50 p.m. daily. Kids love to climb up and down the ladders between decks!

To reach the *Constitution* from Boston, follow the signs that direct you to the Northeast Expressway and the Mystic River Bridge. Before reaching the bridge you will be able to see the *Constitution* and the Navy Yard on your right. If you're coming from north of the city, exit from the bridge at Charlestown. All routes are marked with brown signs showing a three-masted sailing vessel. There is parking at the Charlestown Navy Yard near the *Constitution.* Best bet is to take a sightseeing bus or the MBTA. Try the "T" bus 93 from Haymarket Square. This takes you to City Square, Charlestown, a short walk to the U.S.S. *Constitution* and Bunker Hill. Or take the "T" Orange Line from Haymarket to Bunker Hill Community College, near the Bunker Hill Monument. If you're driving from the *Constitution* to the monument, get instructions from one of the guides at the naval shipyard, since there are narrow one-way streets to cope with.

Also at the Navy Yard is the U.S.S. *Cassin Young,* a World War II destroyer which has been refurbished and is now open to the public. It is docked near the U.S.S. *Constitution.* Admission is free. Call 242-5601 for tour hours.

Note: If you're a naval buff, try a side trip to Heritage State Park at Battleship Cove, Fall River, Mass., 50 miles southeast of Boston, where you can board the attack submarine U.S.S. *Lionfish,* explore the U.S.S. *Joseph P. Kennedy, Jr.,* and the U.S.S. *Massachu-*

setts. For tour information, write or call the Marine Museum at Battleship Cove, Fall River, MA 02723 (tel. 508/678-1100).

The **Bunker Hill Monument,** a 220-foot landmark, was built to honor the men who died in the Battle of Bunker Hill, which took place on June 17, 1775. Although the colonists lost the battle, it speeded the events that eventually pushed the British out of America. Unless you're willing to climb 294 steps—there is no elevator—it's best to observe the tower from the distance.

In the lodge at the base of the monument there are exhibits and talks given by National Park Service rangers from 10 a.m. to 4 p.m. Open daily from 9 a.m. to dusk. Admission is free.

Moored at Griffin's Wharf, where patriots threw tea into the harbor in 1773, is a replica of one of the ships they boarded. The **Boston Tea Party Ship** (tel. 338-1773), a stop on the Harbor Walk Trail, has three main points of interest: the brig *Beaver II,* a full-size working replica of one of the ships involved in the historical event; a museum with copies of historical documents, artifacts, and audio-visual presentations of the period of the 1770s; and a gift shop with Tea Party replicas. And if you really want to get into the spirit of the rebellion, costumed guides encourage you to throw tea chests from the deck into the water. (They're retrieved by their rope harnesses.) The Tea Party Ship is located at the Congress Street Bridge near South Station. Parking in the area is difficult on weekdays (we think if the patriots had to park in the area, the British would still be taxing tea in Boston), so weekends would be your best bet if driving. Or you can take the MBTA Red Line to South Station, or the Tea Party courtesy shuttle at the Old State House from 10 a.m. to 4 p.m. May to October. The Tea Party Ship is open daily from 9 a.m. to dusk. Admission is $3.25 for adults, $2.25 for children 5 to 12, and no charge for those under 5. Complimentary tea is served.

The **Black Heritage Trail** covers sites in the Beacon Hill section of Boston that are part of the history of 19th-century black Boston. You can take one of the guided tours given by the rangers at the **National Visitor Center,** 15 State St., or you can go on your own, using a brochure that includes descriptions of the buildings on the tour. First stop is the 182-year-old **African Meeting House,** 8 Smith Court, Beacon Hill, the oldest standing black church in the United States. It was there that William Lloyd Garrison founded the New England Anti-Slavery Society and Frederick Douglass made some of his great abolitionist speeches. Following extensive restoration work, the Meeting House is now leading a contemporary life with an informative audio-visual presentation, lectures, concerts, and church meetings. Another must on the Black Heritage Trail is a visit to the **Museum of Afro-American**

History at Abiel Smith School, 26 Joy St. (tel. 742-1854). The museum is open Tuesday through Friday from 10 a.m. to 4 p.m. Admission is free.

BEACON HILL

Another historic area that's delightful to walk around is Beacon Hill on the northern side of the Boston Common, an architectural gem from the 19th century crowned by the gold-domed State House. The old brownstone and brick houses are virtually the same as they were when Louisa May Alcott lived at 10 Louisburg Square, Edwin Booth at 29A Chestnut St., and Julia Ward Howe at 13 Chestnut St. Happily, the area has now been designated as a National Historic Landmark and is safely beyond the reach of developers. One of the oldest black churches in the country, the African Meetinghouse, is on the Hill at 8 Smith Court.

The quaint narrow streets have red-brick sidewalks (a second revolution almost occurred when the city dared to suggest repaving in concrete), gaslight lamps, and in spring and summer, flowering windowboxes on most of the town houses. Fashionable **Louisburg Square**, the famed turf of the Boston Brahmins with its cluster of 22 homes and a beautiful central park, is still home to the Old Money. (It was in these environs that the Cabots spoke only to the Lowells and so on.) And the iron-railed square is open only to residents with keys.

When you explore this area, by the way, be ready for a good deal of walking and climbing. Charles Street, with restaurants and boutiques, is at the base of the Hill, and everything else goes up. Tourist buses don't make the rounds there—they probably never could turn the narrow corners—and a parking space is practically impossible to find unless you dare park under a towing sign. And the ever-efficient metermaids do call the tow trucks.

Incidental Intelligence: In Boston's early days, Beacon Hill was one of the three hills, and as the name implies was the site of a beacon. In the early 1800s the ingenious Bostonians, who were becoming cramped for living space, solved their housing problem and unemployment problem with one bold stroke. For a period of 60 years they removed earth from the top of the three peaks on Beacon Hill and built homes on the slopes. And they used that earth to fill in a pond to the north that is now the North Station terminal, and a bay to the west that is now Back Bay.

VISITING BOSTON'S OLD HOUSES

If you're still in the nostalgia mood, you'll enjoy a visit to some of the old houses of Boston that are still standing; here you can get a feeling of what life among the 19th-century aristocrats and upper middle class was like—from the inside. One of the most pleasant of these is the **Gibson House Museum,** 137 Beacon St. (tel. 267-6338; admission is $3, with afternoon tours from 2 to 4 p.m.; open Wednesday through Sunday from May to October, weekends only from November to April). It's full of the kind of curios that our great-grandparents found essential: petrified-tree hat racks, a sequinned pink-velvet pagoda for the cat, a Victrola, gilt-framed photographs of every relative. What must be one of America's oldest telephones is mounted on a second-floor wall, supplementing the internal network of wired bells to summon servants from any part of the house. (Sounds like "Upstairs, Downstairs.") Closed major holidays.

Both the **Nichols House Museum** at 55 Mount Vernon St. (open all year; phone 227-6993 for hours; admission is $2) and **Harrison Gray Otis House** at 141 Cambridge St. (open all year, Monday to Friday, with guided tours at 10 and 11 a.m., and 1, 2, and 3 p.m.; admission is $2.50 for adults and $1.25 for children under 12) were designed by the 18th-century architect Charles Bulfinch and are well worth seeing. (The Otis House is also head-quarters for the Society for the Preservation of New England Antiquities.) Write or call the society at 141 Cambridge St., Boston, MA 02114 (tel. 617/227-3956), for brochures, visiting schedules, and rates for the many historic house museums in the area.

Note: Embedded in the side of the gift shop across from the Hancock House, at 10 Marshall St., is the **Boston Stone,** once the official centerpoint of the city. All distances to and from Boston were measured from this point.

CITY HALL, GOVERNMENT CENTER, AND THE NEW BOSTON

If you remember your history, you know that "Old Boston" was once considered very revolutionary. So just consider "New Boston" as following tradition when you visit **Boston City Hall** (dubbed an "Aztec Tomb" by its critics), which overlooks the Faneuil Hall Marketplace. The main approach is across an eight-acre red-brick plaza, comparable—in size only—to St. Peter's Square in Rome. There are fountains at one end, good for foot-dunking in hot weather, and steps for sitting. But no trees or benches. The plaza comes alive at times with music and dance per-formances sponsored by the city—and with demonstrations and protest rallies not sponsored by the city. City Hall itself is dually regarded as "one of the great civic buildings of the 20th century" and as a cold, concrete-and-brick monstrosity, depending on whether you're talking to architects or plain Bostonians. Office workers and visitors say they get lost in the huge connecting passageways; designers extol the high lobby with its exhibition areas, the huge glass doors, the light shafts, and the imaginative use of space and irregular shapes and surfaces. And there seems to be general agreement that the balcony outside the mayor's office is a great place for visiting royalty—like the victorious Bruins hockey team or the champion Red Sox or Boston Celtics—to greet the cheering throng below. Form your own opinion by taking one of the free guided tours given weekdays from 10 a.m. to 4 p.m. The building is open from 9 a.m. to 5 p.m., and at times there are very good art and photo exhibits in the lobby. To reach Boston City Hall, follow Tremont Street from the Boston Common to Government Center or take the MBTA to Government Center.

Facing City Hall across the plaza are two more new government buildings: the 26-story **John F. Kennedy Federal Office Building** and the **Center Plaza,** one of the country's longest office buildings.

Take a good look at the gleaming aluminum tower at 600 Atlantic Ave., opposite South Station. It's the richest building in town, or more precisely, the center of operations for the **Federal Reserve Bank of Boston.** One of the most striking features in Boston's cityscape, the 604-foot tower has a dramatic glass curtain wall and landscaped plaza leading the visitor to the display area on the ground floor.

In the business wing, glass walls allow tour groups to view coin, currency, check collection, and data services operations. Tours are usually arranged for groups, but you might be able to join one. Call 973-3464 for availability.

An interesting combination of the new and the old is the **Boston Public Library** at Copley Square (tel. 536-5400). The original Italian Renaissance building, said to be modeled after the Chancellory of Rome, is joined to a very functional modern building. Both maintain the same roofline and use pink granite on their façades. The older building has a main staircase lined with murals, and includes artworks by Daniel Chester French, John Singer Sargent, and John Singleton Copley. There is also a tranquil courtyard where you can read, relax . . . or hold a secret rendezvous. In the newer building a Great Hall covered by nine multifaceted windows forms a central core extending the full height of the library. The Research Library building, a national historic site, contains many fine examples of the works of American painters and sculptors of the late 19th century as well as an extensive collection of books from the 18th and 19th centuries. The library has more than 80,000 books in foreign languages for adults and children. Visitors to Boston can make use of a free courtesy card to use the collections or listen to recordings in the audio-visual department. Free concerts, lectures, and films are also offered. Call or write the Public Relations Office, Boston Public Library (tel. 536-5400, ext. 214), for special events and hours. (Look for your hometown paper, in the Newspaper Room.)

The Research Library and the General Library are open Monday through Thursday from 9 a.m. to 9 p.m., on Friday and Saturday to 5 p.m., and on Sunday from 2 to 6 p.m. (closed on legal holidays). During the months of June, July, August, and September, the library is closed on Sunday.

WATERFRONT–FANEUIL HALL MARKETPLACE

This is where the future takes on the shape of the past. Boston's history is tied to the sea—the early fortunes were made via the clipper ship route and colonial commercial life centered around the waterfront. Now, as Boston rebuilds, it turns to the source of its origins for inspiration. A small city within the city is taking shape as the old wharves are rebuilt and the ramshackle warehouses are recycled into chic restaurants, condos, and offices. (You have "arrived" if you have a waterfront address.)

Boston is very proud of its colorful waterfront, and to help visitors become better acquainted with its attractions, the city has a two-mile **Harborwalk,** a trail linking the historic area to the ocean. Just follow the blue line from the Old State House (the red line is for the Freedom Trail) down State Street to Long Wharf and the Aquarium. From there Harborwalk leads to Museum Wharf, site of the Children's Museum and the Boston Tea Party Ship. Get a Harborpass and map at the Information Center on the Common, Bostix at the Faneuil Hall Marketplace, the Old State House, or at the Boston Tea Party Ship. It only costs $1 and offers discounts to spots along the way.

Part of the grand scheme is the **Waterfront Park.** Use the Aquarium subway stop or take the Green Line of the "T" to Government Center and walk down to the sea via City Hall Plaza, Faneuil Hall, and the Faneuil Hall Marketplace. Sit on the terraced steps facing the harbor and dream of the tall ships (perhaps with a picnic lunch and a bottle of wine purchased at the Marketplace or the Haymarket for sustenance). The walks are paved in brick, cobblestone, and granite; the lights have a nautical design; the tot-lot comes with a crow's nest and a wading pool; and there's even a "rest room" for dogs—three brightly painted hydrants!

Faneuil Hall Marketplace, an exciting addition to the Boston landscape, is a miniature city in itself, with stores, restaurants, exhibits, food markets, entertainment, and a swinging nightlife. The three-building complex, which is linked to Faneuil Hall by walkways and a plaza of brick, cobblestone, and granite, is in the National Register of Historic Places, but it is very much alive with people—mingling, shopping, and eating in a bazaar-like atmosphere. The main structure, a three-level Greek revival–style building, opened on August 26, 1976, 150 years after Mayor Josiah Quincy opened the original market. The South Market Building opened on that date in 1977, and the North Market Building on the same date in 1978.

Try to come early in the day to avoid the crush at the copper-domed **Quincy Market Building.** The street level is where the action is, with the Bull Market (shopping stalls and pushcarts) and the glass-canopied sidewalk aisles along either side. Here are the food stalls and market—crafts, craftspeople, and vendors—things to buy and eat. You could treat yourself to a pickup feast from the booths that line the marketplace: turkey sandwich at **Berenson's,** pizza at **Pizzeria Regina,** bagels at **Finagle Bagel,** coffee at **Coffee Connection,** chow mein at **Ming Tree,** shish-kebab at **Aris Barbecue,** tacos at **The Taco Maker,** subs at **Jennetta's,** Kosher franks at the **Brown Derby Deli,** shrimp roll at **Salty Dog,** and cherrystone clams at **The Walrus and the Carpenter.** But be warned: finding a place to sit down to eat is harder than finding a seat on the subway at rush hour. There are benches outdoors and box-like tables and chairs in the rotunda, but sometimes there is no choice but to eat standing or sitting on the floor.

If juggling and balancing plates is not your dish, treat yourself to one of the restaurants. On the top floor, the **Magic Pan** (entrees, desserts, and crêpes) and **Frogg Lane;** on the marketplace level, **Cityside** or **Lily's** sidewalk café for a light lunch; and in the brick basement, **Ashoka** for Indian dining or **Swensen's** for ice cream. Also try **Lily's Piano Bar** and the **Ames Plow Tavern,** a casual pub. Check out the unusual wares on the wooden pushcarts too—baskets, prints, crafts, and even supplies for "lefties" such as scissors, notebooks, and tools. And don't forget to buy some flowers at the stalls or in the **Greenhouse,** open 24 hours.

Now get your breath and try the **South Market Building** on the other side of the promenade—very elegant with expensive gift stores, high-fashion boutiques, and home-furnishing shops (see Chapter VI) adorning its three levels. There you'll find **Seaside Restaurant** (no view of the sea) and the bustling **Cricket's Restaurant** with its glass-canopied "Palm Court." At night the promenade between the Quincy and South Buildings glitters with lights illuminating the shops, the planters of flowers, the trees, and the young entertainers who offer music, mime, and juggling.

The **North Market Building** has posh retail stores, offices, the famous **Durgin-Park Restaurant,** and **Romagnoli's Table** (of TV and cookbook fame).

Hours at the marketplace are 10 a.m. to 9 p.m. Monday through Saturday, and noon to 6 p.m. on Sunday, but some restaurants open early for Sunday brunch and remain open until 2 a.m. daily. There are parking lots nearby, and multilevel parking garages at Dock Square, Haymarket Square, and the Aquarium. Best bet: Take the subway or bus to the State Street, Haymarket, or Government Center "T" station.

TWO WALKING TRIPS: TO LITTLE ITALY AND CHINATOWN

Boston's ethnic neighborhoods are distinct entities working hard to preserve their own cultural identities. Since Boston is such a walkable city, it's worth your while to take a few hours to stroll, browse, and taste (perhaps shop) your way through two of the most colorful enclaves: the North End (Little Italy) and Chinatown. Since the North End backs up to the waterfront, let's start there.

THE NORTH END–LITTLE ITALY: Pushcarts and festivals, old men playing bocce in the "prato," children playing hopscotch on the street, and Italian mamas calling from the windows. That's "Little Italy"—the North End. Here Boston's Italians, packed together in their historic old section, still maintain close family ties and try to keep the "newcomers" out. You see most of the North End when you tour the Freedom Trail (Paul Revere's house and the Old North Church), but there are two other times when you should go there—any weekend, when the pushcarts laden with fruit and vegetables clog the streets, and special weekends in July and August when feasts are held to honor the saints.

Take the subway to Government Center or Haymarket Square for the first stop on your way to the North End, and bring a camera and a shopping bag. This is the historic Haymarket area. On Friday and Saturday, entire families, young business people, students, all wander along the narrow streets, squeezing vegetables, peering into boxes, comparing prices, haggling for bargains. It's a real multimedia experience—sight, sound, smell, and taste. Buy a sub sandwich, a pizza, or hot chestnuts in the winter, or Italian ices in summer, and, eating as you go, explore the tiny narrow streets that have been there for hundreds of years. Buy some cheese, salami, and Italian bread, and perhaps a bottle of wine, and save money on lunch that day.

Use the pedestrian walk under the expressway to get to the residential and restaurant area of the North End, where you'll also find the churches, the focal points of the feast days. When homage is paid to the Madonna or the saints, the streets are blocked off, and the garland-bedecked statues are paraded through the area. There are floats, flowers, and bands, and still more statues, followed by the pious as they wend their way to one of the churches. The local papers carry the listings of feast days in July and August.

Shopping in the North End means shopping for food, so browse through the groceries and little bakeries and buy a few thousand calories: cappuccino or an Italian fruit drink at the **Caffè Paradiso**, 255 Hanover St., or **Caffè Vittoria**, 296 Hanover St. Try one of the little pastry shops for delicious cheese cannolis or macaroons, and indulge in real Italian homemade ice cream at **Caffè Pompeii**, 208 Hanover St. Buy real Italian bread and marvelous cheese to go with it at **J. Pace & Son**, 42 Cross St. And get some of their homemade sauces to take home with you. And don't forget the pizzas!

Pizzeria Regina, at 11½ Thatcher St., makes them crispy and oily and you can even order extra oil. You get a good small pizza at **Circle Pizza,** Hanover and Prince Streets, and family size at the **European Restaurant,** 218 Hanover St.

Follow Salem Street to Charter Street to **Copps Hill,** from which you have a magnificent view of the harbor and the waterfront. You can walk to the waterfront by following **Commercial Street.**

CHINATOWN: Home and shopping center for many of Greater Boston's Chinese families, Chinatown is a tiny, 3-block-long, 12-block-wide area, bounded by the expressway, the downtown shopping district, and the Tufts University medical complex. It's easy to reach by following Stuart Street to Harrison Avenue and Kneeland Street, through the Garment District. Take the Green Line to Boylston Street, and walk one block to Stuart Street. (You can drive to Chinatown following this same route, or turning off the Mass. Pike extension and using the parking garages.) You can also use the parking garage at the Tufts–New England Medical Center on Harrison Avenue. When you see the red phone booths with pagoda tops and bilingual street signs you'll know you're there.

The best place for window shopping is along Beach, Tyler, and Hudson Streets, and Harrison Avenue. Start on Beach Street and walk through the ceremonial **Chinatown Gateway,** which marks the formal entrance to the business district. The gate with its four marble lions is a Bicentennial gift from the government of Taiwan. As you browse, look for the poultry stores with live chickens in coops, waiting to become dinner for some Chinese family. Go into one of the food stores, examine the exotic wares, perhaps choose some dried fish hanging from the racks or "thousand-year-old-eggs" or packaged bird's-nest soup. You may see one of the basements where bean sprouts are grown (they don't always come in cans or packages). You can stop for a snack at **Wai Wai Ice Cream** on Oxford Street and indulge in an iced lichee or iced lotus-seed drink, some almond paste or grass jelly. They also serve chicken, fish bits, and rice dishes. Or have brunch Chinese style at most restaurants. It's called dim sum and consists of assorted Chinese hot hors d'oeuvres. We like **China Pavilion Restaurant,** 14 Hudson St., or **Imperial Tea House,** 70 Beach St. Get there before 11 a.m. if you want to avoid a long wait. Treat yourself to a winter melon dumpling with a delicious creamy filling, steamed sponge cake, moon cakes, or a bag of fortune cookies at **Ho Yuen Bakery,** 54 Beach St., open from 8 a.m. to 7:30 p.m. They'll even bake a birthday cake for you! You can check the schedule at the **China Cinema,** 84 Beach St. (tel. 423-7415), for a movie with English subtitles, browse in the gift shops, or relax at one of the many good Chinese restaurants (see Chapter IV for details).

If you're in Boston at the time of the Chinese New Year (January or February, depending on the moon), join the crowds to watch the traditional festivities, as dragons weave up and down the streets to the accompaniment of Chinese music and very loud firecrackers. In August, try to see the Festival of the August Moon, a local street fair. And don't forget those cameras. Call the Chinese Merchants Association, 20 Hudson St. (tel. 482-3972), for information on special events.

Chinatown Shopping: Ming's Oriental Super Market at 85-90 Essex St., is where the locals shop for daily fare including live fish and imported delicacies such as lichee nuts, preserved strawberries, and Chinese teas. They also have small gifts including teapots, bowls, spoons, and mats at reasonable prices. **Su Sun Market** on Harrison Avenue is another good food market. Buy some Chinese noodles, spices, or hot sauces to try at home.

BOSTON'S GARDENS

Boston's gardens rate a sightseeing trip of their own. They're not all within walking distance of each other, but with a combination of footwork and public transportation or auto, you can see them all in a long afternoon. (Give yourself time to relax and enjoy them.) The **Boston Public Garden,** adjacent to the Boston Common, is one of the prettiest public flower gardens anywhere, especially in the spring when thousands of tulips and pansies burst into delicate bloom. It's ideal for resting, people-watching, or letting the kids (or yourself) have a ride in the famed Swan Boats that move gently along the pond, under the bridge, around the island, and back from 10 a.m. to 5 p.m. The fare is 95¢ for adults, 75¢ for children under 12 and 85¢ for seniors.

Not noted for flowers, but for its trees, is the **Boston Common,** whose beautiful shade trees are identified with botanical labels.

The most spectacular garden of all awaits you at the **Arnold Arboretum** on 125 The Arbor Way, in Jamaica Plains, one of America's oldest parks. Opened in 1872 and often called America's greatest garden, it is open daily from sunrise to sunset. A National Historic Landmark, it is administered by Harvard University in cooperation with the Boston Department of Parks and Recreation. You can have a fine time wandering here through some 265 acres containing over 6,000 varieties of ornamental trees, shrubs, and vines hardy to the Boston area. Spring is heavenly, the air fragrant with the scent of dogwood, azaleas, rhododendrons, and hundreds of varieties of lilacs, for which the Arboretum is especially famous. You'll be sorry if you don't bring those cameras. There is no admission charge, and if you'd like information on what's in bloom, call 524-1718.

You can take the MBTA Orange Line to the Forest Hills stop and follow the signs to the top of a small hill. The Visitor Center is open 8:30 a.m. to 4 p.m. weekdays, and 10 a.m. to 4 p.m. weekends.

And if you'd like to do a little mini-mountain climbing, there's the **Blue Hills Trailside Museum,** Visitor Center for the 6,000-acre Blue Hills Reservation, Rte. 138 off 128, Milton (tel. 333-0690), just a short drive south from Boston. The exhibits are all new and imaginatively designed to reproduce the natural habitats of the Blue Hills. There are lookout towers and slide and crawl spaces designed so that visitors can watch live animals as they go about their everyday lives. A beautiful glass wall overlooks an outdoor pond, and there are trails to climb on the hillsides. Open Tuesday through Sunday from 10 a.m. to 5 p.m. except Thanksgiving, Christmas, and New Year's. Admission is charged.

GUIDED TOURS

WALKING TOURS: If you prefer guided walking tours to hoofing it on your own, **Boston by Foot,** 77 N. Washington St. (tel. 367-2345), conducts architectural tours of Beacon Hill and the Government Center area May through October. The guides, or docents, have taken a special educational program and are very knowledgeable about the architecture and history of the town. In addition to pointing out the distinguishing characteristics of Boston's architecture, they include history and anecdotes in the 1½-hour tours. The "Heart of the Freedom Trail" tour starts at the statue of Samuel Adams in front of Faneuil Hall on Congress Street on Tuesday, Thursday, and Saturday at 10 a.m. and on Sunday at 2 p.m. Tours of Beacon Hill start at the foot of the State House steps on Beacon Street on Tuesday, Thursday, and Saturday at 10 a.m. and on Sunday at 2 p.m. There are also Twilight Strolls through Beacon Hill at 5:30 p.m. on Wednesday and Friday. Other tours include Copley Square in Back Bay and the North End. Rates are $5 for adults and $3 for children.

There are also special tours for children, **Boston by Little Feet,** meeting at the statue of Samuel Adams, in front of Faneuil Hall on Congress Street on Sunday at 2 p.m. The children are encouraged to see, touch, and talk about the buildings they see. The tour takes an hour and costs $3 for children and adults. Call 367-2345 for meeting places and information on custom tours. Tickets may be purchased from the guides or from Bostix in Faneuil Hall Marketplace.

Historic Neighborhoods Foundation, 2 Boylston St. (tel. 426-1885), offers several walking tours that focus on neighborhood landmarks including Beacon Hill, North End, Back Bay (always involving interiors), and the waterfront and financial districts. The "Make Way for Ducklings" tour, very popular with children and adults, includes a ride on the Swan Boats in the Public Garden.

Schedules change with the season, and programs are based on themes, such as social history and topographical development. Write or call Historic Neighborhoods Foundation for current schedules.

You can't pick the flowers, but you can have a wonderful time on the Boston Park Rangers' free guided walking tours of **Boston's "Emerald Necklace,"** a network of green spaces tying the city to the suburbs, designed by landscape architect, Frederick Law Olmstead. This tour covers outstanding parks and gardens, including Boston Common, Public Garden, Back Bay, Commonwealth Avenue Mall, Muddy River in The Fenway, Olmstead Park, Jamaica Pond, Arnold Arboretum, and Franklin Park. You can choose the full six-hour walk or a one-hour tour of any of the sites. For hours and schedules, call 522-2639, 423-4659, or TTY 725-4006 (the phone for hard of hearing and the hearing impaired).

TOURING IN STYLE: Would you like to tour Boston in a private limousine? Visit just those places you really want to see, and search out the "hidden spaces and uncommon places" that make the city so fascinating? This is the type of tour that **Uncommon Boston, Ltd.,** 437 Boylston St., Boston, MA 02116, arranges so successfully. Uncommon Boston is the brainchild of Susan Berk, archivist, historian, and very knowledgeable Bostonian, who shares her love of the city and its special places through these tours. She has arranged visits to artists' studios with an artist as a guide, literary tours with a poet as a guide, ballet and theater tours, pub and tavern "crawls" (which include hors d'oeuvres and a drink), and chocolate tours (with bags for sample goodies). There are shopping trips and culinary events with guest chefs. Special tours of the area's colleges can also be arranged.

A brochure of regular tours plus a calendar of seasonal offerings is available. Call 617/731-5854 for a description of current tours. You can also request a personalized tour tailored to your interests. Prices begin at $135 for three hours for regular tours. Seasonal events are $20 and up; and the cost of individualized plans varies. "Uncommon" tours are also available throughout New England.

TROLLEY TOURS: A narrated tour is a good way to see the town. Take a trolley and sit back in comfort while you see the points of interest and listen to guides relate the history of Boston. The orange-and-green **Old-Town Trolley,** 329 W. Second St. (tel. 269-7010), schedules 1½-hour tours all year long. You can board at or near most hotels and get off at Quincy Market/Aquarium area, Copley Place, or Bunker Hill Pavilion (U.S.S. *Constitution*); and reboard later for the ride back to your starting point. The tour covers over 50 points of interest from Charlestown to Newbury Street, and is priced at $11 for adults, $9 for senior citizens. Children 5 to 12 are $4.

SIGHTSEEING CRUISES AND BOATING: Now if you'd like a change of pace in your sightseeing, we suggest one of the many cruises available. They range from a half-hour lunch trip through the harbor to a cruise to Provincetown or Gloucester. **Bay State Provincetown Cruises** (tel. 723-7800) and **Boston Harbor Cruises** (tel. 227-4321) both sail from Long Wharf, near the Marriott Hotel, and both offer narrated harbor cruises. Their prices and the length of time at sea may vary, so check them both out. Cost is between $3 and $4 for adults, with special rates for children and senior citizens, and sailing times are usually between 10 a.m. and 5 p.m.

You can see part of the Freedom Trail by boat too. The Bay State Provincetown line operates a Freedom Trail Water Shuttle to Charlestown Navy Yard, which goes through the inner harbor and past the airport, as the captain points out historical sights. You can stop at the Navy Yard to tour the U.S.S. *Constitution* and return on a later boat if you wish. Trips are hourly on the half hour from the red ticket office on Long Wharf, and on the quarter hour from the Navy Yard, and take 55 minutes round trip. Rates are $4 for adults, $2 for children under 12. Or combine lunch with the ocean breezes on Bay State's weekday 12:15 to 12:45 p.m. lunch cruise. Use the ship's galley or bring your own food.

Boston Harbor Cruises, 1 Long Wharf (tel. 227-4321), offers narrated cruises of Boston Harbor. You can choose their 90-minute historic cruise, which departs every two hours beginning at 11 a.m., or the 45-minute Constitution cruise, which docks at Charlestown Navy Yard so you can go ashore and visit the *Constitution*. These tours leave every hour on the half hour from Long Wharf, and on the quarter hour from the Navy Yard. There are also trips to George's Island in the outer harbor where you may stay for a few hours exploring the historic forts. (You can even get a free water taxi to visit the many harbor islands.) These boats sail every two hours from 10 a.m. to 4 p.m. A day-long trip for whale-watching leaves daily at 9:30 a.m. from Pier 7, South Boston, and there is a shuttle boat at Long Wharf at 9:20 a.m. to get you there. It returns at 4:30 p.m., and reservations are required for this one. Rates for the 90-minute cruises are $6 for adults, $3 for children under 12, and $5 for senior citizens. The 45-minute cruises are $5 for adults, $3 for children under 12, and $4 for senior citizens. The all-day whale watch is $20 for adults, $12 for children under 12, and $15 for seniors.

If you have the time, take one of the longer trips. The **Virginia C II, A. C. Cruise Line** sails to Gloucester from 28 Northern Ave. (near the Pier 4 restaurant). It leaves Boston Monday through Friday and on Sunday at 10:30 a.m., and returns from Gloucester at 5:30 p.m. The round-trip charge is $16.50 for adults. You'll have time for lunch or browsing at Gloucester's Rocky Neck Art Colony. Call 426-8419 for details. (On Saturday, the *Virginia C II* goes whale-watching.)

And for a full day at sea, there's the **MV Provincetown II** (tel. 723-7800), which sails from Commonwealth Pier daily from mid-June to Labor Day and on weekends in May and September. It's "anchors aweigh" at 9:30 a.m. for the three-hour trip to Cape

Cod's picturesque Provincetown. The sail home starts at 3:30 p.m., giving you a few hours for shopping and sightseeing. Round-trip fare is $20 for adults, $15 senior citizens, $13 for children under 12, and $3 for bicycles each way.

When the sun goes down, the ships don't return to harbor and drop anchor. Instead they take off again on very popular **evening cruises.** *Water Music* (tel. 876-8742) sails into the setting sun four nights a week to the tune of swing, blues, jazz, or chamber music. On Tuesday, the Dreamboat sways with swing and dance music; and on Wednesday, the jazz boat rocks to the rhythm of top bands. Both sail from Commonwealth Pier at 7:30 and 9:30 p.m. The Concert Cruise floats gently over the waves Thursday at 6:30 and 8:30 p.m. from Long Wharf. You can buy advance boarding tickets (that guarantee you a seat), or regular tickets. The Cabaret Jazz Boat, which offers a light supper, swings out on Friday at 7:30 p.m., also from Long Wharf. Purchase advance boarding tickets if you wish table seating.

And you must take at least one turn around the lagoon at the Boston Public Garden on the most famous ride of all—the **Swan Boats.** Built in the shape of a swan, with graceful neck and outspread wings, these pedal-powered boats still look the same as they did when first created in 1877, except they're now made out of fiberglass instead of wood. Oliver Wendell Holmes called them "as native to Boston as baked beans." Sailing along with the real swans and ducks in the lagoon, they operate from mid-April till the last Sunday in September (weather permitting). Hours are 10 a.m. to 6 p.m. (and from noon till 4 p.m. after Labor Day). The fare is 95¢ for adults, 75¢ for children, and 85¢ for seniors.

Boston's **Harbor Islands** are treasures that the locals like to keep to themselves. There are 30 islands in the outer harbor some of which are open for exploring, camping, or swimming—great spots for the day-tripper. George's Island is the most popular, with an old fort built in 1834; it's open for guided tours, and is rumored to have a resident ghost! There is a visitor's center, refreshment area, fishing pier, place for picnics, and a wonderful view of Boston's skyline. From there, free water taxis run to Lovells, Gallops, Peddocks, Bumpkin, and Grape islands, which have picnic areas and campsites (permits are required—call 740-1605 for permits for Bumpkin, Gallops, and Grape islands, 727-5250 for Lovells, and 523-1184 for Peddocks). Lovell's Island has a sandy beach and is the only island with supervised swimming. Boats run from Long Wharf and Rowes Wharf. Adult fare is $6. The islands are part of the Boston Harbor Islands State Park.

LOCAL BREWS: Sightseeing doesn't have to be all historic homes and museums. How about a brewery? Or two? Boston has two small breweries that offer free tours and are fun to visit.

Commonwealth Brewing, 138 Portland St. (tel. 523-8383), takes visitors to the brewery in small wagons drawn by two big shire horses (similar to Clydesdales) that run free shuttle trips from Faneuil Hall Marketplace on Wednesdays, Thursdays, and Fridays from 6 to 9:30 p.m., and on Saturdays and Sundays from 11:30 a.m. to 4 p.m. The brewing equipment is in the basement and guides explain the whole process, from hops to ale. On the street level is a restaurant and bar so that you can buy a glass of their English-style brew right where it is made.

Mass. Bay Brewing Co., 306 Northern Ave. (tel. 574-9551), brews and bottles Harpoon Ale, in small batches without preservatives, and sells it only in New England. Visitors to the brewery can see the various stages of processing, including the bottling and labeling of this handcrafted beer. Free tours are given Tuesday (bottling day) and Friday at 1 p.m., and Saturday at 11 a.m. and 1 p.m. Parking is available.

TIME FOR A SWIM

If you're ready now for a swim, you can take about an hour's drive south on Rte. 3 to **Nantasket Beach,** a large, well-equipped public beach in Hull. Or you can go farther south to Duxbury near Plymouth for a clean, quiet, nine-mile beach with dunes. The beach is located off Rtes. 3A and 139. Public parking is at the north end. Going north from Boston, try **Revere Beach,** which has an expanse of sandy beach and a gentle surf. Parking along the beach is free. Or take the MBTA to Revere Beach or Wonderland stations, 20 minutes from Boston. If you have a car, drive up to the end of the beach, near Point of Pines and the General Edwards Bridge, for less crowded swimming. Even more spacious, with clear, cold water for swimming is **Nahant Beach,** about three miles north. (We should warn you that the temperature of the water at North Shore beaches is apt to be quite low; they're not as cold as the beaches of Maine, but not as warm as those on the South Shore and Cape Cod.) If you're going to Nahant, get there early in the morning, especially on the weekends, since parking is just $1 and spaces fill up fast.

To the North Shore: If you're still in a summertime, beachy mood, you could continue driving north, on a one-day trip, to **Salem,** the original Witch City, where you can explore old houses and some outstanding museums, swim at **Salem Willows,** or take a boat ride to historic **Marblehead,** home of the American navy and now host to the chic yachting set, a great place to walk around, with its quaint streets, vintage houses, and fun shops; on to

Gloucester, home of the fishing fleet; and to the picturesque artists' colony at **Rockport.** But for the very best swimming on the North Shore, you should drive farther (a little over an hour from the city) to Ipswich, to beautiful **Crane Beach,** with its picturesque dunes, miles of white sand, and crisp, cold water. Admission is $6.50 during the week, $10 on weekends, but it's worth it, since many of the other North Shore beaches are for residents only. The drive, incidentally, will take you through what we call "John P. Marquand country," those elegant little villages where the Boston Brahmins have long escaped the summer heat.

If the parking lot at Crane is full (get there by 10 a.m.), try some of the other North Shore beaches. There are two fine places in Gloucester. **Wingaersheek Beach,** which is off Rte. 128 (exit 13), has beautiful white sand, a fantastic view, and sand dunes for climbing or hiding behind to seek privacy. It's open through Labor Day and there's also a charge for parking. **Stage Fort Park,** Rte. 128 (exit 13), is at Gloucester Harbor and has 100 acres of oceanfront with sheltered beaches, playgrounds, picnic and cookout areas, and an old fort site for the kids to explore. And if you'd like a stretch of several beach areas with magnificent dunes and a strong surf (surf fishing is allowed), follow Rte. 1A to Newburyport and **Plum Island,** which is part of the **Parker River Wildlife Refuge** with nature trails, observation towers, and wildlife. No admission or parking charge, but the small lots fill up early —sometimes cars are turned away at 9 a.m.

Just a word of warning: Wingaersheek, Plum Island, and Crane beaches are hosts to Greenhead flies as well as swimmers for a few weeks in late July and early August. Bring insect repellent with you. The beaches have lifeguard services and bathhouses.

Other fine area beaches include **Salisbury Beach,** Rte. 1A, south of the New Hampshire border, which has spectacular surf; and **Good Harbor Beach,** Gloucester, also with a fine surf, on Thatcher Road off Rte. 127A.

BOSTON'S EXTRAORDINARY MUSEUMS

The museums of Boston are among the finest in the country, and they offer a variety of choices for you to visit; museums devoted to art, science, transportation, plant, sea, and animal life are all within easy access of each other. Here's a rundown of what they offer to help you arrange your sightseeing.

Whether or not you're a serious student of art, you should pay a visit to two of the loveliest museums in the country, both of which happen to be in Boston: the Boston Museum of Fine Arts and the Isabella Stewart Gardner Museum.

MUSEUM OF FINE ARTS: Like the Metropolitan Museum of Art in New York (to which it ranks second among all the great museums of the country), the Museum of Fine Arts, 465 Huntington Ave. (tel. 267-9300), is enormously popular, usually drawing long-line crowds for its special exhibits. But even without anything special going on there is enough here to hold your attention for days—or at least many hours. The century-old museum is famous for its Oriental and Old Kingdom Egyptian collections, Medieval tapestries, and Buddhist temple, as well as American and European art. Our particular favorites are the Americans: Whistler, John Singer Sargent, Childe Hassam, with so many superb portraits and paintings that recall the young days of the colony and the country and the lovely days of Old Boston.

The main entrance to the museum is in the **West Wing,** a very contemporary granite I.M. Pei structure which contrasts sharply with the original building. A 200-foot-long curved skylight extends the length of the wing, which has climate-controlled galleries, an auditorium, gift shop, and an atrium with a tree-lined sidewalk café. It's extremely pleasant to sit there and enjoy light refreshments and sip wine. The glass-walled Fine Arts Restaurant, on the second floor of the West Wing, has fine gourmet cuisine. Pick up a floor plan at the Information Desk or take one of the free guided tours. (There's free checking just off the main lobby.)

Museum hours are 10 a.m. to 5 p.m. on Tuesday and Thursday through Sunday, to 10 p.m. on Wednesday. The West Wing and Evans Wing are also open Thursday and Friday evenings from 5 to 10 p.m. The museum is closed Monday and major holidays. Admission is $5 during hours the entire museum is open, and $4 during hours the West Wing only is open. Children under 16 are free, and senior citizens are $4 at all times. Dial ANSWERS (tel. 267-9377) for recorded listing of weekly events, or 267-9300, ext. 363.

The museum is located between Huntington Avenue and The Fenway. Take the "E" car on the MBTA's Green Line. If you're driving, you can park in the lot off Museum Road.

ISABELLA STEWART GARDNER MUSEUM: Stepping into the Isabella Stewart Gardner Museum, at 280 The Fenway (tel. 566-1401), is akin to walking back into the past, into a Venetian *palazzo* of a century ago, right into the middle of a Henry James novel. Mrs. Gardner, the wife of a wealthy Bostonian, lived in this house for 22 years and had it constructed to fit her fondest dreams; much of the art collection within was chosen with the help of her friend, Bernard Berenson. Pièce de résistance of the place is a breathtaking courtyard filled year round with fresh flowers (lilies at Easter, chrysanthemums in the fall, poinsettias at Christmas) and covered by a skylight. Spotted all about, on every floor, are the treasures that Isabella Gardner chose to live with: Whistlers and Sargents, Matisses and Titians; Italian religious masterpieces (including Raphael's *Pietà*); stained-glass windows; exquisite antique furniture. Try to get here for one of the concerts given in the magnificent Tapestry Room, with its heavy-beamed ceiling, superbly tiled floor, and priceless tapestries. They're given at 3 p.m. on Sunday, at 12:15 p.m. on Thursday, and at 6 p.m. on Tuesday (except July and August). All concerts are free.

Hours are noon to 6:30 p.m. on Tuesday (except July and August) and noon to 5 p.m. Wednesday through Sunday. (Closed on Monday and national holidays.) There is a voluntary donation of $3. For recorded information on exhibits and programs, call 734-1359. Lunch and desserts are served in a small café.

INSTITUTE OF CONTEMPORARY ART: Located in a handsomely remodeled Richardson-style building at 955 Boylston St., the Institute of Contemporary Art (tel. 266-5151), across from the Hynes Convention Center, is the showplace for 20th-century art spanning a wide range of stylistic forms, including painting, sculpture, photography, and video. The institute also offers a rich variety of activities—films, lectures, music, poetry, and an educational program for children and adults. Admission is $3.50 for adults, $2.50 for senior citizens and students, and $1 for children under 14. On Friday from 5 to 8 p.m. there is no charge at all. Hours are 11 a.m. to 5 p.m. Wednesday through Sunday, to 8 p.m. on Friday. The museum is closed Monday and Tuesday and major holidays.

NEW ENGLAND AQUARIUM: One of the busiest museums in Boston is the New England Aquarium at Central Wharf (tel. 742-8870). Take the MBTA Blue Line to the stop marked Aquarium, then the long escalator to the street, and you've arrived. And remember—aquariums aren't just for kids! This one will fascinate the whole family. Buy the guidebook, have a look at it, and at the ground-floor display, and then work your way up on the ramp alongside the glass four-story 200,000-gallon Giant Ocean Tank (the largest cylindrical saltwater tank in the world) with a Caribbean Coral Reef.

Five times daily you can watch scuba-divers feed the huge sharks, turtles, and moray eels in the tank. Other exhibit tanks are stocked with over 7,000 specimens of mammals, reptiles, birds, amphibians, fish, and invertebrates. The penguins and harbor seals are always fun to watch; and at the hands-on exhibit, "Edge of the Sea," visitors can pick up tidepool animals, including sea stars, horseshoe crabs, and sea urchins. The 1,000-seat floating amphitheater, Discovery, has dolphin and sea lion shows five times daily.

Summer hours from July to September are 9 a.m. to 6 p.m. on Monday, Tuesday, and Thursday, to 8 p.m. on Wednesday and Friday. Saturday, Sunday, and holiday hours are 9 a.m. to 7 p.m. Winter hours are 9 a.m. to 5 p.m. Monday through Thursday, to 8 p.m. on Friday, to 6 p.m. on Saturday and Sunday. The Aquarium is closed Christmas and Thanksgiving. Admission is $6 for adults, $3.50 for children 4 to 15, $5 for senior citizens, military, and students with ID. Children under 4 are free. If you're driving, take the Dock Square-Callahan Tunnel exit from the expressway, and park in the Harbor Towers garage near the Aquarium.

Note: The Aquarium sponsors whale-watch expeditions daily from early April through mid-October. They take you several miles out to sea to the Stellwagen Bank, feeding ground for the whales as they follow their migratory paths from Newfoundland to Provincetown. Rates are $22 for adults, $18 for senior citizens, and $16 for children 4 to 15 years.

For information about current Aquarium activities, call these numbers: 742-8870 for recorded information, 973-5200 for the main switchboard, 973-5227 for whale-watch recorded information.

MUSEUM OF SCIENCE/HAYDEN PLANETARIUM:

The Museum of Science at Science Park (tel. 742-6088) has a little something for everyone. Little children, teenagers, adults—everyone seems to be fascinated by the exciting, look-and-touch place full of exhibits that engage the visitor personally. This is a look *and* touch museum. You can, for example, pat a reptile, confront a live owl or porcupine eyeball to eyeball, play tic-tac-toe with a computer (which usually wins), weigh yourself on a scale—in moon measurements—or climb into a space module. The West Wing exhibits run the gamut of the ages, including a life-size replica of a tyrannosaurus. Don't miss the adjoining Hayden Planetarium where star shows are usually scheduled twice daily, but extra performances are sometimes added to accommodate visitors. Since the capacity of the Planetarium is limited, we suggest you buy your show tickets (an extra charge) when you enter the museum, even if it's quite some time before the performance. That way you'll be sure to get a seat.

There is also a Theater of Electricity where artificial lightning is produced twice daily, and an exhibit on the human brain where you can test your brain's reactions. The museum is open Tuesday to Thursday from 9 a.m. to 5 p.m., on Friday to 9 p.m., on Saturday to 5 p.m., and on Sunday to 5 p.m. Closed Monday, September through April.

Admission is $5 for adults, $3 for children 4 to 14 and senior citizens. Children under 4 are free. And if you come on Wednesday afternoons September through April, admission is free from 1 to 5 p.m. for everyone. You can walk to the Science Museum from North Station or the MBTA Science Park station. If you drive, the museum has its own parking garage.

MAPPARIUM: You can zoom out of the world at the Planetarium, but if you want a chance to walk right *inside* the world and view it from a new perspective, then take the family to the Mapparium (tel. 450-3790), inside the Christian Science Publishing Society, 1 Norway St., at the corner of Massachusetts Avenue and Clearway Street. You'll find yourself in an enormous room the exact shape of a globe, illuminated from the outside and explored via a bridgeway, under, above, and around which are various parts of the globe. Esthetically, it's a delightful experience; the colors are done in the style of old European stained glass, and the acoustics have a distinct quality, since the hard surface of the room does not absorb sound and one's voice bounces off. Various characteristics of the world are pointed out: where the International Dateline falls, which are the deep-water parts of the ocean. Meridians mark the time zones, so you can check the relative time in any section of the world.

There is also a Bible exhibit, "A Light Unto My Path," which really impressed us. It's the only one of its kind in the world and features a 30-minute film and slide program, an audio-visual time line, and 12 journeys of great figures of the Bible which you can follow on a sculptured map as you listen to the descriptions. The exhibit is at the end of the Christian Science Broadcasting building.

Three tours are given: the Mapparium, the Publishing House, and the church. For the times of the tours, call 450-3794. Admission is free. The Christian Science Complex with its beautiful reflections pool is near the MBTA's Prudential and Symphony stations. Hours are Monday through Friday from 8 a.m. to 4 p.m., on Saturday from 10 a.m. to 3:45 p.m., and on Sunday from 11:15 a.m. to 3:45 p.m. Closed Christmas and New Year's Day.

COMPUTER MUSEUM: It's hard to believe that computers have been around long enough to have a museum dedicated to them, but all those integrated circuits have a past that has been chronicled at the Computer Museum, 300 Congress St. (tel.

426-2800). The museum, located at Museum Wharf next to the Children's Museum, has over a half acre of fascinating displays with "hands-on" as well as historical exhibits. Visitors can use a vintage keypunch machine or the latest personal computer, design a car on a graphics terminal, or have a conversation with a talking computer. (There is another talking computer that gives current listings of lectures and special events when you call 423-6758.)

Museum hours are 10 a.m. to 6 p.m. Tuesday through Sunday, and to 9 p.m. on Friday. Closed Monday except during holidays and Boston school vacation weeks. Admission is $4.50 for adults, $3.50 for students and senior citizens; it's half price on Friday from 5 to 9 p.m. Note: Pick up some chocolate "chips" and microchip jewelry in the Museum Store.

THE CHILDREN'S MUSEUM: The Children's Museum, 300 Congress St. (tel. 426-8855), isn't just for children. Take our word for it, adults have just as much fun as the kids do in this special place where all are encouraged to touch. It's set up so that parents as well as kids can be on their own enjoying an unstructured experience, wandering randomly from one participatory exhibit to another. The possibilities are many: learn all about the human body and health in Mind Your Own Business; test estimating and math skills in the arcade-style Estimating Game; take an alphabetic adventure in the Ark in the Attic; experiment with the ever-changing small science exhibits; try on old clothing from the trunks in Grandparent's House; play games on computers; or explore the manhole beneath a city street. Or visit a Japanese house transported piece by piece from Kyoto, sister city to Boston. The 80-year-old six-room home and shop have been reassembled on the third floor of the museum.

And if you want a great bargain in craft supplies or materials for toys and games, stop at RECYCLE, where you can buy bags of industrial leftovers that can be recycled in many ways. (Admission to RECYCLE and to the museum's Resource Center are free.) Admission to the museum is $4.50 for adults, $3.50 for children ages 2 to 15 and senior citizens. The museum is open from 10 a.m. to 5 p.m. Tuesday through Saturday, until 9 p.m. on Friday (when admission is free from 5 to 9 p.m.). Closed on Monday except during July and August and Boston school vacations and holidays.

The Children's Museum is located on Museum Wharf, and has an unmistakable landmark, a 40-foot red-and-white wooden milk bottle that sits outside the building in a waterfront park. You can drive across the Congress Street bridge from South Station and hunt for a parking space, or take the Red Line to South Station and walk across the bridge.

Note: When the kids get hungry, try the ice cream and sandwiches served from the food stand in the "milk bottle," or hop into the McDonald's adjoining the Museum Gift Shop.

MASSACHUSETTS ARCHIVES: Looking for passenger lists of ships that arrived in Boston between 1848 and 1891? Census schedules dating back to 1840? Or perhaps vital records from all Massachusetts cities and towns, 1841 through 1895? All that information is on hand in the Massachusetts Archives at Columbia Point, 220 Morrissey Blvd. (tel. 727-2816). Here you can also view old documents, maps, charters, and military records going as far back as the Colonial Period (1643-1774). Staff members will also help researchers by mail and phone. The archives are open weekdays from 9 a.m. to 5 p.m. (except legal holidays), and on Saturday from 9 a.m. to 3 p.m.

The **Commonwealth Museum,** in the same building, features permanent and changing exhibitions displaying important artifacts and documents relating to the state's history. The archives and museum are adjacent to the J.F.K. Library.

KENNEDY LIBRARY AND MUSEUM: The Camelot years still live on in Boston at the John Fitzgerald Kennedy Library and Museum at Columbia Point on Dorchester Bay (for visitor information, tel. 929-4567). A combination library, museum, and educational research center, the concrete-and-glass memorial expertly captures the charisma of the Kennedy years. Perched on a hill overlooking Boston Harbor, the $12-million I. M. Pei architectural masterpiece is home to a maze of documents, photographs, recordings, and film clips that commemorate the life and times of the 35th president of the U.S. In addition, all the memorabilia and the historic papers are carefully arranged to give the visitor insight into the American political process and the nature of the presidency.

From the entrance on the mezzanine level, visitors get their first impact of the dramatic tone of the building—the view across the soaring glass-walled pavilion to the sea. That is followed by a poignant 30-minute documentary film which evokes the spirit of Kennedy's "New Frontier" years. The exit from the theater leads to the exhibition area, an artful arrangement of galleries organized around a central area which is a replica of the Oval Office in the White House. There are Kennedy's rocking chair and desk, just as he left them when he went to Dallas on November 22, 1963. The exhibits include some 3,000 items and 750 photographs, and encompass the civil rights movement, the Peace Corps, the space program, and the 1960 presidential campaign. There are dramatic events depicted: the Cuban missile crisis, the Bay of Pigs, the Berlin Wall visit. And political cartoons, favorite books, letters, and audio-visuals with the voices of J.F.K. and Rose Kennedy. Completing the sense of the dramatic quality that prevails throughout the building, the exit corridor echoes with taped sounds of the ocean and gulls, and leads the visitor out to the spectacular atrium.

Outside the building, J.F.K.'s boyhood sailboat *Victura* is on a strip of dune grass between the library and the harbor. Behind is the Archives Tower, nine stories of papers, books, films, and oral histories of J.F.K. and his brother, Robert. The material is available free to scholars and anyone interested in research. A fascinating Ernest Hemingway collection is also in the tower.

You can spend as much time viewing the exhibits as you wish, but count on at least two hours to see all the highlights. Admission is $2.50 adults, $1.50 seniors. Children under 16 with adults are free. Hours are 9 a.m. to 5 p.m. seven days a week. The last film begins at 3:50 p.m.

The getting there is easy. From Boston, drive south on the Southeast Expressway (Rte. 3) to exit 15, which is marked "JFK Library," and follow the signs. There is a large parking lot. And if that is full on weekends, you can use the adjoining University of Massachusetts lot. By public transportation take the MBTA Red Line (Ashmont branch) to the "JFK/U. Mass" stop. A free shuttle bus runs from the station to the library on the hour and the half hour.

Nearby in Brookline

Just a few miles away from the J.F.K. Library, in the suburb of Brookline, is the **John F. Kennedy National Historic Site,** at 83 Beals St. (tel. 566-7937). Restored to the way it was during John's childhood, with a tape-recorded voice of Rose Kennedy describing the rooms, it's pure nostalgia for anyone who grew up in the '20s and '30s and for those interested in the roots of the family. The small, one-family house is open daily from 10 a.m. to 4:30 p.m. Closed Thanksgiving, Christmas, and New Year's Days. Admission is $1 (children under 12 and adults over 62, free). Take the MBTA Green Line to Beacon Street and Coolidge Corner, and walk four blocks north on Harvard Street.

NEW ENGLAND SPORTS MUSEUM: A great place for sports' devotees who relish memorabilia of baseball, football, basketball, and hockey stars is the New England Sports Museum, 1175 Soldiers Field Rd. (tel. 787-7678). Fans can find Ted Williams' original locker from Fenway Park, along with photographs and paintings of New England sporting stars, a video jukebox re-running special moments in sports history, and a videotape collection that contains more than 2,000 hours of great moments in local sports. Admission is $1 for adults; children under 5 and senior citizens are free. The museum is open Wednesday through Saturday from 10 a.m. to 6 p.m., and Sunday from noon to 6 p.m. There are plans to move this museum to the Custom House. Check before you visit.

ART GALLERIES: The big museums are the beginning, but by no means the end, of the lively Boston art scene. There is nothing in the country quite like Newbury Street; the elegant few blocks between Arlington and Exeter Streets house some of the finest contemporary galleries in America, and in such an accessible geographic location! Plan to spend an afternoon taking a leisurely stroll viewing the assorted paintings, sculpture, and prints at the Newbury Street art galleries (there are more than two dozen of them).

THE SIGHTS OF CAMBRIDGE

You can't be in Boston for long without hearing about Cambridge, which bears about the same relationship to Boston as Berkeley does to San Francisco. It's just a short subway ride from the Park Street station of the MBTA across the Charles River, and every visitor should see it.

To get an overall picture of Cambridge, stop first at the **Cambridge Discovery Booth** at the Harvard Square subway entrance. The blue information booth is staffed by trained volunteers who will give you maps and brochures and answer questions about the city. From June through mid-October, it is open from 9 a.m. to 6 p.m. Monday through Saturday, and during the rest of the year until 5 p.m. Hours on Sunday are 1 to 5 p.m. Also from mid-June through Labor Day there are guided tours that include the entire old Cambridge area. Check at the booth about meeting places and times, or call them (tel. 497-1630). Rates for tours are $4 for adults and $2 for children and senior citizens. If you prefer sightseeing on your own, you can purchase an Old Cambridge or East Cambridge walking guide prepared by the Cambridge Historical Commission for $1. If you would like to arrange a special tour, write to Cambridge Discovery, Inc., P.O. Box 1987, Cambridge, MA 02238.

You will, of course, want to explore **Harvard Yard,** which you can do by wandering about on your own, or by taking a free guided tour from the Information Center, Holyoke Center, Massachusetts Avenue (tel. 495-1573). Some of the highlights include the ultra-space-age **Carpenter Center,** designed by Le Corbusier, which manages to be both circular and square at the same time; the **Science Center,** an enormous structure modeled after a Polaroid camera (look for the silver shutter); **Memorial Hall,** with its breathtaking stained-glass windows and vast ceilings; the eight residential houses for undergraduates, styled in Georgian tradition with domes and bell; the imposing **Widener Library** with its 2½ million books (second in size only to the Library of Congress), built by Mrs. Widener in memory of her son who went down on the *Titanic.* (The tours do not go into the libraries as it is felt that groups would disturb the readers. You can visit Widener on your own; for the other libraries, you need a Harvard ID.) You may also want to visit Yamasaki's **William James Center for the Behavioral Sciences.** Take the elevator up to the 15th floor for a spectacular view of Cambridge. Also worth seeing are the **Loeb Drama Center,** home of the American Repertory Theater, and the **Gutman Library,** at the School of Education (across the street from the Loeb), the recipient of many architectural awards. You can also get maps, illustrated booklets, and self-guided walking-tour directions at the Information Center.

The **Harvard University Museums of Natural History,** 24 Oxford St., are four famous museums under one roof: the Museum of Comparative Zoology, the Botanical Museum, the Geological and Mineralogical Museum, and the Peabody Museum of Archeology and Ethnology. They offer a wonderful range of exhibits from pre-Columbian art to dinosaurs, and including rare gems and the famous "glass flowers." Hours are Monday through Saturday from 9 a.m. to 4:30 p.m., on Sunday from 1 to 4:30 p.m. Admission is free on Saturday mornings from 9 a.m. to 11 a.m. At other times the fee is $2 for adults, $1.50 for students and seniors, 50¢ for children 5 to 15; children under 5, free. One fee covers admission to all the buildings.

Most unusual of the museums in this complex is the **Botanical Museum,** Oxford Street, but you don't have to be a botanist to appreciate it. The highlight here is the stunning **Ware Collection** of glass flowers, the most unusual—and durable—flower garden in the world. At first glance, it's almost impossible to tell that the flowers and plants are not real; even when you *know* they're not, you still want to bend over and sniff the perfume. The flowers are considered the finest example of decorative glasswork ever done, the masterpieces of two Germans, father and son, Leopold and Rudolf Blaschka, whom Harvard hired to work at their home near Dresden, Germany, from 1887 through 1936. Since Rudolf's death in 1939, no one has been able to duplicate the artistry of the Blaschkas, who "combined the mind of naturalists and the skill of artists in glass." The museum is open from 9 a.m. to 4:30 p.m.

Monday through Saturday, from 1 to 4:30 p.m. on Sunday. Closed New Year's Day, July 4, Thanksgiving, and Christmas.

The **Harvard University Art Museums**—the Fogg and the Arthur M. Sackler—house some 100,000 works of art in their collections. Both of these distinguished teaching museums are near the Harvard Yard, and just a short walk from the MBTA station at Harvard Square.

The **Fogg Art Museum,** 32 Quincy St. at Broadway, is best known for its collection of British and American 19th-century paintings and drawings, French paintings and drawings from the 18th century through the impressionist period, and late medieval Italian paintings.

The **Arthur M. Sackler Museum,** 485 Broadway at Quincy Street, is the newest museum in Greater Boston, and houses Harvard's collection of Oriental, ancient, and Islamic art. Included are ancient Chinese jades and cave reliefs, Japanese woodblock prints, Roman sculpture and Greek vases, and Persian miniature paintings and calligraphy.

The art museums are open Tuesday through Saturday from 10 a.m. to 5 p.m., Thursday until 9 p.m., Sunday from 1 to 5 p.m.; closed Monday and major holidays. Admission to the three museums is $3 for adults, $1.50 for students and senior citizens, and free for children up to age 18. Admission is free to all on Saturday mornings. One-hour guided tours of the Fogg and Sackler are available every weekday. For tour information call 495-9400.

Harvard Semitic Museum, 6 Divinity Ave. (tel. 495-5656), features artifacts from the museum's archeological collection that focus on the Middle East, as well as special items relating to the history and culture of Semitic peoples. Hours are 11 a.m. to 5 p.m. Monday through Friday, 1 to 5 p.m. on Sunday; closed Saturday and major holidays. Admission is free, but donations are accepted.

Do a little exploring of **Harvard Square.** Here you can buy a newspaper from anywhere in the world, and shop at the big Harvard Coop (rhymes with soup). Then wander through Brattle Street, with its great little bookstores and boutiques, perhaps have tea and pastry or lunch at the charming Blacksmith House near the spot where Longfellow's Village Smithy once stood. Farther along, at 105 Brattle St., is **Longfellow House,** where books and furniture have remained unchanged since the poet died there in 1882 (open daily from 10 a.m. to 4:30 p.m., except Thanksgiving, Christmas, and New Year's Days; admission is $2 for adults, free for children under 12 and adults over 62). The house was also Gen. George Washington's headquarters in 1775–1776.

On adjoining Mount Auburn Street, you might look in at the old cemetery where Longfellow, Oliver Wendell Holmes, and Mary Baker Eddy are buried. And opposite Harvard Common, north of the square, is the 18th-century **Christ Church,** used as a barracks during the American Revolution.

If you'd like to visit the **Massachusetts Institute of Technology** campus on the Cambridge side of the Charles River, facing Boston, you're perfectly welcome to wander around on your own. Ask for the "Walk Around MIT" map-brochure at the Information Center, 77 Massachusetts Ave., Cambridge (tel. 253-4795), which describes the environmental sculpture collection and outstanding architecture. And if you have time, take one of the student-guided tours of the campus (85 minutes long, at 10 a.m. and 2 p.m.). You'll see the two Saarinen buildings on Kresge Plaza, the Nautical Museum, Hayden Library, and several buildings designed by I. M. Pei.

Harvard and its museums are reached by taking the MBTA Red Line subway to Harvard Station. Take the same line to MIT, but get off at Kendall station. If you're driving, follow Storrow Drive to Cambridge, or cross the Longfellow Bridge at Massachusetts Avenue and you're at MIT on Memorial Drive. Continue along the drive to your left for the scenic approach to Harvard, or drive straight ahead from the bridge through the traffic of Massachusetts Avenue for the stores-restaurants-theater approach.

THE BIGGEST SHOW IN TOWN: The only theater of its kind in New England and one of only 12 in the country, the **Mugar Omni Theater** at the Museum of Science, Science Park (tel. 617/523-6664), is the biggest show in town. That is, it has the world's largest film format—10 times larger than conventional 35-mm. film; a four-story domed screen 76 feet in diameter; and a sound system with 84 speakers inside the screen. Images wrap around on all sides of the viewer, creating a "you are there" sensation, whether it's riding the white waters of the Grand Canyon or whizzing through outer space in a dazzling 3-D original film. Presentations change every six months. Admission prices for the Omni show are $5 for adults; $3 for children 4 to 14; and $3 for senior citizens. There are several combination tickets that include admission to both the exhibit halls and a laser show for $7.50 and $10. Showings are Tuesday through Sunday, with Monday presentations added during summer months. It is best to call ahead for reservations and choice of time and date. Garage parking is available.

CHAPTER VI

SHOPPING IN BOSTON

□ □ □

The quality of Boston shopping can be summed up in just one word: great. For when you shop in this town, you're benefiting from two of the secrets of Boston's success: its very chic, very contemporary sophistication, and its centuries-old heritage of shrewd Yankee trading. As a result, Boston has some of the finest specialty and department stores, some of the most imaginative boutiques, and—in particular—some of the sweetest bargains to be found anywhere.

There are, roughly, three major shopping areas in Boston, and others close by. The first is Downtown Crossing, the large, traffic-free pedestrian mall along Washington, Winter, and Summer Streets, near the Boston Common. (The MBTA has arranged special shuttles to take shoppers around the district. Taxis are permitted after 7 p.m.) This is where you find the major department stores, Filene's and Jordan Marsh, and the little bargain emporiums, as well as the shops of Lafayette Place. Most stores are open every evening until 7 p.m. The second is the Back Bay area, long famous for its specialty shops and art galleries. Lord & Taylor and Saks Fifth Avenue have branches here. The mammoth Copley Place, with a three-story Neiman-Marcus showpiece and 100 chic shops in its two-level shopping mall, is also in this area. The third is Faneuil Hall Marketplace, where you can find everything—from status boutiques to pushcarts.

A ten-minute subway ride to Cambridge takes you to a colorful, boutique-filled shopping world in and around Harvard and Charles Squares. And if you're visiting historic Salem, Marblehead, Gloucester, or Lexington, you can conveniently detour at several remarkable discount and bargain establishments and shopping malls.

Note: Massachusetts has no sales tax on clothing (less than

$175) and food. All other items are taxed at 5%. Restaurant meals and food prepared for take-out are also taxed at 5%.

And so—to work. Let's begin at the place where society matrons and secretaries and local housewives meet and compete for the most remarkable bargains in town—at **Filene's Basement.**

THE DOWNTOWN BARGAINS

To look at the upper floors of **Filene's,** a calm, pleasant department store at 426 Washington St., you would never have any idea of what goes on beneath the first floor. But walk downstairs to the basement level and pow! it seems as if every other shopper within a 500-mile radius of Boston has also descended on the area. The reason, of course, is that the "Original Basement" is famous the world over. When the most fashionable stores in the country —Neiman-Marcus, Bergdorf Goodman, Bloomingdale's, Saks Fifth Avenue, to name a few—need to clear out their overstock, when a store goes out of business, when manufacturers have extra merchandise, they sell the lot to Filene's Basement. The result is one of the Basement's famous specials, advertised in advance in the Boston papers. There they are—scads of Neiman-Marcus $500-and-up women's dresses each about $100; $200 pants suits from SFA at $80; $50 name-brand bathing suits at $25. Men's quality leather shoes are $49 a pair. Children's $15 slacks are $7. Wedding and evening gowns are especially good buys. And so it goes: clothing for everybody, luggage, pocketbooks, lingerie, cosmetics, linens, a miscellany of items at phenomenal savings. And the automatic markdown policy keeps lowering the prices over a 35-day period, at the end of which the merchandise is given away to charity. Look for the automatic racks for your best values. The crowds are fierce, the competition keen, and the race is not for the faint-hearted. Get there early, sharpen your elbows, and good luck! There are no dressing rooms, by the way, but nobody minds if you slip things on over your clothes. And—an unusual policy for a discount operation—everything is returnable: you can even mail the merchandise back!

Note: Filene's has expanded its basement operation so that there are now departments in some of the suburbs and in other states. But none of them can compare with the original.

In the heart of Downtown Crossing, at the corner of Summer and Washington Streets, is **Jordan Marsh Company,** New England's largest store. Inside the handsome brick façade you can find ready-to-wear and designer fashions, gift boutiques, housewares, furniture, unique gifts, and a fashion basement too. Plus a bakery that has a secret recipe for blueberry muffins that are famous throughout New England.

Between Filene's and Jordan Marsh is a brick-paved mall with benches where you can rest or have a snack after jostling through the respective basements. Across the street is a vertical shopping mall, "The Corner," and several small stores. In the middle of that block is *the* bargain bookstore, **Barnes & Noble,** 395 Washington St. It's big and crowded, and you check out supermarket style, but you can save a few dollars on many current books and records and quite a bit on publisher's overstocks. And if you have any money left, proceed to the world's biggest **Woolworth's,** at 350 Washington St., which has huge souvenir sections as well as clothing, housewares, and—very important in Boston—a parking garage.

Stoddard's, 50 Temple Pl., between Washington and Tremont Streets, and at Copley Place, is the oldest cutlery shop in the country and has been selling quality merchandise since 1800. The variety of items is amazing. You can choose from about 100 kinds of sewing scissors and 25 styles of nail scissors. (We have given their Swiss army knives for Christmas gifts for many years.) Stoddard's also has shaving brushes, binoculars, fine fishing tackle, and fly rods. Open 10 a.m. to 7 p.m. Monday through Saturday and noon to 5 p.m. on Sunday.

Tired and hungry? Follow the aroma of freshly baked bread to **Wharburton's Hot Bread Bakery,** at the corner of Bromfield and Washington Streets, for over a dozen varieties of bread, rolls, and muffins. Grab a fast pickup between shopping sprees at one of the many fast-food restaurants in "The Corner." Choose from pizza, Japanese food, hot dogs, hamburgers, or ice cream.

And for the pause that adds calories, treat yourself to the most delicious hot-fudge sundae anywhere at **Bailey's,** 26 Temple Pl. or 74 Franklin St. They also gift-pack candies for you to send home —or keep. There are other locations at Faneuil Hall Marketplace and in Harvard Square to satisfy sweet-tooth cravings.

BACK BAY SHOPPING
(Newbury, Boylston, Charles Streets, and Copley Place)

COPLEY PLACE: Start your Back Bay shopping excursion at Copley Place and you may never leave, for there are also two hotels (the Westin and the Marriott), a nine-screen cinema complex, full-service restaurants (including Durgin-Park), and several food shops. This is a mecca of retailing elegance appealing to the affluent shopper who can stroll from the three-level Neiman-Marcus to Tiffany, Gucci, Ralph Lauren, Louis Vuitton, and Saint Laurent

Rive Gauche, with perhaps a stop at Godiva Chocolatiers or Williams-Sonoma gourmet cookware. The 100 shops radiate from a skylit atrium with a 60-foot-high waterfall sculpture circled by pink marble floors. Shop for men's and women's apparel, jewelry, music boxes, gift items, and home furnishings; order customized jewelry at The Goldsmith, or custom-made men's and women's shirts at The Custom Shop Shirtmakers. For your sweet tooth there are four candy shops and Mrs. Field's Chocolate Chip Cookies. Escalators move shoppers (and sightseers) from level to level, but elevators are also tucked into the corners of the building. The shopping galleries are open Monday through Friday from 10 a.m. to 7 p.m., on Saturday to 6 p.m., and on Sunday from noon to 5 p.m. Neiman-Marcus is open the same hours as the galleries, but is closed on Sunday. Some stores have extended hours, and the cinemas and some restaurants are open through late evening.

Even if you don't plan to shop Copley Place, it's worth a visit. The six-block city within a city utilizes air space over the Massachusetts Turnpike extension, uniting the Back Bay and the South End neighborhoods which had been split by the turnpike. Total cost was over $500 million.

The exterior of the vast complex is pink and buff stonework designed to fit into the historic neighborhood of Trinity Church, the Boston Public Library, and the Copley Plaza Hotel. It is connected by glass-enclosed pedestrian bridges to the Westin and Marriott hotels, and to the Prudential shopping center with its retail shops, as well as Lord & Taylor and Saks Fifth Avenue—and from there to the Hynes Convention Center.

Copley Place can be reached by MBTA's Green Line (Copley stop). An underground connection from the Orange Line and from Amtrak's Back Bay Station is now available. If you're driving, take the Copley Square exit eastbound from the Massachusetts Turnpike. Park in the Copley Square garage on Huntington Avenue, corner of Exeter Street. If that's full, use the John Hancock garage or one of the nearby hotel garages. Since they're all expensive, and you'll want to spend hours there, we suggest public transportation.

Note: There is also a bank at Copley Place—in case you need to negotiate a loan for diamonds at Tiffany's.

THE BOUTIQUES: From the glamour world of Copley Place, move on to the boutiques of **Newbury Street,** whose old brownstones that once were home to high society now house elegant shops, art galleries, sidewalk cafés, and chic restaurants. You'll find **F.A.O. Schwarz** for children's toys; **Brooks Brothers** for perfectly tailored clothes; and at the corner of Newbury and Berkeley Streets, housed in a handsome building that was once the Museum of Natural History, **Louis,** the ultra-prestigious men's store where $1,500 suits are coordinated with handmade shirts, silk ties, and Italian shoes. There is also a **Louis for Women** division catering to an elegant female clientele. We suggest starting your shopping spree at the corner of Newbury Street near the Ritz-Carlton Hotel, and strolling and browsing where fancy chooses. Be sure and stop at some of the art galleries and sidewalk cafés. Herewith a sampling of some of our favorite shops:

If you're in the market for a magic carpet, or just a tapestry or hand-woven rug, stop in at **Decor International,** 171 Newbury St., for the finest collection of unique hand-woven rugs anywhere —imported from over 41 countries. Wall hangings are priced from $40, and there are Oriental rugs, quilts, bedspreads, pillows, folk art, and ethnic jewelry too.

The scent of herbs and dried flowers greets you as you enter **La Ruche** (which translates as "beehive"), 174 Newbury St. The shop features unusual decorative accessories, French and Italian faïence, silk flowers (made to order as well), hand-painted baskets and linen, and potpourri. One specialty of the boutique is painted furniture in faux finishes.

Also on Newbury Street, at number 83, is **Laura Ashley, Inc.,** which features a line of the fresh, innocent country prints in dresses, blouses, shirts, and accessories.

Peking Oriental Imports, at 159 Newbury St., features imports from the People's Republic of China—straw baskets, brocade bags, jewelry boxes, silk jackets, fans, and kites.

And topping it all off at the corner of 360 Newbury St. and Massachusetts Avenue is **Tower Records,** claimed to be the largest record store in the country, and perhaps the world, with three floors of records, tapes, and compact discs. It's colorful with banks of neon and noisy with blasting stereos. Open from 9 a.m. to midnight, except Sunday when it opens at noon.

One more stop before you leave the area should be the **Women's Educational and Industrial Union,** at 356 Boylston St. We've found lovely handmade children's clothes there, as well as needlepoint designs, yarns, beautiful gifts, and antiques. This nonprofit educational and social service organization has been part of the Boston scene since 1877.

Note to antique aficionados: Charles Street, which starts at the intersection of Boston Common and the Public Garden, boasts many high-quality antique shops.

THE BOOKSTORES: If your shopping list includes books combine your browsing with refreshments at **Harvard Bookstore Café,** 190 Newbury St., an upscale gathering place where literati meet at tables among the stacks. There's a good variety of selections on both the shelves and the menu.

Further along the street, **Trident Booksellers and Café,** 338 Newbury St., has a tiny café with simple fare, a relaxed atmosphere, and a large selection of books on philosophy, meditation, and macrobiotics along with mainstream novels and paperbacks. Sunday afternoons there are often readings by the Writers League of Boston. For schedules phone 617/267-8688.

If you're into nostalgia you'll enjoy **Avenue Victor Hugo Bookshop,** 339 Newbury St., where its musty shelves stretch to the ceiling and cling to the brick walls. Most of the 100,000 volumes are "previously owned," as are the magazines, comic books, sheet music, and other memorabilia.

FANEUIL HALL MARKETPLACE

You already know about the Faneuil Hall Marketplace as a food and entertainment center; it should also be part of your Boston shopping experience. There are three buildings in the market, separated by brick-and-stone malls. The Central Building (see Chapter V on sightseeing) has the food stalls, pushcarts, craftspeople, little stores, and novelties. The South and North Markets have the boutiques and clothing stores.

The Arcade in the South Market is a treasure trove of little boutiques with unusual wares. At **Have A Heart,** everything from jewelry, stationery, and gift wrappings to quilts, pillows, and baby T-shirts has a heart motif.

Folklorica has an exquisite selection of jewelry, antique and contemporary. Not to be missed!

And **Bear Necessities** specializes, of course, in bears: stuffed polar bears, teddy bears, Goldilocks bears, and even totebags and notepaper with the bear motif.

Move on to **Celtic Weavers** for handmade items imported from Ireland, England, Scotland, and Wales.

For decorative pieces for the home, browse through the little shops such as **Brass'n Bounty.** Or explore the vast assortment of furnishings and kitchenware at **Crate and Barrel.** Buy soaps, jellies, or dried petals and oils to make your own potpourri at **Crabtree and Evelyn,** and original scrimshaw at **Boston Scrimshanders.**

We think the concept of a gallery of museum shops, where you can find gifts and art reproductions from several museums all in *one* place, is the answer to an art lover's shopping dream. The **Gallery of Museum Shops** on the second floor of the South Market building features items from the Museum of Fine Arts, Thoreau Lyceum, Old Sturbridge Village, and other cultural centers.

Now to the North Market. Several fine restaurants are here, including Romagnoli's Table (of TV and cookbook fame), and the ever-popular original Durgin-Park (see Chapter IV). We suggest starting at one end of the building and browsing through, upstairs and downstairs, stopping at little shops for children's clothes, toys, and games. And if you know you're going to jog off the calories, try **Sweet Stuff,** a candy store with unusual treats including chocolate pizzas and dozens of varieties of jelly beans, or **Seréndipity** for fabulous chocolate sodas.

There are so many shops that we're only able to recommend a few of our favorites. It's fun to wander through and make your own discoveries, or you can pick up a brochure that lists all the shops and eateries (over 150) at the information center beneath the rotunda of the Quincy Market Building.

MAIL-ORDER OUTLETS: If you're like us, you might enjoy receiving mail-order catalogs but hesitate to order without actually seeing the merchandise. To our delight, we've found several mail-order firms that have retail stores in the Boston area where you can see before you buy.

In Boston: With locations at 29 School St. and at the new Marketplace Center (adjacent to the Faneuil Hall shopping area), **Brookstone** has a fascinating selection of unusual and high-quality tools, housewares, travel accessories, and garden items. **Sharper Image of San Francisco,** also in the Marketplace Center, sells very upscale electronic items and merchandise you usually won't find in your local shopping malls. **Markline,** another supplier of high-quality electronics, watches, and audio equipment, has a retail store at 1 Federal St., near the Federal Courthouse. And at the Marketplace Center and Copley Place shopping mall, **Williams-Sonoma** sells the kitchen wares featured in its very popular catalog.

Beyond Boston: On Rte. 1 in Danvers (north of the city) and Rte. 9 in Framingham (south of the city), **Deerskin Trading Post** offers the leather coats and jackets, accessories, and boots highlighted in the catalog. And they also have great reductions in their catalog surplus section in Danvers. **Appleseed's,** famous for classic women's fashions, has its retail headquarters in Beverly at 54 Dodge St., off Rte. 1A North.

SHOPPING IN CAMBRIDGE

Cambridge is located just across the Charles River from Boston. It's about a five-minute drive, but since parking is as hard to find as tuition money for Harvard, take the Red Line of the "T" to the Harvard/Brattle stop, and start your shopping at **"The Coop,"** the famous Harvard Cooperative Society, at 1400 Massachusetts Ave., across from the subway station. This is *the* meeting place in the square. It's a complete department store, and you can buy everything from stationery (with Harvard insignia) to clothes to stereos. And of course, books. The annex to the Coop has three floors of books, including the required texts for Harvard classes.

Crate and Barrel, 48 Brattle St., with its dramatic glass front, is the other large store in the square. It has a Scandinavian accent with beautiful glassware, kitchenware, and Marimekko fabrics. (And if you're in the mood for a good buy, try their warehouse store at 171 Huron Ave., a few minutes from Harvard Square.)

We like **Ann Taylor,** 44 Brattle St., for women's clothes, and we always check the sale racks in back of the store. The values are great. **Clothware,** 52 Brattle St., is a specialty shop with a contemporary line of women's dresses, lingerie, and fun accessories. They also have their own private label line. And for men's wear with the Harvard look, there's **J. August Co.,** 1320 Massachusetts Ave., and the **Crimson Shop,** 12-18 Dunster St.

One store that still retains old Cambridge elegance is **J.F. Olsson,** at 43 Brattle St. The collection of pins, necklaces, and earrings is delightful. And we always find distinctive greeting cards there. It's been several years since we first discovered **Colonial Drug,** 49 Brattle St., and we're still working our way through the more than 600 fragrances they feature at the perfume counter. No fancy displays, no pressure, just a lovely place to shop.

You can go antique hunting on Brattle Street too. **Bernheimer's Antique Arts,** 52C Brattle St., specializes in antiquities, European, Asiatic, and primitive art; and also carries beautiful antique jewelry. **Cardullo's Gourmet Shop,** 6 Brattle St., is a gourmet's delight with fine food specialties from all over the world. If you can't afford the truffles, buy some imported crackers or cheeses.

Now, from Harvard Square to nearby Charles Square. The stores at Charles Square, Bennett and Eliot Streets (just look for the colorful flags) are pure "yuppie" heaven. There are fashionable boutiques for clothing, gifts, novelties, and accessories, clustered around an atrium. An adjacent courtyard is used for dining, concerts, festivals, etc. Among our favorite things at Charles Square

are the quality fashions at **The Talbots,** which has a wonderful store for petites; the greeting cards and stationery at **Papermint;** and the travel and safari clothing at **Banana Republic.** And of course, the enclosed parking garage for 700 cars under the central courtyard. The shops are open from 10 a.m. to 9 p.m. weekdays, to 6 p.m. on Saturday, and from noon to 6 p.m. on Sunday.

On John F. Kennedy Street (the old Boylston Street with a new name), you'll find **The Garage,** another complex of shops and eating places. Savor a roast beef sandwich with boursin cheese at **Formaggio,** and you shouldn't leave without sampling a cup of fresh-ground, freshly brewed coffee at the **Coffee Connection.**

DOLLAR-WISE SHOPPING: You'll love shopping in Boston's elegant stores, but you'll probably want to pick up a few bargains too. Try **John Barry Ltd.,** 75 Kneeland St., which discounts quality women's wear from many manufacturers. Nearby at 50 Essex St., **New England Textiles** has tremendous values on fabrics, by the bolt or by the yard. In the suburban malls, look for **Loehmann's,** which has great buys in women's clothes; and **Marshall's,** one of the large discounters of clothing, linens, gifts, and shoes. Check the phone books for their locations north and south of the city. **Syms,** 637 Lowell St., off Rte. 1, West Peabody, has a well-deserved reputation for good buys in men's and women's clothing. And the expensive Joan and David shoes found in chic shoe salons can also be found at the **Joan and David outlet,** 1935 Revere Beach Parkway in Everett. Call 387-5005 for current hours.

The **Blacksmith House Café,** 56 Brattle St., is a delightful spot for coffee and Viennese pastries. And **Bailey's,** at 21 Brattle St., has our four-star rating for hot-fudge sundaes.

A short distance from Harvard Square at 11 Divinity Ave., the **Peabody Museum Gift Shop** has folk art and handmade crafts from all over the world, from primitive African sculpture to delicate Chinese porcelain, all at excellent prices. The shop is open Monday through Saturday from 10 a.m. to 4:30 p.m., on Sunday from 1 to 4:30 p.m.

CHAPTER VII

BOSTON AFTER DARK

□ □ □

All through the year there's enough activity to keep the nightowls busy, from jazz and rock clubs to romantic cocktail lounges for drinks and dancing, even dinner-theaters presenting Broadway musicals.

Boston, however, is not a particularly late town. The bars do stay open until 2 a.m. (1 a.m. on Saturday nights), but the public transportation systems shut down quite a bit before. Some of the MBTA lines start closing at midnight, and all trolleys and buses are safely tucked away for the night by 1:30 a.m. After that, you'll have to depend on your own wheels or on a cab.

CULTURAL BOSTON

MUSIC: The **Boston Symphony Orchestra.** A child growing up in Boston is likely to be under the impression that there is only one really great symphony orchestra in the world—the Boston Symphony, of course. Bostonians are justifiably proud of that remarkable orchestra, and they've been "going to Symphony"—that is, to Symphony Hall, 301 Huntington Avenue at Massachusetts Avenue (tel. 266-1492)—for over 100 years now. No matter what season of the year you're in town, you should be able to see the Boston Symphony in one of its varied manifestations.

The winter season of the Symphony runs from September through April, and although most tickets are taken by subscription, the house is not completely sold out. For Friday-afternoon and Saturday-evening performances, "rush seats" are available, one to a customer, to a limited, lucky few. They cost $5.50 each and go on sale in the Cohn Annex Lobby at 9 a.m. on Friday and 5 p.m. on Saturday. Good seats are available for almost all performances. The BSO performs most Tuesday, Thursday, and Saturday evenings, Friday afternoons, and a few Friday evenings.

Beginning in early May until early July, everybody goes to "Pops"—that's the **Boston Pops Orchestra.** During Pops season, Symphony Hall is decorated in garden tones of green, the orchestra seats are taken out and replaced with tables and chairs, punch and light beverages are sold (the Pops name comes from the sound of popping champagne corks during concerts), and the music ranges from light classical to popular. It's marvelous and you've got to go. Performances are Tuesday through Sunday and tickets are $9 to $26.

Tanglewood, the home of the **Berkshire Music Festival** in Lenox, MA (tel. 413/637-1940), is summer headquarters for the Boston Symphony. From Boston you can drive there in 2½ hours on the Massachusetts Turnpike. BSO Tanglewood concerts run from the end of June through the end of August, and they feature outstanding conductors and soloists on Friday and Saturday evenings and Sunday afternoons. Best accoustical seats are in the "shed" but it's great fun to pack a picnic supper, bring a blanket, and buy the inexpensive lawn seating. There are open rehearsals on Saturday mornings and student concerts on some evenings.

Other Music Groups

Over 300 free concerts featuring faculty and students are presented during the academic year at the **New England Conservatory of Music,** 290 Huntington Ave. (tel. 262-1120). **Berklee College of Music,** 1140 Boylston St. (tel. 266-1400), presents free student and faculty concerts every weekday afternoon and evening in its recital halls. In addition, the Berklee Performance Center, one of the finest auditoriums in the country, hosts a wide variety of concerts by major performers throughout the season.

The glorious **Isabella Stewart Gardner Museum,** 280 The Fenway (tel. 734-1359), features soloists and chamber music in the Tapestry Room on Tuesday at 6 p.m., Thursday at 12:15 p.m., and Sunday at 3 p.m., except in July and August. Suggested donation is $3.

The **Hatch Shell** along the Charles River, near Arlington Street, is the scene of many free programs during the summer, including the Boston Pops, the Boston Ballet, chamber music, rock groups, bands. Check the newspapers for listings.

THEATER: Theater in Boston runs the gamut from professional Broadway shows to improvisational and experimental works and college productions. The name theaters that often host Broadway tryouts are the **Shubert Theater,** 265 Tremont St. (tel.

426-4520); the **Wilbur Theater,** 246 Tremont St. (tel. 423-4008); and the **Colonial Theater,** 106 Boylston St. (tel. 426-9366).

Bostix: Theater tickets at half price? Symphony, too? The brightly lit Bostix kiosk in the heart of Faneuil Hall Marketplace offers a "daily menu" of entertainment events. Choose from the well-balanced diet of discounts on more than 100 theater, music, and dance events, as well as museums, historical sites, and tourist attractions in and around Boston. Half-price day-of-performance tickets, subject to availability, as well as full-price advance ticket sales are featured. (There is a small service charge.) Discount-coupon packets for reduced rates on museums, films, and tourist sites are also available. Sorry, you can't use credit cards, and there are no refunds or exchanges. Bostix is open Monday through Saturday from 11 a.m. to 6 p.m., on Sunday from noon to 6 p.m. Call 723-5181 for recorded information on the day's offerings.

Boston has excellent local theater companies. Consider the **Huntington Theater Company,** 264 Huntington Ave. (tel. 266-3966); **Charles Playhouse,** 74-76 Warrenton St. (tel. 426-6912); **Lyric Stage,** 54 Charles St. (tel. 742-8703); **Boston Shakespeare Company,** 52 St. Botolph St. (tel. 267-5600); and the **American Repertory Theater,** at Harvard's Loeb Theater, 64 Brattle St., Cambridge (tel. 547-8300). The **Terrace Room** at the Boston Park Plaza Hotel, 64 Arlington St. (tel. 357-8384), is a good choice if you like musical comedy in the dinner-theater format. The **Wang Center for the Performing Arts,** 268 Tremont St. (tel. 482-9393), is host for the really big shows such as opera, ballet, and touring groups.

College theater is quite good in Boston as well. The **Loeb Drama Center** at Harvard, **Tufts Arena Theater** in Medford, **Spingold Theater Center** at Brandeis in Waltham, and **MIT** can all be counted on for good offerings.

LECTURES: Boston and Cambridge always attract top-name celebrities to the many lecture platforms in the area. To find out who's speaking where, check the "Calendar" section of the *Boston Globe* on Thursday, the *Boston Herald* on Friday, or the weekly *Phoenix.* One of the best series in town is that presented by **Ford Hall Forum,** the oldest continuously operated public lecture series in the country. Tickets are sold on a subscription basis, but there are usually extra seats in the large lecture halls, and the public is admitted free of charge 15 minutes before the program begins.

Lectures are held Sunday evenings at 8 p.m. at Alumni Auditorium, Northeastern University, Suite #240, 271 Huntington Ave., near the Museum of Fine Arts; and Thursday evenings at 7:30 p.m. at Faneuil Hall. For advance program information, write or phone Ford Hall Forum, 8 Winter St., Boston, MA 02108 (tel. 617/437-5800).

Whodunit?: The villain may change with each performance of *Shear Madness*, the comedy-murder mystery at the **Charles Playhouse, Stage II**, 74 Warrenton St. (tel. 426-5225), because the audience is part of the action, which takes place in a unisex hairdressing salon, and they can question suspects, reconstruct events, and then name the murderer. It's been a show-biz institution in Boston since it opened in 1980 in the cabaret-style playhouse, and broke the record for the longest-running nonmusical play in theater history in November, 1987. Performances are Tuesday through Friday at 8 p.m., on Saturday at 6:30 and 9:30 p.m. and on Sunday at 3 and 7:30 p.m. Tickets are $16 to $19 and a special dinner or Sunday brunch package is available for $22.95.

CINEMA: Cinema in Boston is alive and vigorous. In addition to the many movie houses that show first-run films in "Cinemas 1, 2, 3, 4, 5, 6" compartmented into one building, there are theaters specializing in film festivals, revivals of the classics, and avant-garde films.

To catch all the goodies that you missed years ago, try the **Brattle Theater,** 40 Brattle St., Cambridge (tel. 876-4226), which presented revivals when the current batch of oldies were new. The Brattle shows award-winning classics. Both the **Boston Public Library** (tel. 536-5400) and the **Museum of Fine Arts** screen oldies. There is a charge for the museum's film series (call 267-9300 for details), while the library's flicks are free.

The city's colleges and campus organizations sponsor independent film programs. Most of them are open to the general public. The prices are low, and students often get special rates by showing ID cards. Some of the colleges offering film series are: Boston College, Boston University, Harvard University, the MIT Film Society, Northeastern University, and Tufts University.

THE CLUBS

You can enjoy just about any type of club scene you want in Boston (until 2 a.m. "last call"). From one end of town to the other you can find concert clubs, rock, disco, punk, and good jazz for listening and dancing. The following is a sampling of some of the best in town.

GLITZY DISCO: **The Channel,** 25 Necco St. near South Station (tel. 451-1905), is Boston's largest live rock'n'roll concert club, with the ability to pack in 1,500-plus fans. **Metro,** 13-15 Landsdowne St. (tel. 262-2424), near Fenway Park, goes for the gimmicks—videos, lasers, and a 15-foot video screen. **Axis,** 13 Landsdowne St., (tel. 262-2437), is a new rock club that is dance oriented and requires "creative dress."

ALL THAT JAZZ: Boston and Cambridge are in the midst of a jazz revival. Many first-rate musicians perform regularly in lounges and clubs throughout the area. Fortunately, most lounges do not have a cover charge (except for special events), but you might find the music competing with the din of the crowd on a busy night.

The best jazz nightclub in town is the **Regattabar** at the Charles Hotel, 1 Bennett St., Cambridge (tel. 864-1200), which features local and national artists. The large third-floor room has a 21-foot picture window from which you can look out on the flag plaza of Charles Square and the bustle of Harvard Square while enjoying drinks and an unlimited buffet. Tuesday through Friday Regattabar opens at 4 p.m. daily, and performances are 9 and 11 p.m. There is no cover from 4 p.m. until showtime. Buy tickets at the door or in advance from Concertix (tel. 876-7777).

Other fine spots for listening and dancing are the lounge at **Zachary's** in the Colonnade Hotel, 120 Huntington Ave. (tel. 424-7000); **Copley's Bar** at the Copley Plaza Hotel in Copley Square (tel. 267-5300); and **Turner's Bar** at Turner Fisheries, 10 Huntington Ave., in the Westin Hotel (tel. 424-7425). All three feature top musical groups with lots of jazz. And there's big-band music at **Last Hurrah** in the Omni Parker House, 60 School St. (tel. 227-8600).

COMEDY CLUBS: Treat yourself to a few good laughs at the area's comedy clubs: **Stitches,** 969 Commonwealth Ave. (tel. 254-3939); **Comedy Connection,** Backstage, Charles Playhouse, 76 Warrenton St. (tel. 391-0022); **ImprovBoston,** Crossroads, 405 Beacon St. (tel. 576-2306), an improvisational comedy troupe; and **Catch a Rising Star,** 30 John F. Kennedy St., Cambridge (tel. 661-9887). These clubs are not open every evening, so call for hours and "open-mike" nights—tryout times for new comedians.

THE HOTEL AND RESTAURANT LOUNGES— Entertainment and Drinks

Many of Boston's most popular nightspots are associated with the major hotels and restaurants (see Chapters III and IV). But some of them are interesting enough to be listed separately:

The Bar at the Ritz, 15 Arlington St. (tel. 536-5700), is elegance personified. The club-like setting with rich walnut paneling, a gleaming fireplace, a magnificent view of the Public Garden, and national awards for the perfect martini—all make it one of Boston's favorite lounges. And for the first time in the Bar's history, there is a pianist with wonderful jazz music on the baby grand each evening from 8:30 p.m. to 12:30 a.m. The Bar is open Monday through Saturday from 11:30 a.m. to 1 a.m., and on Sunday from 4 p.m. to midnight. Lunch is served Monday through Saturday from noon to 2:30 p.m. There are also several nonalcoholic drinks on the menu.

The **Plaza Bar** in the Copley Plaza Hotel, Copley Square (tel. 267-5300), is a splendid setting for romance. It's dimly lit with luxurious wide leather chairs and couches. The palms, ceiling fans, ivory-tusk lamps, and deep, cushioned armchairs are reminiscent of the days of the British Empire in India. Drinks are excellent, and there's no need to leave for supper. A two-course meal with an appetizer plus an entree is offered Monday through Thursday from 5 to 10:15 p.m., and Friday and Saturday from 5 to 8:15 p.m., for $18 per person. (The hors d'oeuvres are complimentary from 5 to 6 p.m.) Keyboard master Dave McKenna works his piano magic from 9 p.m. to 1 a.m. Monday through Saturday. The Plaza Bar is open daily from 5 p.m. to 2 a.m.

The **Bristol Lounge** at the Four Season's Hotel, 200 Boylston St. (tel. 338-4400), is a perfect choice after the theater, after work, or any time at all. An elegant room with soft lounge chairs, a fireplace, and fresh floral arrangements, it features a fabulous weekend dessert buffet. You can relax to the keyboard harmonies of some of Boston's foremost pianists on weekends as well.

The **Custom House Lounge** at the Bay Tower Room, 33 floors above Faneuil Hall Marketplace at 60 State St. (tel. 723-1666), is one of the most romantic places in town. The spectacular view includes the harbor, the airport, and Faneuil Hall Marketplace. There's entertainment and dancing from 8:30 p.m. nightly, and a fine selection of hors d'oeuvres, wines, and cocktails are served from 5 p.m.

THE SINGLES SCENE

No problem finding a good singles bar or dance spot in Boston. The scene is a varied one and the "in" places shift from season to season, from the Waterfront to Back Bay to Cambridge. Here are a few spots that are continuing favorites:

The Boston Marriott Hotel at Long Wharf, 296 State St. (tel. 227-0800) resembles a cruise ship as it faces the harbor, and **Rachael's,** the sleek lounge with an ocean view, has a continuous bon-voyage party beginning at 11:30 a.m.. Unlimited hors d'oeuvres are served from 5 to 7 p.m. for $1.

Friday's (from Thank God It's . . .), 26 Exeter St. (tel. 266-9040), has an interesting decor, too. Or so we've been told. But we've never been able to see through the crowd of spirited young singles sampling the spirits to find out. They start coming about 5 p.m. and in a few hours the line goes halfway around the block. The attraction? Mainly the people, but there's also a bountiful hors d'oeuvres buffet, large drinks, and music on the tapedeck.

Friday's is a good dining choice too, with a big selection of snacks and appetizers, salads, omelets, burgers, steaks, and seafood, plus desserts and ice cream and fruit dessert drinks. Food prices range from $4 to $12. Open from lunchtime until the bar closes. The glass-enclosed sidewalk café facing Newbury Street is perfect for observing the scene—or being observed.

TAKE A SPIN: If you leave your table at **The Spinnaker,** at the Hyatt Regency, 575 Memorial Dr., Cambridge (tel. 492-1234), for a few minutes and it's not there when you come back—don't worry! The core of this glass-walled rooftop lounge revolves, and it will return in about 50 minutes. Catch up with your friends and enjoy the view of Boston's skyline and the Charles River over your drinks—all the regulars plus some specials like strawberry daiquiris and ice-cream cocktails. Decorated in shades of coral and gray, with soft lounges and cane-backed chairs, Spinnaker is also open for lunch ($8.50 to $13.50) from 11:45 a.m. to 2 p.m. (except Saturday and Sunday), and dinner (around $20), nightly from 6 to 9 p.m. Cocktails are served till 1 a.m. daily, until 2 a.m. on Friday and Saturday. Sunday brunch is 10 a.m. to 3 p.m.

When the sun sets, the **Faneuil Hall Marketplace** becomes one long dating bar from Lily's and Crickets at one end to Seaside and Cityside at the other, with Houlihans, the Boston Beach Club, and lots of smaller cafés in between.

And on and near the waterfront there's lots of mingling going on at **The Winery,** on Lewis Wharf (tel. 523-3994); and the **Black Rose,** 260 State St. (tel. 742-2286), which harks back to Boston's Irish roots. The music concentrates on ancestral tunes and ballads, and "Mother Sweeney's" food is justly famous.

The **Hub Cap Lounge,** at the Top of the Hub, 52 stories up in the Prudential Building (tel. 536-1775), has music and dancing nightly from 9 p.m. Dress is neat-casual, but the panoramic view of Greater Boston is truly elegant.

The most famous pub in town is the **Bull & Finch Pub,** 84 Beacon St. (tel. 227-9605), the inspiration for the TV hit "Cheers." The outdoor scenes were filmed at this popular bar downstairs at the Hampshire House, and thousands of tourists come each year hoping to find the cast regulars there. They're back in Hollywood, of course, but their TV followers do find good food, drinks, and "Cheers" souvenirs. Casual pub fare is served from noon to midnight, and drinks are poured till 2 a.m.

AND IN CAMBRIDGE

The Cambridge nightlife scene is different—more cerebral, with the conversation punctuated by talk of literature, art, philosophy, and politics. The dress is casual.

The **Harvest,** 44 Brattle St. (see Chapter IV), is a most sophisticated Cambridge watering spot, attracting celebrities, young professionals, and local faculty. The decor features crisp Marimekko prints against light woods. The outdoor terrace, with its umbrellas and trees strung with tiny lights, is delightful on a warm summer evening.

MUSIC: Cambridge nightlife is not limited to just talk—there is some fine music here as well. Serious jazz fans like **Ryle's,** 212 Hampshire St., Inman Square (tel. 876-9330), with its choice of bands in both the upstairs and downstairs rooms. Downstairs, where dinner is served, you can socialize with music as the background. (Between sets, spin a few tunes on the jukebox—it's one of the best around.) Upstairs has great acoustics and the audience there comes to listen to the gamut of first-rate jazz sounds. . . . **Willow Jazz Club,** 699 Broadway in nearby Somerville (tel. 623-9874), features contemporary jazz. Its close proximity to the Tufts University campus makes the Willow a popular student nightspot, but the top-notch musicians who play here lure jazz aficionados from miles around. . . . **Nightstage,** 823 Main St. (tel. 497-8200), at Central Square, has established a solid reputation for booking exciting talent and has the largest room in the area—225 seats.

COFFEEHOUSES: If you want a less frenetic scene and your tastes lean to folk music, or you want a cozy place for hand-holding, try one of the many coffeehouses in town.

Best known of the group is **Passim,** 47 Palmer St. (tel. 492-7679), behind the Coop. It was the focus of the folk boom in the '70s and still has a national reputation as an outstanding show-case for folk musicians. When it's not being a concert room (five nights a week), it's a charming coffeehouse which offers lunch and light meals, plus selected artwork and jewelry. Open Monday through Saturday from 11:30 a.m. to 11 p.m.

The Nameless Coffee House, 3 Church St. (no phone), at-tracts an enthusiastic young crowd that dotes on the wide range of music presented, the storytelling, and on the free refreshments—coffee, cider, tea, cocoa, and cookies. There is no admission charge, either. Open only Friday and Saturday evenings, September to May, from 7:30 p.m. to midnight.

And if you want a place to sit and chat over a cup of coffee (no entertainment), try **Café La Ruche,** 24 Dunster St. (tel. 497-4313), where you can sip Viennese coffee and foamy cappuc-cino at candlelit tables; or the **Coffee Connection** in the Garage, 36 John F. Kennedy St. (tel. 492-4881), specializing in superb coffees and teas.

Note: To find out who's performing where and when, call **Concert Line** (tel. 353-3810) or **Jazzline** (tel. 262-1300).

SPORTS

Since many of the Boston teams play their games at night, consider them part of Boston nightlife. And depending on when you're in town, try and see at least one team in action.

The **Red Sox** play baseball out at Fenway Park, near Kenmore Square. Take the bus to Kenmore Square or the "T" to Fenway Sta-tion. The **Celtics** (basketball) and the **Bruins** (hockey) play in the Boston Garden, next to North Station. Walk from Haymarket Square, or take the "T" to North Station. If you're a greyhound fan, there's racing at Wonderland Park, Revere, reached via the "T" on the Blue Line. And the thoroughbreds race at Suffolk Downs, in East Boston, which can also be reached on the Blue Line.

The **New England Patriots** play football in Foxboro, which is on Rte 1. Buses leave from the South Station entrance, Riverside "T" Station, and Shopper's World in Framingham. Call Sullivan Stadium for times (tel. toll-free 800/542-1776).

CHAPTER VIII

BEYOND BOSTON

□ □ □

Outside of Boston lies the rest of the Commonwealth of Massachusetts, and what a treasurehouse of sights and attractions it is! To limit your choice to manageable proportions we survey, first, three major locations: (1) The Paul Revere Trail (Lexington and Concord); (2) Boston's North Shore Resorts and Cape Ann; and (3) Plymouth. Finally, we take you on a trip to one of the most attractive vacationlands in the United States, just a few hours away from the Hub: (4) Cape Cod.

THE PAUL REVERE TRAIL

One of America's major historic routes—and one that almost all visitors want to retrace—is the journey of Paul Revere on the night of April 18, 1775: the ride westward from Boston to Lexington and Concord to warn the colonists that the British were coming. Local residents joke that if Paul Revere were to make the ride today, he'd get stuck in traffic and reach Lexington after the Revolution was over. *Be forewarned:* Avoid the rush hours as you drive through Cambridge and on to Lexington.

LEXINGTON: Lexington is now almost absorbed into Boston as a suburb, but it still has the awesome feel of history about it, and the flavor of a small country town, with an open common on which stands the country's oldest Revolutionary War monument. This was the spot where the growing tension between the British occupiers and the independence-seeking rebels first came to a head with shots being fired. Hard on the heels of Paul Revere came more than 400 British soldiers, and fewer than 100 American patriots stood their ground and returned shot for shot. Nobody knows who set off the first musket, but the result of the crossfire was eight dead and ten more wounded. The battle continued through the day, and, indeed, for the next several years.

The Chamber of Commerce operates a **Visitor Center** (tel. 617/862-1450) at the corner of the Village Green, 1875 Massachusetts Ave. Here you can see a diorama outlining and explaining the Battle of Lexington. The **Minuteman Statue** on the Green is said to be of Capt. John Parker whose words, perhaps more than any other, provided the rallying cry for the Revolution to follow: "Stand your ground, don't fire unless fired upon, but if they mean to have a war let it begin here!"

Apart from the Town Common, the major historic sights in Lexington are the **Buckman Tavern,** 1 Bedford St., which has been restored to its original state and was the rendezvous for the Minutemen on that fateful battle day; the **Munroe Tavern,** 1332 Massachusetts Ave., where the British troops maintained their headquarters; and the **Hancock-Clarke House,** 36 Hancock St., where Samuel Adams and John Hancock were sleeping when Paul Revere arrived to warn them of the imminent arrival of British troops. This house, furnished in colonial style, was originally built in 1738 and is now a museum of the Revolution.

All three buildings are operated by the Lexington Historical Society, which conducts guided tours. Hours are Monday to Saturday from 10 a.m. to 5 p.m., and Sunday from 1 to 5 p.m., April 18 to November 1. Admission is $2 each house, $4.50 for a combination ticket for all three.

Minuteman National Historical Park (tel. 484-6156) encompasses both the Lexington and Concord areas, and features two visitors' centers which present exhibits and films retelling the story of the Minutemen and the Battle of Concord Bridge. The **Battle Road Visitor Center** in Lexington is on Rte. 2A in a beautifully landscaped park. The **North Bridge Visitor Center** in Concord overlooks the river and the historic bridge from a hilltop location. There's a grand view from the top and it's a great spot to view fall foliage (you can picnic in the shade of the trees too). The North Bridge Visitor Center is open daily from 8:30 a.m. to 6 p.m. The Battle Road Center has the same hours, but is closed from December to mid-April. Admission is free.

At the **Museum of Our National Heritage,** corner of Massachusetts Avenue and Marrett Road (tel. 861-6559 or 861-0729), the emphasis is on the development of the United States from its founding, with changing exhibits on dramatic events and turning points in this country's history. Open Monday through Saturday from 10 a.m. to 5 p.m., and on Sunday from noon to 5 p.m. Closed Thanksgiving, Christmas, and New Year's Days. Free admission and parking. Sponsored by the Scottish Rite of Freemasonry.

Where to Stay

Visitors staying over in Lexington will want to consider the 96-room **Battle Green Inn,** 1720 Massachusetts Ave., Lexington, MA 02173 (tel. 617/862-6100), or toll free 800/343-0235), a pleasant two-level motel with a year-round pool right in the heart of town near the Minuteman National Park. Singles cost from $54; doubles, from $56. Efficiencies are also available.

Where to Dine

One of the loveliest restaurants in Lexington is the **Hartwell House,** 94 Hartwell Ave. (tel. 862-5111), at exit 31B off Rte. 128. Lunch is served Monday through Friday; dinner is served Monday through Saturday. Right in town there's **Corey's,** 20 Waltham St. (tel. 861-7549), for continental lunch and dinner; and **Le Bellecour,** 10 Muzzy St. (tel. 861-9400), which serves French and nouvelle-American cuisine and is also open for lunch and dinner.

CONCORD: What had happened earlier in the day at Lexington was to be repeated, but greatly magnified, in the little town of Concord, and today tourists visit this town to examine the site of the first pitched battle of the Revolution.

After the Lexington affair, Minutemen from all over the countryside converged on Concord, each bearing the musket that was allowed him by English law, and by the morning of April 19 several hundred had assembled. The first flare-up occurred at one of the bridges over the Concord River, which British officers felt had to be held to cut the rebels off from town. As the redcoats began to tear up the planks of the bridge, the Minutemen advanced on them. When the redcoats fired, the Minutemen returned the fire, killing three British regulars. Beside the bridge there is now a statue bearing the famous ode:

> *By the rude bridge that arched the flood*
> *Their flag to April's breeze unfurled*
> *Here once the embattled farmers stood*
> *And fired the shot heard round the world.*

Worried by the growing strength of the rebel force, the British began to march back to Lexington, but this was definitely a mistake. Less than a mile out of town, as the British column was plodding along, their red uniforms making only too clear a target, the crackle of musketry opened up on them from three sides. From behind houses and trees, from behind walls and from rooftops, hidden rifles picked off the column one by one. By the end of the day the British had lost 290 men, the Americans fewer than 100.

The anniversary of Revere's ride is today a state holiday called Patriot's Day, and is observed on the third Monday in April with local parades. A rider in colonial dress leaves Boston on horseback and retraces the trip. Everyone turns out in the streets of Arlington and Lexington to watch and recall this important date in U.S. history.

A Side Trip to Lowell

As far as we know, Paul Revere never went to Lowell, but we think you'd enjoy the **Lowell National Historical Park,** less than an hour north of Boston. From Lexington, take Rte. 95 North to Rte. 3 North to Lowell. This is a revitalized old mill town that is keeping its past alive through the historical park. You can visit the old textile mills, and take a fascinating two-hour trip by trolley and canal boat. And it's free! Since it's so popular, reservations are necessary; and the rangers at the National Park Services Center, 15 State St., Boston (tel. 242-5642), can help you with your plans. Or you can call the Lowell Park directly at (508)459-1000. While there, visit the museum on millgirls and immigrants, the waterpower exhibit, and take a ride along the canals in a barge, a real treat on a hot day.

BOSTON'S NORTH SHORE RESORTS AND CAPE ANN

Cape Ann is a smaller Cape Cod, known mainly to Bay Staters and artists. This is New England's rock-bound coast, where Yankee fishermen and clipper-ship captains made their homes. Now a busy resort area, its beaches, seaports, and shops attract tourists, artists, and antique hunters. You can drive there directly from Boston in about an hour by following Rte. 128. It takes a bit longer if you follow Rte. 1A, the winding scenic route, but it's worth it, since you can explore the North Shore towns of Swampscott, Marblehead, Salem, Essex, and Gloucester before reaching Rockport, the famous artists' colony on the tip of Cape Ann.

The **North of Boston Tourist Council,** P.O. Box 3031, Peabody, MA 01960 (tel. 508/532-1449), has a free map and 56-page guidebook to the area; and you may also write directly to the chambers of commerce in the towns you wish to visit.

THE ROAD TO CAPE ANN: Since the trickiest part of getting to Cape Ann is finding your way out of Boston, some driving instructions are in order so you won't waste precious time getting lost. (On summer weekends this area is incredibly crowded, by the way; try to make this drive on a weekday.) First find your way to the Callahan Tunnel by following the maze through the market district. If you take a left at the wrong place and find yourself on the Northeast Expressway instead, don't panic. Just take the Mystic River Bridge to Rte. 1A in Revere, where the scenic drive begins. (Take the exit marked "Revere" if you're on the bridge; the tunnel takes you directly to Rte. 1A.)

Revere (named after guess who?) has a long, sandy beach, crowded but good for swimming, with a sheltered harbor, and free parking along the ocean. At night the crowds block traffic for miles, heading for greyhound racing at Wonderland Dog Track. We skip all that now, though, and continue north on 1A to Lynn. Pick up Rte. 129 where you see the signs for Swampscott and Marblehead, and follow the shoreline.

In Swampscott, you might visit the **Mary Baker Eddy Historic House,** 23 Paradise Rd., open Monday to Saturday from 10 a.m. to 5 p.m. and on Sunday from 2 to 5 p.m., and Tuesday through Sunday from 1 to 4 p.m. November to May. Admission is charged. Closed in February. You can watch the boats in the cove at **Fisherman's Beach,** fish from the town pier, or go swimming right in Swampscott or at nearby **Nahant Beach.**

Marblehead is the next town along the coast, and we suggest you stop here for a while and wander through "Old Marblehead," with its winding, narrow streets and 18th-century homes bordered by hollyhocks and curio shops. This is the "Yachting Capital of the World," and in summer the boats in the inner harbor are packed together in their moorings like sardines. (The Marblehead fishermen specialize in flounder, mackerel, and lobster.) In the outer harbor, there is sailboat racing all summer, and the popular "Race Week" in July attracts enthusiasts from all over the country.

Marbleheaders are very proud of their historical background. This has been a seafaring town from the time it was a colonial fishing village, deriving its name from the rock, marble-like cliffs that protect it from the sea. (Walk along Front Street to Fort Sewell, and you can climb right out on the cliffs and soak up the sun and sea breezes.) Merchant ships sailed around the world from here, and the wealthy sea captains built beautiful mansions, some of which still stand. Its citizens were active in the Revolution, and Washington and Lafayette were guests at the **Col. Jeremiah Lee Mansion,** which you can visit at 161 Washington St. This is one of the finest examples of Georgian architecture in America, and has original colonial furnishings and decorations. Open 10 a.m. to 4 p.m. except Sunday from mid-May to mid-October. Closed holidays. Admission is $2.25. For more information, write Marblehead Historical Society, P.O. Box 1048, Marblehead, MA 01945.

King Hooper Mansion, 8 Hooper St. (tel. 631-2608), built between 1727 and 1747, is now the headquarters of the Marblehead Arts Association. It was the home of merchant prince Robert Hooper, known as "King" because of his generosity to the town. Splendidly decorated and furnished, it includes ballroom, slave quarters, and wine cellar. Open 1 to 4 p.m. Tuesday through Sunday (closed in January and February). Adults pay $1 (children, 50¢) for a tour of the mansion. There's free admission to the two rooms of changing exhibits.

Another interesting house is the **Lafayette Home,** at the corner of Hooper and Union Streets. One corner of the house was bizarrely chopped off—to make room for the passage of Lafayette's carriage when he visited the town in 1824.

On the hill at Washington Square is **Abbot Hall,** the town hall, where you can see the original of the famous painting, *The Spirit of '76.* Open 8 a.m. to 5 p.m. on Monday and Friday, and 8 a.m. to 9 p.m. Tuesday through Thursday; closed holidays. Saturday hours are 9 a.m. to 6 p.m.; and Sunday it is open 11 a.m. to 6 p.m. from May 30 through the end of October. Free admission.

Dining in the Swampscott-Marblehead Area

Two of the largest and best-known restaurants on the North Shore are in Swampscott—**Hawthorne by the Sea** and the **General Glover House,** both operated by the owner of Boston's famed Pier 4, with prices in the same upper range. The Hawthorne, on Humphrey Street (tel. 595-5735), which perches on a cliff alongside the ocean, specializes in seafood. (We also love their fabulous baked Alaska.) The colonial-style Glover, at Vinnin Square, Rte. 1A (tel. 595-5151), is famous for roast beef from the open hearth; and we usually feast on marinated mushrooms and popovers while waiting for the entree.

For exceptional Italian meals in Marblehead, or anywhere, it is hard to beat **Rosalie's,** 18 Sewall Ave. (tel. 631-5353), which has been named best restaurant on the North Shore by many restaurant critics. It is decorated with antiques, stained-glass window panels, and early Victorian memorabilia.

Rosalie's pasta is made fresh each day in her kitchen. The "angel hair" pasta, cappelli d'angelo alla Rosalie, served with her special sauce, is our favorite. We have a weakness for the veal scaloppine in marsala sauce, but also find it hard to resist the seafood combinations, the boneless breast of chicken served with a Grand Marnier sauce, or the filet mignon topped with spinach, crabmeat, and béarnaise sauce. All entrees include salad, and are served with linguine and mixed vegetables. The dinner price range is $11.95 to $16.95 for entrees, $3.75 to $7.95 for appetizers and pastas. Prices at lunch are $4.95 to $6.25. And you must try Rosalie's famous "no crust" spinach pie, served at lunch and Sunday brunch. The restaurant is open for lunch from 11:45 a.m. to 2:30 p.m. Monday through Saturday, and for dinner from 5:30 to 10 p.m. nightly. The very popular Sunday brunch is served from 10:30 a.m. to 2:30 p.m. Ask for directions to the restaurant when you call for reservations.

In Old Marblehead, we recommend four eating spots on the harbor. **The Landing,** at 81 Front St. (tel. 631-1878), the most expensive of the group, is pleasantly appointed and has an open deck for warm-weather dining. It's very popular with the boating crowd who drop anchor at the adjacent town dock. (If you're driving rather than sailing, there's valet parking.) **The Barnacle,** at 141 Front St. (tel. 631-4236), is another good place for viewing the harbor, either from the large windows in the casual dining room or from the deck. Hearty seafood chowder—New England style, of course—and fish dinners are featured. Entrees are in the moderate range. **Brewer's Unforgedible Edibles,** 78 Front St., a popular informal spot opposite the town pier, is the place for light, inexpensive meals including chili, tacos, excellent salads, vegetarian dishes, sandwiches, and filling homemade soups. And adjacent to the town pier is **The Driftwood,** 63 Front St. (tel. 631-1145), small and crowded but with good, inexpensive fish dinners that you can also order for take-out. Get a platter of clams and enjoy them while watching the boats from the town pier or from the hilltop at nearby Crocker Park.

Marblehead Notes: Take some time to shop and treat yourself to a silkscreened tote bag at the original **Marblehead Hand Prints** store, 111 Washington St.

STAYING IN MARBLEHEAD AND SWAMPSCOTT

Cap'n Jack's, 253 Humphrey St., in nearby Swampscott, MA 01907 (tel. 617/595-7910), describes itself as "a salty waterfront inn," and that it is. There's a tree-shaded lawn overlooking Massachusetts Bay, a sundeck for resting or sunbathing, Jacuzzi, and a pool. All 33 rooms have a refrigerator and TV. From May 1 through October 31, apartments cost $450 to $600 weekly; rooms, $36 to $80 daily. Off-season rates drop to $32 to $66 daily.

Nautilus, 68 Front St., Marblehead, MA 01945 (tel. 617/631-1703), is a guesthouse where you're really treated like a guest. It's located on the harbor, and some of the rooms have ocean views. And as it's right in the heart of "Old Town," you can easily browse in the little shops, go antiquing, and stroll the winding streets of the town. Rates are $50 to $55 a day for doubles. All rooms have semiprivate bathroom facilities.

When you're finally ready to leave this area, look for the signs that lead to Salem (and watch out for the one-way streets).

SALEM: Since it's not able to live down its reputation as the city where witches were hanged, Salem has capitalized on it instead. There's a Witch House, a Witch Museum, and even the Witch Trail, with signs showing a witch on a broomstick pointing the way. But although the witchcraft hysteria of 1692 brought Salem to the attention of the world, it is famous for much more than witches. Salem is one of the oldest of American cities, and parts of it have retained much of the former flavor. Streets are lined with 18th-century homes, some preserved with their original furnishings. Chestnut Street, with its homes of the wealthy merchants of the China Trade era, is considered one of the most architecturally beautiful streets in the country, and the residents must, by legal agreement, follow the colonial theme in their decorating and furnishings.

Twenty historic points are listed on Salem's **Historical Trail,** but there are at least twice as many attractions—cultural and recreational included—that are worth visiting. Most of them are within walking distance of each other. If you prefer driving to walking, you can get a map with directions for covering the city at information centers at Riley Plaza, Central Wharf, the Chamber of Commerce, or Old Town Hall, 32 Derby Square.

At Riley Plaza you can also board the **Salem Trolley,** which will take you through the town, let you off for shopping, dining, and sightseeing, and then back on again for only one ticket which can be used all day from 10 a.m. to 4 p.m. Fares are $5 for adults and $2 for children. Salem Trolley is operated by Hawthorne Tours, Inc., 59 Wharf St., Pickering Wharf (tel. 744-5463).

We suggest beginning your tour at the wharves, from which Salem vessels set off to sail the world. They are now part of the **Salem Maritime National Historic Site,** 178 Derby St. (tel. 744-4323), nine acres of historic waterfront representing a cross section of the commercial foreign trading port of Salem. National Park rangers provide tours and programs around the site explaining the maritime history. Tours and buildings open to the public vary according to seasonal schedules, but they usually include the following places of interest: Derby Wharf, the 1819 Custom House, West India Goods Store, the Bonded Warehouse, the Scale House, Derby House, and Central Wharf (where there is a Visitor Center). The site is open daily from 8:30 a.m. to 5 p.m. except Thanksgiving, Christmas, and New Year's Days.

Turning right two blocks farther down brings us to the famous **House of Seven Gables,** on Turner Street (tel. 744-0991). This impressive 1668 structure, built by Capt. John Turner and the inspiration of Hawthorne's novel, has six rooms of period furniture and a secret staircase.

Guided tours consist of an introductory audio-visual program, a visit to the House of Seven Gables, and to Nathaniel Hawthorne's birthplace (c. 1750), which is on the grounds. The House of Seven Gables is open daily from 10 a.m. to 4:30 p.m. Labor Day to July 1, and in the summer from 9:30 a.m. to 5:30 p.m. Admission is $4 for adults, $2 for children 6 to 17.

The **Peabody Museum of Salem,** 161 Essex St., at East India Square (tel. 745-1876 for live information or 745-9500 for recorded information), was founded by the East India Marine Society in 1799. Four interconnected collections—Maritime History, Asian Export Art, Ethnology, and Natural History—are exhibited in over 30 galleries in a complex of seven connected buildings. Figureheads, ship models, scrimshaw, rare cultural objects, and the flora and fauna of Essex County are displayed.

The new Asian Export Art Wing has the world's largest collection of objects made in Asia for Western markets between 1500 and 1940. The 1,000 pieces displayed include porcelain, paintings, silver, gold, and ivory.

Admission $4 for adults, $3 for students and senior citizens, and $1.50 for children ages 6 to 16. Museum tours are given daily at 2 p.m. Hours are Monday through Saturday 10 a.m. to 5 p.m. and Sundays noon to 5 p.m. Open Thursday evenings until 9 p.m. Closed Thanksgiving, Christmas, and New Year's Day.

The **Essex Institute Museum Neighborhood,** 132 Essex St. (tel. 744-3390), consists of a museum, a research library, and historical houses. The institute has an extraordinary collection of Salem memorabilia, portraits, dolls, household objects, books, manuscripts, and actual witchcraft trial records. The fully furnished period houses in the complex, dating from 1684 to 1818, are shown on the guided tours. Essex Institute is open year round, Tuesday through Saturday from 9 a.m. to 5 p.m. and on Sunday and holidays from 1 to 5 p.m. Closed Thanksgiving, Christmas, and New Year's Day. Open on Monday from June 1 through October 31. Admission is $3 for adults, $2.50 for senior citizens, and $1.50 for children. Tickets for the house tours must be purchased at the museum.

The **Witch House,** 310 ½ Essex St. (tel. 744-0180), was the home of Jonathan Corwin, who, in 1692, conducted some of the early examinations of the accused witches in this house, along with John Hawthorne (a member of the same family as Nathaniel Hawthorne). It's an eerie-looking dwelling that has probably changed but little since those days. The Witch House is open March 15 to June 30 and Labor Day to December 1 from 10 a.m. to 4:30 p.m.; July 1 to Labor Day from 10 a.m. to 6 p.m. Admission is $2.50 for adults; $1.25 for youths five to 16.

PICKERING WHARF: Pickering Wharf, at the corner of Derby and Congress Streets, is based on a delightful concept: town-house condominiums, a yachting marina, fine ships, and restaurants in a harmonious setting between the ocean and the city. And it works!

The boutiques have Boston and Cambridge origins; the little gift stores, bakeries, candy stores, and ice cream parlors are charming. (Make your own smörgåsbord sundae at **Putnam Pantry.**) **Victoria Station,** the **Chase House,** and **Topsides** restaurants, facing the harbor, draw the crowds for the food and the social scene, and have outdoor terraces for summer drinks and snacks. Victoria Station (tel. 745-3400) has lunch and dinner plus a Sunday brunch served from 11 a.m. to 3 p.m.

Pickering Wharf is a lovely place to stroll, day or evening. The seawalk is softly lit at night. Admire the yachts anchored along the pier, take a cruise yourself on one of the excursion boats that tour the harbor, or go out to sea on a whale watch.

And for a change of mood, have a picnic at **Salem Willows,** the waterfront amusement park just a few minutes away from the center of town. Free admission and free parking.

Accommodations in Salem and Danvers

Centrally located is the **Hawthorne Hotel,** On the Common, 18 Washington Square, Salem, MA 01970 (tel. 508/744-4080). It's an attractive hotel within walking distance of the waterfront and Salem's museums. Rates start at $75 for singles and $85 for doubles. There is also a fine dining room and a tavern in the hotel.

Not far from Salem harbor is the charming **Coach House Inn,** 284 Lafayette St., Salem, MA 01970 (tel. 508/744-4092), a ship captain's mansion and carriage house dating back to the middle of the last century. The elegance of that time is preserved in the furnishings, high ceilings, and lavish fireplaces, many of marble or carved ebony. Rooms here run $62 to $80 with continental breakfast.

Right in the heart of downtown Salem, just a block away from the shopping center and near all the historical attractions, is the **Salem Inn,** 7 Summer St. on Rte. 114, Salem, MA 01907 (tel. 508/741-0680). This three-story red-brick building, a restored sea captain's house, may not be too impressive on the outside as it's on a busy street. But walk through the front door and the scene changes. The atmosphere is bright and cheery, and there is a secluded garden and brick terrace in the rear of the building. All 23 rooms have king- or queen-size beds, antique fireplaces, air conditioning, and direct-dial telephones.

Rates are $79 for accommodations with bath (tub or shower) in the room, and $69 for room with private bath across the hall. Suites with kitchen are available at $85 and $90.

And in nearby Danvers, **King's Grant Motor Inn,** Rte. 128, Danvers, MA 01923 (tel. 508/774-6800), has 125 spacious rooms with color TV, phone, and Inn-room movies. There's also a tropical garden with a lounge, indoor pool, and whirlpool. Prices start at $65 for a single, $80 for a double, and $88 for a twin. Suites are $250.

About 40 minutes from Boston, **Appleton Inn,** 275 Independence Way, Danvers, MA 01923 (tel. 508/777-8630 or toll free 800/78-APPLE), is an attractive three-story red-brick building with green shutters, white portico, bell tower, and an outdoor swimming pool. It's located off Rte. 128 at exit 24 near the Liberty Tree Mall, where, by the way, you'll find some of the best shopping bargains around. From Appleton Inn, it's easy to scoot up to the North Shore or down to Boston.

The rooms all have TV, individual climate control, two phones, and bathrooms with heating lamps and shower massage units. Forty nonsmoking rooms are set aside on the second floor; and there are five rooms equipped for the disabled on the first floor.

Rates go from $85 to $89 single, and $95 to $99 double. The two-room executive suite that accommodates one to four persons is $135. One of the best deals is the weekend price of $55 single or double, valid for a Friday, Saturday, or Sunday evening. Children under 16 stay free with parents and complimentary cribs are provided. Parking is free and a coin laundry is on the first floor.

Dining in Salem and Danvers

Salem has some excellent restaurants in all price ranges and ethnic styles located in the center of town along Derby Street, and at Pickering Wharf (see description above).

One of the nicest places in Salem is the **Lyceum,** 43 Church St. (tel. 745-7665), in the building where Alexander Graham Bell made his first public demonstration of the telephone. There's a fireplace in the dining room, a large glass-enclosed patio with hanging plants, and a pub. Prices are moderate. The Lyceum is open weekdays from 7 a.m. for breakfast, till midnight. Brunch is served on Saturday and Sunday mornings.

The **Bull & Finch Pub,** 195 Derby St. (tel. 744-8588), at Pickering Wharf, is a casual spot serving pub fare and seafood. Under the same management as the Boston Bull & Finch (which was the inspiration of the TV series "Cheers"), it has a great view of the historic Derby Waterfront.

Roosevelt's, 300 Derby St. (tel. 745-9608), is an excellent moderate-priced restaurant serving dinner and Sunday brunch. The salad bar is the most bountiful in the area and comes free with your dinner or separately for $3.95. (Be sure to sample the baked beans.) Dinner hours are 3:45 to 10 p.m. Early-bird specials served 5:30 to 7:30 p.m. include dinner and salad bar for around $10.

Stromberg's, on the bridge between Salem and Beverly, Rte. 1A (tel. 744-1863), is one of the most popular seafood restaurants on the North Shore. The drawing card is the combination of top-grade fish and low-grade prices. The flounders are taken straight from the fishing boats. There are always several daily specials in addition to the regular menu, and complete dinners start at $7. Lunch specials begin at $4.75. Hours are 11 a.m. to 8:30 p.m. daily except Monday. (On long holiday weekends, they close on Tuesday.) Incidentally, Stromberg's is located on the spot where Roger Conant and his followers landed in 1686.

For an international setting, try **Saignon Mha Hang,** 6 Hawthorne Blvd. (tel. 741-1533), for excellent, moderately priced Vietnamese dinners.

Incidental Intelligence: If you drive on to nearby Beverly, you can catch **Le Grand David and His Own Spectacular Magic Company,** one of the top-rated classical magic productions in the country (they entertain at White House Easter parties), who perform wizardry mixed with singing and dancing on Sunday at 3 p.m. at the Cabot Street Cinema Theater, 286 Cabot St., Beverly (tel. 927-3677). Tickets are $7 for adults and $5 for children. It's a good idea to call or write for reservations since most performances are sold out well in advance.

ON THE ROAD TO GLOUCESTER: You have several routes to choose from as you head to Gloucester, including the ocean route. Take the boat from Pier 1, Northern Avenue, at the bridge at 9:30 a.m. (see Chapter V). If you don't have much time, Rte. 128 through Danvers and Beverly (where George Washington commissioned the schooner *Hannah,* the first vessel to fly the Continental flag) is the fastest way. If you have time to explore, exit from Rte. 128 at Rte. 133 to Essex, one of the country's earliest shipbuilding centers, now known for seafood restaurants, Essex clams, and antique shops.

On Main Street on the Causeway, you'll find some excellent places to eat, including full-service restaurants and take-out spots. For both good food and a fine river view, we like **Callahan's** (tel. 768-7750), and the excellent **Tom Shea's** (tel. 768-7669). And for a good buy, the **Village Restaurant** (tel. 768-6400), at the end of the Causeway, is top-rated for inexpensive dinners and fried clams (there's also take-out service). The most famous of the Essex restaurants is **Woodman's** (tel. 768-6451), where according to local historians, the first clam was fried when it was accidentally dropped into heated batter. It's a rustic, self-service eatery with long lines attesting to its popularity. The portions are generous: the large clam chowder can really serve two people.

HAMMOND CASTLE
Well worth a stop is Hammond Castle, also known as Hammond Museum, 80 Hesperus Ave., Gloucester (tel. 283-2080). You reach it by following scenic Rte. 133 (exit 14 on Rte. 128) onto Rte. 127. Turn left onto Hesperus Avenue, and follow the road to the castle. Financed (at a cost of over $6 million) and planned by the late inventor John Hays Hammond, Jr., the medieval castle was constructed of Cape Ann granite. There are towers, battlements, stained-glass windows, a great hall 60 feet high, and an enclosed "outdoor" pool and courtyard lined with foliage, trees, and medieval artifacts. Many 12th-, 13th-, and 14th-century furnishings, tapestries, and paintings fill the rooms. A pipe organ with over 8,200 pipes is used for concerts. Write for a copy of their calendar. There are guided tours of the castle every day from 10 a.m. to 4 p.m., and candlelight tours are given Wednesday evenings in July and August from 5 to 9 p.m. Admission is $3.50 for adults, $3 for senior citizens, and $2 for children ages 6 to 12; candlelight tours are $5.

GLOUCESTER: Now on to the Cape Ann town of Gloucester, where the famed bronze statue of the **Gloucester Fisherman** overlooks the ocean as a memorial to the more than 10,000 fishermen who went "down to the sea in ships" and did not return. The city's history goes back to the Norsemen who skirted the coast in 1001, and to Champlain, who founded what is now Eastern Point. A more recent claim to fame is the invention here of the process for blast-freezing foods by Clarence Birdseye.

Gloucester still retains as close an association with the sea and seafarers as it did when it was founded almost 350 years ago. It has a large Italian and Portuguese fishing colony, and their annual St. Peter's Fiesta (at the end of June or beginning of July), when the boats are blessed, brings tourists from all over the country for the event. There are parades, floats, marching bands, and a 600-pound statue of St. Peter which is carried through the streets.

The **Rocky Neck Art Colony** in East Gloucester is one of the oldest-established art colonies on the East Coast. Primarily a working center for artists, not just a series of shops selling their wares, it's on a tiny jetty of land connected to the mainland by a causeway. About two dozen galleries are located in its colorful alleys and piers along with fishing boats, appealing shops, and restaurants. To reach Rocky Neck, take Rte. 128 to East Gloucester, exit 9, and follow East Main Street to Rocky Neck Avenue. (Rudyard Kipling worked on his book *Captains Courageous* on Rocky Neck.)

The Sights of Gloucester

Beauport, the Sleeper-McCann House, 75 Eastern Point Blvd. (tel. 283-0800), was designed by interior decorator Henry Davis Sleeper to house his vast antique collections. From 1907 to 1934 he designed over 40 unusual rooms, decorated in different periods, of which 26 are open to the public. The Golden Step Room, with a breathtaking view of the harbor; the Pine Kitchen, in the style of an old pioneer home; the Tower Library, with an immense collection of antiquarian books; and the Paul Revere Room are among the most popular. Weekday tours are given 10 a.m. to 4 p.m. from May 15 to October 15. There are also weekend tours from 1 to 4 p.m., mid-September through mid-October. Admission is $5 adults, $2.50 children.

Cape Ann Historical Association, 27 Pleasant St. (tel. 283-0455), is the museum of Cape Ann's history, combining a historic furnished house with a modern addition. Exhibition areas include the Capt. Elias Davis House (1804), decorated and furnished in the Federal style with furniture, silver, and porcelains;

plus the nation's single largest collection of paintings and drawings by Fitz Hugh Lane, the American luminist painter. The Maritime Room features an exhibit on the fishing industry, ship models, and historic photographs of the Gloucester waterfront and fishing fleet. Open Tuesday through Saturday from 10 a.m. to 5 p.m. Admission is charged. Closed in February.

North Shore Harbor Cruises and Whale Watches

For cool ocean breezes, sightseeing, a sunset cruise, or whale-watching, take an excursion boat from either Gloucester or Salem. In Gloucester, an oldtime paddleboat named *Dixie Belle* sails from Seven Seas Wharf at the Gloucester House Restaurant on the hour from 10 a.m. to 5 p.m., and from Rocky Neck in East Gloucester, near the Rudder Restaurant, on the half hour, for a 45-minute narrated tour. At Pickering Wharf, Salem Willows, and Central Wharf at the Derby waterfront in Salem, you can choose from a variety of cruises around Salem and Marblehead Harbors.

The most exciting excursions are the whale-watching trips that take you 15 miles out to sea to Stellwagen Bank, which runs from Gloucester to Provincetown. It seems that millions of sand eels and other fish that whales dote upon have gathered along this bank, and the whales gobble them up during their north-south migrations. The whales often perform for their audience too, by breaching (jumping out of the water), and occasionally dolphins join the show.

Check the local marinas for sailing times, prices (around $15 for adults, less for children and senior citizens), and reservations. In Gloucester, call **Seven Seas Whale Watch** (tel. 283-1776), the **Yankee Fleet** (tel. 283-6089), **Cape Ann Whale Watch** (tel. 283-5110), **Capt. Bill's Whale Watch** (tel. 283-6995), or **Whale Safaris** (tel. 281-4163). In Rockport, call **Capt. Ted's Whale Watch** (tel. 546-2889). Or write or call the **Cape Ann Chamber of Commerce,** 128 Main St., Gloucester, MA 01930 (tel. 283-1601), for information and brochures from the whale-watching fleet.

Dress warmly for these cruises as it's much cooler at sea than in town, and take sunglasses, a hat, rubber-soled shoes, and a camera with plenty of film. And it might be helpful for some to take a seasickness pill before boarding.

Other Sights

Take time to visit these other points of interest, if you can. **Stage Fort Park** is the site of a historical fort with ancient cannons. It's on Hough Avenue (off Western Avenue) and has picnic areas and beaches open to the public. **Harbor Loop** is where band concerts are held. **Eastern Point Lighthouse and Breakwater** has a magnificent view of the ocean. In good weather you can walk to the end of the breakwater. On **State Fish Pier,** Parker Street, fishermen unload their catches every morning.

Accommodations in Gloucester

One of the friendliest motor inns we know is the **Atlantis,** Atlantic Road, Gloucester, MA 01930 (tel. 508/283-5807), in the Bass Rocks section of Gloucester. It has the charm and warmth of a guesthouse, yet it's a large up-to-date facility with Danish-modern decor, wide picture windows, private sundecks, color TVs, and a landscaped heated swimming pool. Rates are based on double occupancy and range from $85 to $90. There's an $8 charge for an extra person. These rates apply from June 18 through Labor Day. Lower fees are in effect from March to mid-June and from after Labor Day through November.

Another outstanding motel directly on the oceanfront is **Bass Rocks Motor Inn,** Atlantic Road, Gloucester, MA 01930 (tel. 508/283-7600). With its stately white columns and red-brick walls, it has the appearance of a southern mansion transplanted to the rocky coast. A rooftop sundeck, balconies, and swimming pool all offer excellent views of the surf. In-season rates are $105 to $115, double occupancy. The motor lodge is open April to November, and has lower rates off-season.

Blue Shutters Inn, 1 Nautilus Rd., Gloucester, MA 01930 (tel. 508/281-2706), is a charming New England inn, white with blue shutters, with sweeping views of Good Harbor Beach and the ocean from the large, sunny rooms. Accommodations include deluxe apartments completely equipped for four, two-room suites with private bath, and doubles with either private or shared bath. A large living room with fireplace, sofas, rockers, TV, and books is available for guests; and an excellent complimentary breakfast is served daily by owners Paul and Pat Earl. The inn is open May through October. From the end of June to Labor Day double rooms are $45 to $70 per night, and $85 for suites. Weekly rates are $310 to $510. Rates are lower in May and early June, and after Labor Day.

Dining in Gloucester

The seafood at the outstanding **Gloucester House Restaurant,** Seven Seas Wharf (tel. 283-1812), is brought directly from the fishing boats tied up at the pier to the kitchen, where specialties such as baked stuffed scrod and lobster stuffed with lobster are prepared. You might even sample native squid or an octopus salad. There are picture windows all around giving you a panoramic view of the harbor and the fishing fleet. And after dinner, you can stroll along the wharf. Entrees range from $8 to about $20. Lobster prices are seasonal. And there's a special menu for children. Open daily from 11:30 a.m. to 9 p.m.; until 10 p.m. weekends. In the summer, clambakes are served outside on Seven Seas Wharf.

Every table at **Captain Courageous,** the excellent restaurant at 25 Rogers St. (tel. 283-0007), has a view of the harbor. On the menu are steaks, chops, and seafood with dinners going for $9.95 to $16.95. Early dinner specials, served from 3 to 7 p.m., are priced from $6.95. Lunch, Monday through Friday from 11:30 a.m. to 4 p.m. is $3.95 up. Captain Courageous is open Monday through Thursday from 11:30 a.m. to 9 p.m., until 9:30 p.m. on Friday and Saturday. Sunday hours are noon till 9 p.m.

ROCKPORT: Rockport is a few miles from Gloucester along Rte. 127. If you stop to do all the sightseeing we've suggested, it will probably take you three days from Boston. If you just view the scenery from the car window, it will take less than 90 minutes. Best known for its artists' colony, Rockport is also a lovely, picturesque little town. Weekend parking can be a terrible hassle, so go on a weekday if you can. We suggest circling the square once (meters have a two-hour limit), and if there's no place to park try the back streets, even if they're some distance from the center of town. Or use the parking lot on Upper Main Street, Rte. 127. It's a short distance from the tourist information booth, and the $5 fee includes all-day parking and free round-trip shuttle service from 11 a.m. to 7 p.m. daily.

You can also get to Rockport via train from North Station (45 minutes each way; phone 617/227-5070 for details). It's about $6 for the round trip. A possible return stop might be the **Beverly Depot,** 10 Park St., Beverly, a 19th-century station converted into an attractive steak and seafood restaurant.

Even though there are many charming areas in Rockport, the one that stands out most is the wooden fish warehouse on the old wharf in the harbor, since it probably has been the subject of more paintings than anything since the Last Supper. The red shack, known as **Motif #1,** is a fitting symbol for this beautiful fishing town. Destroyed in the blizzard of 1978, it has been rebuilt through donations from the local community and tourists. And it stands again on the same pier, duplicated in every detail, reinforced to withstand future northeast storms.

It's easy to see why aesthetes are captivated by the town's charm: the picket-fenced Colonial houses; the narrow, winding streets; the crash of waves against the rocky shore and the ever-present squeal of swooping seagulls. Rockport's pride and joy is **Bearskin Neck,** a narrow peninsula of one-way alleys lined with galleries, antique stores, and ancient houses, set so close together that neighbors could almost lean out of their upstairs windows and shake hands across the street. Bearskin Neck was supposedly named after an unfortunate bear which drowned and was washed ashore here almost 200 years ago.

Part of the fun in Rockport is shopping along Bearskin Neck where there are about 100 little shops carrying clothes, gifts, toys, inexpensive novelties, and expensive handmade crafts and paintings. And there are plenty of places to snack too; take your choices from lobster in the rough to Austrian-style strüdel in four delicious flavors.

Well over two dozen art galleries in town display the works of both local and nationally known artists. And the **Rockport Art Association,** 12 Main St. (tel. 508/546-6604), open daily year round, sponsors major exhibitions and special shows throughout the year. In October there's an Amateur Art Festival, and in the winter a live Christmas pageant, a holiday highlight that attracts big crowds.

Be sure to ask at the Rockport Chamber of Commerce office for one of its colorful maps of the town. In the bottom right-hand corner it bears the warning: "Our sea serpent visits only every 25 years." How reassuring!

Staying in Rockport

Just north of town on the road to Pigeon Cove is the luxurious **Yankee Clipper,** Rte. 127, Rockport, MA 01966 (tel. 508/546-3407), on extensive lawns overlooking the sea. There are actually three different buildings, of which the inn is the most attractive: Georgian architecture, a heated saltwater swimming pool, and rooms with private balconies. From almost all parts of the property there are excellent views of the sea, especially from the extensive and attractive dining room. Rates begin at $85 for a double, bed and breakfast, and $70 per person per day, Modified American Plan, with various prices according to season, type of room, etc. The Clipper is open year round. Sunday brunch is served from 11:30 a.m. to 2 p.m. at $12.95. Reservations a must.

Somewhere in the old guest register of the **Ralph Waldo Emerson Inn,** Phillips Avenue, Rockport, MA 01966 (tel. 508/546-6321), you might find the name of Emerson himself, for the distinguished philosopher was a guest in the old section of the inn in the 1850s. Of course, there have been changes made since then in this lovely resort on Pigeon Cove in Rockport, but it still retains the charm of a gracious era. The view of the ocean from Cathedral Rocks is magnificent. Guests can enjoy the heated outdoor saltwater swimming pool or the indoor whirlpool and sauna, go fishing, sightseeing, shopping, or just relax in the comfortable chairs on the old fashioned veranda. The inn offers a Modified American Plan with breakfast and dinner for $65 to $109 single, $108 to $135 double. Without meals, rates are $45 to $89 single, $68 to $95 double. The dining room is open to the public on an availability basis. Breakfast is served from 8 to 10 a.m., and dinner from 6 to 8 p.m. Open May to October 31.

Back in town at 37 Mt. Pleasant St., Rockport, MA 01966 (tel. 508/546-2701), is the **Inn on Cove Hill,** built in 1791 from the proceeds of pirates' gold found a short distance away. We don't know if any gold is hidden on the grounds, but we do know that this attractive Federal-style home, operated by Marjorie and John Pratt, is an excellent vacation hide-away from April to October. Many of the colonial features have been preserved or restored in this white three-story inn. The guest rooms have colonial furnishings, handmade quilts, some canopy beds, fresh flowers in summer, plus the modern features of baths and television. In warm weather, continental breakfast with home-baked breads and muffins is served on bone china at the garden tables; and in inclement weather, the hosts bring you breakfast in bed on individual trays. In-season rates are $52 to $75 double with private bath, $45 with shared bath. Lower rates apply off-season. If you're coming by train from Boston, the hosts will meet you at the station; if you drive, parking is provided.

For those who want modern hotel comfort and a beachfront location, **Captain's Bounty Motor Inn,** 1 Beach St., Rockport, MA 01966 (tel. 508/546-9557), is the place. Ocean breezes provide natural air conditioning, since each room overlooks the water and has its own balcony and sliding glass wall. All comforts, such as TV, soundproofing, ceramic tile baths with tub and shower, are provided. Kitchenette units are available. In-season doubles cost $80; kitchenettes, $82 to $95.

There are two "Peg Legs" in town. One is **Peg Leg Motel,** 10 Beach St., Rockport, MA 01966 (tel. 508/546-6945), operated by Jim and Polly Erwin. This attractive motel is on a quiet knoll overlooking Rockport Harbor and directly across the street from the public beach. The rooms are decorated with Ethan Allen furniture, some with rocking chairs or "overstuffed" comfortable chairs. All have double beds, TV, and ceramic tile bath with tub and shower. In-season rates are $85 to $95 double. There is plenty of free parking at the motel. Open May 1 to October 31. If you prefer colonial atmosphere, **Peg Leg Inn** is just down the street at 18 Beach St., Rockport, MA 01966 (tel. 508/546-2352), a group of Early American houses with front porches, attractive living rooms, and well-kept flower-bordered lawns. Rates are $45 to $85 double, in-season. All rooms have private bath and TV, and some have excellent ocean views.

Old Farm Inn, 291 Granite St. at Pigeon Cove, Rockport, MA 01966 (tel. 508/546-3237), is a 1799 saltwater farm with charming antique-furnished rooms in the Inn and the Barn Guesthouse. Rooms are $63 to $73 in season and $53 to $63 off-season. A room with a kitchenette is $78, and a two-room suite runs $115. Small refrigerators are available. An ample continental breakfast is included in the room rate.

Dining in Rockport

Although most visitors to Rockport go to the **Blacksmith Shop,** 23 Mt. Pleasant St. (tel. 546-6301), primarily for the excellent food, some connoisseurs choose this fine restaurant overlooking Rockport Harbor for the atmosphere—the antique furnishings, chairs from Italy, lights from Spain, paintings in the gallery, and the old forge, anvil, and bellows preserved from the shop where Rockport's village smithy stood. The main dining room, resting on stilts in the harbor, has been enlarged many times since its establishment in 1927, and now accommodates 200. Seafood is the specialty, and owner Larry Bershad goes to the docks every morning to select the best of the local catch. In season he brings back swordfish, halibut, and lobster from Rockport lobster pots. And the menu always features Gloucester scrod (with or without lobster sauce), broiled yellowtail, baked stuffed Alaskan king crab, scallops, and clam chowder, as well as meat and poultry specials. Dinner entrees range from $7.95 to $20.95, and are served from 5 p.m. The luncheon menu, available all afternoon, has seafood specials plus sandwiches, salads, and quiche. A late-supper menu is offered from 9:30 to 11:30 p.m. with lighter fare. You can also come in the afternoon for dessert and coffee. The Blacksmith Shop is open daily from the last week in May until the third week in October, 11 a.m. to 11:30 p.m.

For lunch or dinner in a greenhouse, complete with hanging baskets, five-foot geranium trees, and flowers all around, walk through town to the end of Main Street to **Peg Leg,** 18 Beach St. (tel. 546-3038), where both the food and the surroundings are superior. The greenhouse, very romantic in the evening with its recessed spotlights and candles, is behind the cozy and attractive main restaurant. Peg Leg is open for breakfast, lunch, and dinner, serving from 8 a.m. to 9 p.m. weekdays, and from noon to 9 p.m. on Sunday. It is closed Tuesday. Dinner entrees include chicken pie, Maryland softshell crabs, steaks, and lobsters. Dinner prices run $8.95 and up; at luncheon, $5.95 up. Baking is done on the premises, and breadbaskets always have sweet rolls and treats such as fresh cranberry bread or blueberry muffins. The service is excellent; owner Robert H. Welcome exemplifies his name.

It looks like a coffeeshop in front, but don't let that fool you. **Oleana** (tel. 546-2049) is a Rockport institution with excellent food and a magnificent harbor view from the windows in the rear of the restaurant at 27 Main St. Choose seafood or chowder from the moderately priced à la carte menu.

Note: Rockport is a "dry" community and restaurants are forbidden by law from serving alcoholic beverages, but you can brown-bag it with your own bottle.

And if you'd like to find a way to recycle that brown bag or want some tips on what to do with old newspapers, visit the **Rockport Paper House,** 50A Pigeon Hill St., Pigeon Cove. It was built in 1922 entirely out of 100,000 newspapers—walls, furniture, everything! Every item of furniture is made from papers of a different period. Admission is charged.

ON THE WAY BACK: If you'd like to do some more exploring after leaving Rockport, take Rte. 128 to Rte. 1A to **Ipswich,** another historical town, probably best known for magnificent Crane's Beach, and then on to Newburyport, with elegant 19th-century homes and a history of waterfront shipyards. Or you can take Rte. 128 back to Boston. Just follow the signs.

Take scenic Rte. 1A on your return to Boston through Hamilton and Wenham and visit the fascinating doll collection at the **Wenham Historical Association and Museum,** 132 Main St., Wenham (tel. 468-2377). The world-famous collection of over 5,000 dolls includes a 3,000-year-old Egyptian doll, several porcelain Parisian fashion plates, and adorable little Kewpie dolls. Open Monday through Friday from 11 a.m. to 4 p.m., on Saturday from 1 to 4 p.m., and on Sunday from 2 to 5 p.m. Admission is $1.50 for adults and 50¢ for children 6 to 14.

While in Wenham, stay for lunch and tea at the lovely **Wenham Tea House** on Old Bay Road, Rte. 1A at the Village Green (tel. 468-1398). It's a charming place and the food is good and reasonably priced. Open Monday through Saturday from 11:30 a.m. to 2:30 p.m. for lunch, and from 3:15 to 4:30 p.m. for tea. Closed Sunday and holidays and the last two weeks of February. Browse through the little gift shops before you leave.

Back on the road to Boston, you drive through Hamilton and by the very posh Myopia Hunt Club, where you might want to buy tickets for the polo matches on Sunday at 3 p.m. from late May to October.

PLYMOUTH

The historic town of Plymouth (pop. 44,000) is where the U.S. began (in spirit—Jamestown preceded it by 11 years); it's hard not to be awed by reminders of the more than 3½ centuries of history that have accumulated there. When the Pilgrims first set up their encampment at this site in December 1620 (after a preliminary but unsatisfactory landing at Provincetown), all was bleak and uninviting. But the hardy adventurers built homes, planted crops, and established friendly relations with the natives; and the seeds they planted have, in more ways than one, endured to this day. (To reach Plymouth from Boston by car—about 40 miles—follow the Southeast Expressway to Rte. 3. Take exit 6 to Plymouth, turn right onto Rte. 44, and follow signs to the historic attractions. Buses operated by the Plymouth and Brockton Street Railway leave the Greyhound Terminal; tel. 749-5067.)

The Plymouth of today is an attractive seafaring town with much to occupy your attention. Even if you're just passing through, you'll at least want to inspect the famous Plymouth Rock on which the first Pilgrims made their initial contact with the land. You should also find time to examine *Mayflower II*, a full-scale reproduction of the ship that brought them to this country, and Plimoth Plantation, which gives an idea of what life was like in those rugged days. Possibly your first stop should be the town's **Information Booth** on South Park Avenue, just below the intersection of Rte. 44 and Court Street (tel. 746-4779), where hotel and motel reservations can be made and all your questions answered. Open daily from 8 a.m. to 6 p.m. April through November.

If you'd like to plan ahead, call the office of the **Plymouth Area Chamber of Commerce** (tel. 508/746-3377), Monday through Friday from 9 a.m. to 5 p.m.

The large, new **Regional Information Center** at exit 5 off Rte. 3 (tel. 508/746-1150) dispenses information and brochures on Plymouth, Cape Cod, and Boston, along with free cranberry juice (what else?) seven days a week from 9 a.m. to 5 p.m. The restrooms there are open all night for the convenience of travelers.

PLYMOUTH SIGHTS: The most logical place to begin your tour of Plymouth is where the Pilgrims began—at **Plymouth**

Rock. The Rock, accepted as the landing place of the *Mayflower* passengers, was originally 15 feet long and 3 feet wide. It was moved on the eve of the Revolution and several times thereafter, before acquiring its present permanent position at tide level, where the winter storms still break over it as they did in Pilgrim days. The present portico which enshrines the Rock was a gift in 1920 of the Colonial Dames of America.

Cape Cod was named in 1602 by Capt. Bartholomew Gosnold, and 12 years later Capt. John Smith sailed along the coast of what he named "New England" and designated "Plymouth" as the mainland opposite Cape Cod.

The passengers on the *Mayflower* had contracted with the London Virginia Company for a tract of land near the mouth of the Hudson River in "Northern Virginia"; in exchange for their passage to the New World, they would work the land for the company for seven years. However, on November 11, 1620, falling among perilous shoals and roaring breakers, with the wind howling, they had to make for Cape Cod Bay and anchor there. Subsequently, their captain announced that they had found a safe harbor and refused to continue the voyage farther south to their original destination. They had no option but to settle in New England, and with no one to command them, their patent from the London Virginia Company became void and they were on their own to begin a new world.

The **Mayflower II,** berthed at State Pier in Plymouth, only steps from Plymouth Rock, is a full-scale reproduction of the type of ship which brought the Pilgrims from England to America. Although there is little technical information known about the original *Mayflower,* William A. Baker, designer of *Mayflower II,* incorporated the few references in Governor Bradford's account of the voyage with other researches to re-create as closely as possible the actual ship. Exhibits on board show what life was like during that 66-day voyage in 1620 on a vessel crowded with 102 passengers, 25 crewmen, and all the supplies needed to sustain the colony until the first crops were harvested. Trying to imagine the hardships of that voyage, when one sees how little room there was for so many people, boggles the mind.

Men and women in period costumes on board the ship talk about the crossing of the *Mayflower,* answer questions, and dispatch little-known but interesting pieces of information.

You will not want to miss a tour of the ship. The *Mayflower II* is open to the public from the end of March to November 30 from 9 a.m. to 5 p.m. daily. During July and August, tickets are sold until 6:30 p.m. every night. Admission is $3.75 for adults, $2.75

for children 5 through 12; under 5, free. The vessel is owned and maintained by Plimoth Plantation which is three miles south of the ship. A combination ticket including *Mayflower II* and Plimoth Plantation is $10 for adults, $7.50 for children.

Right alongside the *Mayflower II* there are replicas of early Pilgrim dwellings from 1620–1621. Open daily from 9 a.m. to 5 p.m.

Apart from the *Mayflower* and the Plimoth Plantation, possibly the town's major attraction is **Pilgrim Hall Museum,** 75 Court Street (tel. 746-1620), open all year from 9:30 a.m. to 4:30 p.m. Admission is $3 for adults, $2.50 for senior citizens; children, $1. The oldest public museum in the United States, on the National Register of Historic Places, it is replete with original possessions of the early Pilgrims and their descendants. The building itself dates from 1824. Among the exhibits is the skeleton of the *Sparrowhawk,* a ship wrecked on Cape Cod in 1627, which lay buried in the sand and undiscovered for more than 200 years.

PLIMOTH PLANTATION: Plimoth Plantation is a worthy recreation of a 1627 Pilgrim village. You enter by the hilltop fort that protects the "villagers" and then walk down the hill to the farm area, visiting the homes and gardens along the way that have been constructed with careful attention to historic detail. It's great fun to talk to the Pilgrims, people who, in speech, dress, and manner, assume the personality of a member of the original community. You can watch them framing a house, splitting wood, shearing sheep, preserving foodstuffs, or cooking a pot of fish stew over an open hearth, all as it was done in the 1600s. And they use only the tools and cookware available at that time. (It's a challenge to try and get them to acknowledge modern phrases such as airplane, camera, silverware, and ice cream.) Sometimes you can join in the activities—perhaps planting, harvesting, a court trial, or a wedding party.

The community is as accurate as research can make it: eyewitness accounts of visitors to the original Pilgrim colony were combined with archeological research, old records, and the 17th-century history written by the Pilgrims' leader, William Bradford, who used the spelling "Plimoth" for the settlement. There are daily militia drills with matchlock muskets which are fired to demonstrate the community's defense system. In actual fact, little defense was needed as the local Indians were friendly. These Indians included the Wampanoags, who are represented at a campsite near the village, where the museum staff demonstrates native foodways, agricultural practices, and crafts.

At the main entrance to the plantation you'll find two modern buildings with an interesting orientation show, exhibits, gift shop, bookstore, cafeteria, and nearby picnic area.

To reach Plimoth Plantation (tel. 746-1622) from Rte. 3, take the exit marked "Plimoth Plantation Highway." The village is open daily from the end of March through November 30 from 9 a.m. to 5 p.m. The Wampanoag campsite is open daily May 1 to October 31. Admission to both exhibits is $8.50 for adults, $5.25 for children 5 through 12; under 5, free. A combination ticket for Plimoth Plantation, the Indian campsite, and the *Mayflower* is $10 for adults, $7 for children 5 through 12. (Note: Wear comfortable shoes. There's a lot of walking involved and, naturally, it isn't paved.)

If you like cranberries—cranberry sauce, cranberry bread, or even cranberry sherbet—you'll be fascinated by the exhibits at **Cranberry World,** 225 Water Street (tel. 747-1000), where there are outdoor working bogs, antique harvesting tools, and a scale model of a cranberry farm. September and October are harvest time. In addition there are daily cooking demonstrations and free refreshments. Hours are 9:30 a.m. to 5 p.m. daily April 1 through November 30, later in July and August. Admission free. The Cranberry World Visitor's Center is about a ten-minute walk from Plymouth Rock.

Note: Cranberry juice was named the official beverage of the Commonwealth of Massachusetts in 1970. We'll drink to that!

You can walk along the waterfront to Cranberry World, but it's more fun to take the picturesque open-air trolley which runs frequently to the points of interest in town. Trolley markers indicate the stops.

And if you'd like to see one of the original church bells cast by Paul Revere, stop by the Revere Factory Store, at the corner of Lothrop and Water Streets, across from Cranberry World. This is an outlet for the famous Revere Ware copper and brass pots and pans, and you can get very good buys on factory irregulars. Open Monday through Saturday from 9:30 a.m. to 5:30 p.m.

Now take some time away from the bustle of the waterfront and relax at **Town Brook Park** at Jenny Pond, across from the Governor Carver Motor Inn. This is a beautiful tree-lined pond, and you can stretch out on the grass or feed the ducks and swans. Across from the pond is **Jenny Grist Mill Village,** a reconstructed Early American water-powered mill and a cluster of specialty shops. A large waterwheel powers the mill, and you can watch as corn, wheat, and rye are ground into grain. You can also purchase stone-ground grains for your own baking, or buy breads, cakes, and natural food products. And they say that the fish ladder at the mill is the best place to see the spring herring run. The grist mill (tel. 747-0811) and shops are open seven days a week from 10 a.m. to 6 p.m. Plenty of parking and free admission.

You can shop at the **Village Landing Market,** overlooking the Plymouth waterfront. The specialty shops and boutiques are clustered along cobblestone walkways bordered with benches, trees, and flowers. Summer band concerts are held in the gazebo, and it's a charming place for shopping or browsing.

HISTORIC HOUSES: You can't stay at the beautiful historic houses of Plymouth, but you should visit them to see the changing styles of architecture and furnishings since the 1600s. Costumed guides explain the homemaking details and the crafts of earlier generations. There are six homes which can be visited during a walking tour: Richard Sparrow House (1640), Howland House (1667), Harlow Old Fort House (1677), Spooner House (1749), Antiquarian House (1809), and Mayflower Society Museum (1754–1898). Combination tickets for tours of all the houses are available; consult the Information Booth, discussed above, for details.

STAYING IN PLYMOUTH: The **Sheraton Plymouth,** 180 Water St., Plymouth, MA 02360 (tel. 508/747-4900, or toll free 800/325-3535), is a very attractive new facility facing the harbor. Located at the Village Landing, it shares the charming ambience of the marketplace with its little shops and park. The 177 guest rooms have climate control, color TV, in-room movies, and direct-dial/message-service phones. Some have balconies that overlook the swimming pool and whirlpool, located in a colorful garden setting. The hotel also has a fine restaurant, Apricots, which serves a delicious Sunday brunch. Room rates are $95 to $100 single, $105 to $110 double, April 1 to November 15. At other times the rates are $80 to $85 single, $90 to $95 double. An additional adult in the room (18 and older) is $10.

One of the finest hotels in Plymouth, the **Governor Bradford Motor Inn,** Water Street, Plymouth, MA 02360 (tel. 508/746-6200), is beautifully situated right on the waterfront and only one block's walk from Plymouth Rock, the *Mayflower,* and the center of town. The 94 rooms, each with two double beds, are attractive in the modern style, with wall-to-wall carpeting, TV, individually controlled air conditioning, heating, and a small outdoor pool. Rates vary according to the season, the highest being from June 15 to October 26—$80 to $85 for a single, $90 to $98 for a double—with varying scales in winter, spring, and fall. Children under 14 are free.

A sister hotel to the Governor Bradford, the **Governor Carver Motor Inn,** 25 Summer St. at Town Square, Plymouth, MA 02360 (tel. 508/746-7100), is an impressive Colonial-style building, with excellent modern accommodations, large pool, color TV, free cribs, and all the amenities. It is also within walking distance to the main attractions, and in-season rates run $76 to $78 in a single, $88 to $90 in a double. Again, open all year and very comfortable. Pick your Governor.

Located midway between Plymouth Rock and Plimoth Plantation is the **Colonial House Inn,** 207 Sandwich St., Plymouth, MA 02360 (tel. 508/746-2087), whose quiet, secluded grounds offer a picturesque view of Plymouth Bay plus a swimming pool. All rooms have Early American decor, private bath, cable TV, and air conditioning, and are quite pleasant and home-like. In season, double rooms are $50 to $70.

The **Cold Spring Motel,** 188 Court St., Rte. 3A, Plymouth, MA 02360 (tel. 508/746-2222), is a pleasant, quiet motel, convenient to all historic sites. There are 31 air-conditioned rooms with color TV, wall-to-wall carpeting, and private bath. There's parking at your door, and a picnic area on the grounds. Summer rates are $48 to $61; off-season, $38 to $48.

A most attractive vacation spot outside town, yet within walking distance of the Plimoth Plantation, is the **Pilgrim Sands Motel,** 150 Warren Avenue, Plymouth, MA 02360 (tel. 508/747-0900). There are 64 ultramodern units, located right on the ocean, all with tile bath and shower, individually controlled heating (most with air conditioning), TV, wall-to-wall carpeting, and tasteful furnishings. In summertime you can enjoy the private beach, terraces, whirlpool spa, and outdoor and indoor pools too. Most rooms have two double or two queen-size beds, and double-occupancy rates in season are $78 to $96 (the higher rate for oceanfront rooms). In spring and fall, the tariff goes down.

Note: On busy summer weekends, every room in town is often taken. Make reservations in advance, or you may have to sleep in your car.

DINING IN PLYMOUTH: Seafood, of course, is the specialty at almost all Plymouth restaurants, where much of the daily catch goes right from the fishing boat to the kitchen. Two choice places along the town wharf are **McGrath's Harbour Restaurant** (tel. 746-9751) and the **Fisherman's Dinners Restaurant** (tel. 746-1704).

To the rear of Fisherman's Dinners is the **Mayflower Seafoods Fish Market**—self-service, no tipping. Choices range from fish and chips to baked stuffed lobster, with all kinds of fish and chicken in between. If you'd like to eat on the wharf, just ask that your order be prepared for take-out. Also on the waterfront is **Scruples,** 170 Water St., Village Landing (tel. 747-3200), an up-scale, contemporary restaurant serving breakfast, lunch, dinner, and Sunday brunch, open from 6:30 a.m. to 11 p.m. And in town at 51 Main St. is **Station One Bar & Restaurant** (tel. 746-6001), once Plymouth's central fire station, with the oldtime atmosphere still preserved, and now an excellent place for lunch and dinner.

Bert's, on Warren Street, Rte. 3A (tel. 746-3422), is also on the ocean, three miles from the center of town, opposite Plimoth Plantation. It's a popular, attractive spot with a view of the beach and has two lounges and dancing. Service is fast and efficient, the food is good, and the portions are generous.

A SIDE TRIP TO EDAVILLE: Before you leave Plymouth County to see Cape Cod, take a ride on the **Edaville Rail Road** on Rte. 55, South Carver, where a restored two-foot-gauge steam rail-road tours 5½ miles of an 1,800 acre cranberry plantation. In the fall you can watch the harvesting. Open daily 10 a.m. to 5 p.m. Admission is $8.50 for adults, $6 for seniors, and $5.50 for chil-dren. To reach Edaville, take exit 6 on Rte. 3 (Plymouth exit), then Rte. 44 west to Carver and Rte. 58 south to Edaville.

A TASTE OF THE GRAPE: It doesn't quite fit in with the his-toric image of Plymouth, but the **Commonwealth Winery,** 22 Lothrop St. (tel. 746-4138), has created its own niche in town. The winery is open for tours, free tasting, and retail sales Monday through Saturday from 10 a.m. to 5 p.m., and on Sunday from noon to 5 p.m. The equipment is a blend of stainless-steel fermen-tation tanks and recycled oak barrels. The grapes are French-American hybrids that thrive in New York, and which create some excellent wines. There is also a new cranberry wine.

Commonwealth Winery is near Cranberry World Visitor Cen-ter. Follow the signs.

CAPE COD

Cape Cod—pine-scented, sea-swept, cranberry-bogged—is one of the most popular vacation lands in the Northeast and one of the most amenable anywhere. Here, where the Pilgrims made their first landing (at Provincetown, before they sailed to Plymouth looking for a better harbor), thousands of Bostonians now maintain beach homes; New Yorkers and Philadelphians and people from the Midwest love it for summer vacations, as do ever-increasing throngs of Canadians. And there is plenty to attract the visitor in this bent-at-the-elbow peninsula which juts out into the Atlantic 57 miles south of Boston pointing its tip northward to the city. This old seafaring corner of New England (whaling ships once put out from its ports, and fishing is still a big industry) boasts a landscape that includes 300 miles of sparkling, sandy white beaches, as well as marshlands, meadows, pine forests; quaint New England towns with their trim architecture, their old saltbox houses and winding, tree-shaded lanes; scores of art galleries, museums, summer theaters, historical attractions; facilities for a dozen different sports; plus some of the best antiquing and most diversified shopping anywhere.

There are hundreds of restaurants and hotels to feed and house the almost half million people on the Cape any given summer day, and accommodations run the gamut from cozy guesthouses run by oldtime Cape Codders, where the landlady fixes you coffee in the kitchen in the morning, to shiny new motels complete with heated year-round pools, saunas and Jacuzzis, and individually controlled air conditioning and heating. It's a modern, bustling, heavily crowded summer resort area, but with enough salty New England flavor still left to make it a rather unique spot on this globe.

If you're in Boston in the summer, you must certainly go "down the Cape" for a few days, or better yet, a few weeks; if you have the kids with you, it's a good place for them to let off some steam. In the spring and fall, the Cape is particularly lovely: not warm enough for swimming, but brisk and clear, uncrowded, and fine for sightseeing, shopping, sports. And there are those who also dote on it in winter, when they can sit by the fire in a quaint guesthouse and perhaps watch a famed New England "nor'easter" lash the streets. A word about the weather: Don't expect perfection, even in summer, but a rainy day on the Cape can have its own windy charm.

BEACHES: You can't miss them, and you have your choice of either bathtub bathing in the warm waters facing Buzzard's Bay and Nantucket Sound or the more traditionally nippy Massachusetts waters on the oceanside shore. Most Cape towns have both ocean and bay beaches, and some have lakes and freshwater ponds as well. Many of the smaller towns require resident stickers to use their beaches (you get one for your car when you check into your hotel), but there are also many beaches open to the general public, like **Craigville Beach** at Barnstable and the enormous, well-equipped **Scusset State Beach Reservation** near Bourne (access via Rtes. 3, 6, and South Sagamore Circle). The National Seashore maintains some of the best beaches of all: try **Head of the Meadow** in North Truro, **Coast Guard Beach** in Eastham, **Herring Cove** in Provincetown. There's a daily parking fee, or you can get a seasonal pass.

CAMPING:
Cape Cod's major camping sites are the **Shawme Crowell State Forest** at Sandwich, **Scusset State Beach** at Sagamore; and a larger site, the **Roland C. Nickerson State Forest** at Brewster, where there are freshwater ponds stocked with trout. Many fine private campgrounds are also open from Bourne to Wellfleet.

BIKING AND HIKING:
There's good biking on the **Bourne bike path** which goes along the Cape Cod Canal. This is the canal's service road and is closed to vehicular traffic, making it a very pleasant trail for cyclists. Falmouth has the **Shining Sea Bike Trail,** which starts at Woods Hole Road outside the center of town and leads to the Woods Hole Steamship Authority terminal on the harbor. Other bike paths follow trails in the **Cape Cod National Seashore,** where there are also hiking routes. (See the Cape Cod National Seashore section, or call 508/349-3785 for specific locations.)

FOR BIRDWATCHERS:
Cape Cod is a birdwatcher's delight. In the autumn migratory season the coast becomes a major flyway. And in some years observers have tallied more than six million birds in a single night!

GETTING TO CAPE COD:
Here you have several choices:

By Car
Take the Southeastern Expressway from Boston and follow Rte. 3 south through Plymouth and to Sagamore, where the Cape Cod Canal officially marks the beginning of the Cape. If you're headed directly to Provincetown or the other north Cape towns like Wellfleet or Truro (where half the psychoanalysts of New York retreat for the month of August), you can make better time by

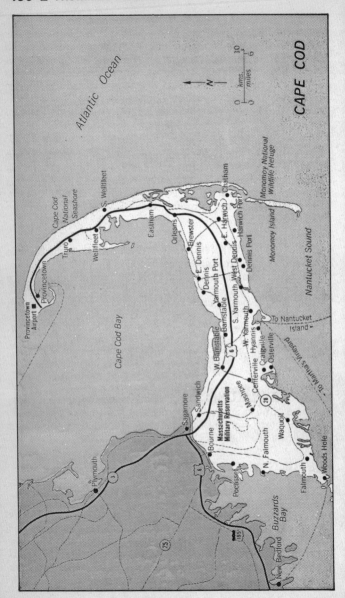

driving the fast Mid-Cape Highway (U.S. 6), but we think it's a shame to miss the charms of such graceful villages as Barnstable, Dennis, Brewster, and Chatham, through which you will pass by taking the very scenic Rte. 6A, along the north shore.

If you're headed for Hyannis, or for Harwich with its cranberry industry, for Falmouth or for Woods Hole (where you pick up the boats to Nantucket and Martha's Vineyard), head south after you cross the Cape Cod Canal and take Rte. 28 eastward.

By Air

Daily flights from Boston to Provincetown and Hyannis by **Continental Airlines,** Logan Airport, Eastern Terminal, Boston (tel. 617/569-8400). Conveniently scheduled flights daily. Travel time is only half an hour to Provincetown and 45 minutes to Hyannis.

By Train

The **Cape Cod and Hyannis Railroad** has a train that runs from the Braintree MBTA station to Sandwich, Hyannis, and Falmouth, mid-May through October. You can take the Red Line "T" to Braintree or drive south on the Southeast Expressway to Rte. 3 exit 17. There's parking at the station. Fares start at $7. Write or call the Cape Cod & Hyannis Railroad, 252 Main St., Hyannis, MA 02601 (tel. 508/771-1145), for schedules.

By Bus

Plymouth and Brockton Street Railway Co. (tel. 617/773-9400), Park Square, Boston, at the Greyhound Terminal, and at South Station Transportation Center, Atlantic Avenue, runs buses to Hyannis from 6:40 a.m. to 12:15 a.m. daily. Buses leave hourly during the week, and on a special schedule weekends. **Cape Cod Bus Lines** runs from Hyannis to Provincetown twice daily, connecting with the Boston bus. Call the company in Hyannis (tel. 508/775-5524) for schedules. **Bonanza Bus Company** (tel. 617/423-5810), also at the Greyhound Terminal in Boston, takes the route to Falmouth, Wareham, Buzzard's Bay, and Woods Hole, and connects with the ferry to Martha's Vineyard.

By Ship

Bay State Provincetown Cruises, 20 Long Wharf, Boston (tel. 617/723-7800), has a round-trip boat to Provincetown daily in mid-June, July, and August, and weekends in late May and early September. It sails from Commonwealth Pier, 1 South Boston (next to Anthony's Pier 4 Restaurant), at 9:30 a.m., and arrives in Provincetown at about 12:30 p.m. The return trip leaves at 3:30 p.m. Round-trip tickets (same-day return) cost $20 for adults, $13 for children. One way is $13 for adults, $10 for children. There's a band on board, and sandwiches and snacks are available.

A CAPE COD CANAL CRUISE: Most tourists barely see the Cape Cod Canal as they drive over the Bourne or Sagamore Bridge on their way to or from the Cape. But this 17-mile-long waterway is worth a visit of its own. We suggest a canal cruise sometime during your Cape vacation as a relaxing and informative way to spend a day or evening. There are several choices: a two- or three-hour sail, a sunset cocktail cruise, or a Moonlight 'n Music outing. On most of the trips a narrator describes the history of the canal, which was built in five years (from 1909 to 1914) at a cost of $16,000! If your timing is right you can watch the vertical-lift railroad bridge at Buzzard's Bay being lowered for the Cape Cod and Hyannis Railroad train, and then being raised again for boats after the train passes through. The canal boats sail from the Town Pier in Onset, a mile from the rotary at junction of Rtes. 6 and 28 in Wareham. Prices start at about $5.50 for the two-hour cruise. There are discounts for seniors on Monday and Friday, and special rates for families on the 4 p.m. cruise. For a schedule and current prices write or phone **Cape Cod Canal Cruises,** Onset Bay Town Pier, P.O. Box 3, Onset, MA 02558 (tel. 508/295-3883). Combinations of train rides and cruises are available through the Cape Cod and Hyannis Railroad (see the Hyannis section).

INFORMATION, PLEASE: For help, advice, driving directions, information on hotels, restaurants, sports facilities, beaches, shops, whatever, consult any of these three major information centers maintained by the **Cape Cod Chamber of Commerce.** They are located at the junction of Rtes. 6 and 132, Hyannis; South Rotary, at Bourne Bridge; and Sagamore Rotary, at Sagamore Bridge. Or you may write in advance for information to Cape Cod Chamber of Commerce, Jct. of Rtes. 6 and 132, Hyannis, MA 02601 (tel. 508/362-3225).

Because of the seasonal nature of resort areas and the many changes from year to year we suggest that you also check with the aides at the local information booths in each town for up-to-the-minute details on beach parking fees, farmers' markets and summer fairs, chowder suppers, and band concerts. They can also tell you where to find quiet beaches and hidden trails known only to the locals.

At the information centers or at your hotel get a free copy of the "Cape Cod Guide," and check for discount coupons for restaurants, museums, and entertainment. You really can save money that way. Also check the town newspapers for sales and coupons.

Since restaurants often change hours and policies, call ahead for reservations and at the same time ask questions about dress policy, charge-card or cash options, nonsmoking sections, and the availability of alcoholic beverages.

And watch your parking meters! We've picked up a few "souvenir tickets" that cost as much as a really fine souvenir.

SANDWICH: The Cape really begins at the Cape Cod Canal, completed by the army Corps of Engineers in 1914 to save southbound ships a lengthy and often dangerous journey round the tip and out to sea. (The bones of many an old ship lie deep in Cape Cod waters.) Just south of the canal, on Rte. 6A, is the town of Sandwich, a remarkably serene little village that always reminds us of the English countryside, complete with a meandering stream and several swans. The time-honored visitor attraction is the internationally renowned **Sandwich Glass Museum** on Rte. 130, in Town Hall Square, a repository of the exquisite Sandwich glass that was made here from 1825 to 1888. (Open April 1 to October 31, 9:30 a.m. to 4:30 p.m. daily. For winter hours, call 888-0251 or write P.O. Box 103, Sandwich, MA 02563. Admission for adults is $2.50; children under 12, 50¢.)

A newer attraction, and also an outstanding one, is the absorbing museum of Americana, **Heritage Plantation of Sandwich,** located in a beautifully landscaped setting at Grove and Pine Streets (tel. 888-3300), three miles from the Cape Cod Sagamore Bridge. It has something for every member of the family: antique autos, a military museum with 2,000 military miniatures, one of the finest collections of Currier and Ives lithographs in existence, an operating windmill, and an original 1912 carrousel. Admission is $6 for adults, $2.50 for children 6 to 12, and free for under-6s. In addition there are picnic facilities and 76 acres of nature trails and landscaped grounds with thousands of Dexter rhododendrons and over 750 varieties of daylilies. Bring your camera!

Other historical sites to note include the 300-year-old **Hoxie House** (open mid-June through September, 10 a.m. to 5 p.m.; admission is $1 for adults and 50¢ for children; in combination with the Grist Mill, $2 and $1), an early saltbox furnished in period style by Boston's Museum of Fine Arts; **Thomas Dexter's Grist Mill** (open mid-June through September, daily; admission is $1.25 for adults, and 75¢ for children), restored to 17th-century style and offering cornmeal for sale; **Yesteryears Doll and Miniature Museum,** Main and River Streets (open May 15 to October 31 Monday through Saturday from 10 a.m. to 4 p.m. and on Sunday from 1 to 4 p.m.; admission is $2.50 for adults, $1.50 for children under 12, and $2 for senior citizens). The collection fills two floors in the First Parish Meeting House, established by the Pilgrims in 1638.

In these days of mechanical processing, we were delighted to find the **Green Briar Jam Kitchen** on Discovery Road in East Sandwich almost unchanged since it was opened in 1903. Here jams and jellies are cooked in small batches in the old-fashioned way without any pectins or artificial preservatives—just fresh fruit and sugar. And in the summer months, jams are "sun cooked" for about three days on a shelf placed under an awning of slanted glass. There is no charge for admission, but you probably won't be able to leave without buying at least one jar of that delicious jam. Green Briar is run by the Thornton W. Burgess Society, and there are nature trails behind the house, where you might find descendants of Thornton Burgess's Peter Cottontail who roamed the briarpatch long years ago. Nearby is the **Thornton W. Burgess Museum** at 4 Water St. (tel. 888-6870), open daily from 10 a.m. to 4 p.m., on Sunday from 1 to 4 p.m., April to December.

Staying in Sandwich

For accommodations, the **Earl of Sandwich Motor Manor,** East Sandwich, MA 02563 (tel. 508/888-1415), just north of town on Rte. 6A, is a very comfortable, Tudor-designed motel, attractively landscaped, and complete with all the comforts, including soundproofed rooms, color TV, electric heat. Doubles cost $50 to $70, with complimentary continental breakfast in season. Lower rates off-season.

The **Dan'l Webster Inn,** 149 Main St., Sandwich, MA 02563 (tel. 508/888-3622), has an oldtime buggy at the front entrance, and the colonial theme is carried out through the inn and restaurant. Built in 1971 on the site of the original 1692 inn, it comprises 37 guest rooms and five suites with whirlpool tubs. The decor is colonial with some canopy beds, rockers, and original oil paintings. On the modern side, there's individually controlled heat and air conditioning, baths with tub/shower, color TV with in-room movies, and an outdoor pool and patio. Summer rates are $89 to $165 double; winter, $65 to $135. The Modified American Plan includes breakfast and dinner for an extra $36 a day per person.

Wingscorton Farm Inn, 11 Wing Blvd., East Sandwich, MA 02537 (tel. 508/888-0534), is a centuries-old Cape Cod manse (circa 1758) with just enough modern amenities to make it a wonderful vacation spot.

Set back from Rte. 6A, with lawns, gardens, orchards, and a private ocean beach nearby, Wingscorton offers accommodations in the Main House, Carriage House, and Cottage. The rooms have restored antique furnishings, working fireplaces, and private baths. Rates for doubles range from $115 to $150 and include a full farm breakfast with fresh produce from the gardens. Singles are $90 with breakfast. The Cottage rents for $650 per week and sleeps six. (Breakfast is extra for Cottage guests.) Hosts Dick Loring and Sheila Weyers also welcome "well-trained" pets.

Dining Along Route 6A

One of the pleasures of driving along Rte. 6A is discovering some of the finest restaurants on the Cape. Starting at Sandwich and continuing along the scenic route to East Brewster, you can enjoy everything from dinner "in the rough" to the finest haute cuisine.

For gracious dining at a leisurely pace when the rush of sightseeing gets a bit too much, we recommend the restaurant at the **Dan'l Webster Inn,** 149 Main St., Sandwich (tel. 888-3622). The furnishings are in colonial style, the tables beautifully set with fine glassware and china, and there are some extremely comfortable high-back plush dining chairs. There are three different dining rooms, each with its own charm. Our favorite is the Conservatory, the glassed-in room that looks out on the landscaped courtyard with its huge linden tree. Inside there are Oriental rugs, chandeliers and more plush furnishings.

As for the food, it's excellent. Beef, veal, chicken, and seafood specialties are offered in a price range from $10.95 to $23.95. Entrees include a cheese dip, vegetable sticks, salad, potato, and delicious warm bread. At lunch you can have a complete meal or choose a salad or omelet. Serving is continuous from 8 a.m. to 10 p.m. A very special buy is early dinner from 4:45 to 6 p.m. for $10.95.

Also in Sandwich is **Sandy's,** a popular local restaurant in a white building along Rte. 6A (tel. 888-6480). There's a large menu to choose from, and usually a long line at the door since prices are moderate, from $6 to $16. And they also serve children's portions to anyone (a great idea if you have a small appetite)! Sandy's is open from 11:30 a.m. to 9:30 p.m. seven days a week in summer.

Note: Some restaurants in town are closed on Monday; others don't open until lunch. So if you don't want to hunt all over town for breakfast as we did, ask for advice at your motel.

We know some people who make the trip from Boston to the Cape just to dine at **Chillingsworth,** Rte. 6A in East Brewster (tel. 896-3640). This award-winning French restaurant has five candlelit dining rooms with fresh flowers at each table and a view of a carefully tended garden. Dinner is table d'hôte from $32.50 to $44, with five full courses prepared from top-quality ingredients and served by attentive personnel. The menu changes nightly but usually includes filet of beef Kempinski, rack of lamb, and several fish, chicken, duck, and meat selections. There is usually a hot and cold soup (we can recommend carrot and leek and the melon soup), well-prepared fresh vegetables and salads, and a splendid array of desserts including cake, sherbet, and several mousses laced with liqueur. There are two dinner seatings every day but Monday. An à la carte lunch that meets Chillingsworth's standards is also served.

HYANNIS: Hyannis became famous because it once housed what in effect became the summer White House, the Kennedy home. Crowds would throng the streets of the little south-shore village in the town of Barnstable content to bask, however tenuously, in the glamour of the region.

Today, although much of the summer tourist boom remains, Hyannis evokes sadness for those who revered the Kennedy legend. Many visitors drive down Ocean Street to pay a brief tribute to its memory by observing the J.F.K. memorial, a plaque on a stone wall looking over the Atlantic.

To reach Hyannis, take the Mid-Cape Highway, Rte. 6, to exit 132, which passes the airport on the way into the town. Traffic usually backs up on this road, so if you can, ask at one of the service stations for directions to the bypass roads used by the local residents.

The village itself, although small, boasts two harbors and six public beaches for which you must pay a parking fee unless you receive a sticker from your motel. There are also many fine beaches in Yarmouth, just a few miles from Hyannis.

Hour-long harbor cruises leave from the Ocean Dock in Hyannis Port starting at 9 a.m. and every 30 minutes thereafter from May through October (call Hy-Line, tel. 775-7185). In addition to passing neighboring islands, these cruises offer what is probably the best view of the Kennedy estate compound (on land, guards discourage visitors from approaching too closely). There are also two sunset cocktail cruises. At the same dock there are several daily sailings, May to October, to Nantucket and Martha's Vineyard that allow about four hours ashore on either island. Sailing time to

Nantucket is two hours; to the Vineyard, 15 minutes less. For exact times, spring and fall schedules, and current rates, call 775-7185.

A NOSTALGIC TRAIN RIDE: Take a nostalgic trip from Hyannis to Sandwich to Buzzards Bay on an old-fashioned 1920s railroad coach, chugging through cranberry bogs, dunes, farmlands, and the great salt marshes. The **Cape Cod & Hyannis Railroad** runs several excursions daily from mid-May to October, leaving from Hyannis, Sandwich, or Buzzards Bay. You can choose a trip that crosses the canal railroad bridge at Buzzards Bay, one that connects with the Martha's Vineyard Ferry in Hyannis, or one that goes to Heritage Plantation in Sandwich. Most rides are round trips, but one-way trips are available if you'd like to stay a while. Reservations can also be made for the first-class parlor car for lunch, and for cocktails in the tavern car. Fares range from $9 to $25, and children's and senior citizen fares are available. For current schedules write or call the Cape Cod & Hyannis Railroad, 252 Main St., Hyannis, MA 02611 (tel. 508/771-1145).

Shopping in Hyannis

There are three major shopping areas in Hyannis: the **Cape Cod Mall, Main Street,** and the area near the **West End Rotary.** The mall, located on the outskirts of Hyannis beyond the airport, is a large complex of some 100 shops following the pattern of a typical suburban mall. Main Street is touristy with many little shops and boutiques, gift stores and eating places—some of them open until 10 or 11 p.m. each night. Buy taffy there, or fudge, or popcorn in dozens of delicious flavors including amaretto and watermelon. Stop at the **Picadilly Deli** for a light meal, quiche, salad, or muffins. And for a cool oasis on a hot day, seek out **The Courtyard,** a cluster of eating places and gift shops in a flower-bedecked courtyard with a fountain and white tables and chairs. It's hidden from the crowds on Main Street, so look for the small alley across the road from the West End plaza.

And in downtown Hyannis at Stevens and North Streets, near the West End Rotary, is the **Chart House Village Market Place,** with fine specialty shops, galleries, and restaurants grouped to resemble an 18th-century brick market.

Note: Visit Hyannis's candle factories on free tours, and watch candles being made from fragrant bayberries. **Colonial Candle Company** is at 238 Main St., and **Old Harbor Candle** is on

Rte. 132 across from the Sheraton Regal Inn. And at Old Harbor's **Cracker Barrel** you can grind your own peanut butter.

Staying in Hyannis

Hyannis seems to have motels, hotels, and tourist homes just about everywhere you look; yet on a busy summer weekend, it's hard to find a room. We suggest making reservations either in Hyannis or nearby Yarmouth/West Yarmouth well in advance. You might want to choose accommodations in one of the following specific areas.

If you'd like to avoid driving and the hunt for parking spaces, the motels and guesthouses along the harbor, Main Street, and the adjacent streets put you in walking distance of the shops and ocean. Route 128 in the direction of Yarmouth and Bass River is lined with motels, gift shops, and restaurants; and the streets branching off the highway lead to the beaches. Beyond the airport and the Cape Cod Mall, along Rte. 132, are the big-name hotels favored by convention groups and tourists seeking the fancy touches.

If you like a resort hotel that has everything (including convention groups), there's the **Hyannis Regency Inn,** Hyannis, MA 02601 (tel. 508/775-1153), on Rte. 132, and **Tara Hyannis Resort,** West End Circle, Hyannis, MA 02601 (tel. 508/775-7775). Both have golf courses and tennis courts (Regency's are indoors), health clubs, indoor and outdoor pools with whirlpool, lounges, and restaurants. The guest rooms naturally have all the amenities, including cable TV. The in-season rates at Tara are $125 to $190 double; and at the Regency, $89.95, double only. Check on off-season rates and package deals.

Also very nice is the **Iyanough Hills Motor Lodge and Golf Club,** Hyannis, MA 02601 (tel. 508/771-4804), with large, comfortable rooms. There's also an indoor pool, whirlpool, sauna, and playground. It's set well back from the road on Rte. 132. Doubles are $69.95 in season. Efficiency units available.

And across the road on Rte. 132, the **Rainbow Motel,** Hyannis, MA 02601 (tel. 508/362-3217), has 45 comfortable units on a lake, where you can go boating or fishing. There's a small outdoor pool and picnic areas. Rooms are air-conditioned, with phones and cable color TV. Rates run $54 to $64 double in season.

The **Inn on Sea Street,** 358 Sea St., Hyannis, MA 02601 (tel. 508/775-8030), is a very special place—a small, elegant Victorian inn on a quiet street that is near the beach and within walking distance of the town. The 1850 home has been completely restored by innkeepers J.B. Whitehead and Lois Nelson, and furnished with antiques, Oriental rugs, and period furniture, including a four-poster bed with canopy. A full complimentary breakfast is served each morning at individual tables set with flowers, the hosts' finest sterling silverware, crystal, and china. It includes fruit, cheese, eggs, granola, and home-baked muffins, coffee cake, and wheat toast. Guest rates are $55 to $75 year round.

Dining in Hyannis

The **Paddock,** at the West End Rotary (tel. 775-7677), is one of the favorite spots in town, featuring fresh fish, prime ribs, Long Island duckling, and two-pound live lobsters. Menu choices range from standard baked or broiled items to imaginative fare such as breast of chicken Calcutta (the chicken is stuffed with dates, walnuts, and oranges, and served with curry sauce and fresh fruit). All entrees include a relish tray, salad, and a choice of potato, pilaf, or vegetable. At dessert time, forget the calories and try poached pears with ice cream or cranberry apple pie. Prices range from $12 to $18.

The decor is turn-of-the-century with mahogany paneling, Victorian antiques, and fresh flowers on linen-covered tables. Jackets for gentlemen are preferred. The Paddock serves dinner from 5 to 10 p.m.; lunch, noon to 2:30 p.m.

We found one of the best moderately priced meals in town at **"Up The Creek,"** 36 Old Colony Rd., Hyannis (tel. 771-7866), away from the center of town, but worth looking for. Lunch, dinner, and Sunday brunch are served, and they're always busy. At lunch, you can get baked scallops or a petit sirloin for under $6. At dinner, veal dishes are less than $10 and seafood entrees are priced from $7.50 to $10.95. A terrific Sunday brunch is available from 11:30 a.m. to 2:30 p.m., with a cocktail, appetizer, and entree of fish, meat, or eggs for $7.50. Be sure and make reservations. Hours for lunch are from 11:30 a.m. to 2:30 p.m. Monday through Friday. Dinner hours are from 5 to 9 p.m. Sunday through Thursday, and until 10 p.m. on Friday and Saturday.

When you're watching your budget, there's the **Lobster Hut,** Rte. 28 in West Yarmouth (tel. 771-0571). Service is cafeteria style in two cheerful orange-and-brown rooms facing the highway. The broiled scrod lunch and the fish and chips are good values. So is the lobster roll. Open daily from 11 a.m. to 10 p.m. in season.

And in Yarmouthport, look for **"Jack's Out Back,"** 161 Main St. (tel. 362-6690), for a quick, inexpensive breakfast or lunch. Using the menu over the counter you write your own order. Help yourself to coffee and soft drinks as well. Try soup and garlic bread, and a veggie or roast beef pocket for lunch. If you leave a tip in the big kettle on the counter, Jack will ring the large bell on top to let everyone know of your generosity. *Note:* Jack's is hard to find. Look for the antique shops at 161 Main St. and walk through the parking lot behind them. Jack's is the yellow building "out back."

And if you like the salt air to spice your seafood, **Baxter's,** 177 Pleasant St. (tel. 775-4490), serves fried clams and other fresh fish on the wharf or the ferry boat. It's very much a Hyannis landmark.

Note: For a quick, do-it-yourself meal, head for the salad bar at any of the big supermarkets. Great for picnics or eating in your room.

MID-CAPE MUSEUMS: Brewster is a small town that's big on museums—there are three of them on Rte. 6A: The **Drummer Boy Museum** follows the story of the American Revolution via life-size panoramas and guided tours, daily, May to October, from 10 a.m. to 4 p.m. A restored 18th-century windmill, the most photographed structure on Rte. 6A, is part of the complex. Call 896-3823 for tour rates. The four-acre **New England Fire & History Museum** features antique fire-fighting equipment and related memorabilia, plus a 19th-century blacksmith shop, a Victorian apothecary shop and a diorama of the Great Chicago Fire. There is a gift shop and a picnic area and guided tours daily. Open Memorial Day weekend to mid-September from 10 a.m. to 5 p.m., plus weekends till Columbus Day. Call 896-5711 for admission charges. And at the **Cape Cod Museum of Natural History,** guided tours on the marsh trails are conducted throughout the year. Call 896-3867 for hours, fees, current exhibits, lectures, and film schedules.

FALMOUTH: Falmouth is a charming seacoast town, 68 miles south of Boston, with beautiful harbors and beaches and a Village Green surrounded by historic homes and churches. Falmouth celebrated its 300th birthday in 1986. There are the usual bustling tourist areas, and a busy harbor from which a ferry sails to Martha's Vineyard several times daily; but there are also quiet streets for strolling, with lovely old homes that once belonged to whaling skippers.

To find your way around, pick up a "Walking Guide" at your motel. Or take a trolley (really a bus that looks like a trolley) that goes through the town and along the oceanfront. Some drivers include a running commentary of all points of interest, and you can note those you'd like to visit later.

Historical sites open to visitors are: the **Saconesset Homestead** in West Falmouth, a 300-year-old Cape Cod farmstead with exhibits, gardens, animals, and a Sunday flea market; the **home of Katherine Lee Bates,** author of "America the Beautiful," at 16 Main St.; and the **Falmouth Historical Society Building** on Palmer Avenue at the Village Green, noted for its Colonial rose and herb gardens, and for the restored kitchen with open hearth and Early American cooking utensils.

Of course you'll want to try one of the warm beaches. Most require resident or guest stickers (check at your motel), but the famous **Old Silver Beach** in North Falmouth offers general parking for a daily fee.

Dining in Falmouth

For your very special dinner in Falmouth, we suggest the **Regatta of Falmouth By-the-Sea,** at the end of Scranton Ave. (tel. 548-5400), one of the most beautiful waterfront dining locations on Cape Cod. Fresh seafood from all over the world, creative French and American cuisine, and extraordinary wines are presented in the pink-and-mauve dining rooms, where candles glow on each table. Try the lobster bisque with lobster-filled ravioli, the grilled shrimp, and the homemade fresh sorbets. Dinner is served nightly from 5:30 p.m. to "10-ish," May through October. Price range is $17 to $26.

And to make sure that Cape Codders and visitors will be able to enjoy Regatta dining all year, owners Wendy and Brantz Bryan recently opened a second restaurant, **The Regatta of Cotuit at the Crocker House,** Rte. 28 in Cotuit (tel. 428-5715), which is on the road that connects Hyannis and Falmouth. Located in a Federal mansion that has been carefully restored, Regatta has nine gracefully styled dining rooms and lounges. Local produce, game, fish, and fowl are featured on a menu that is based on modern cuisine. The entrees are served on Limoges plates. Price range is $17 to $26. Open for dinner 5:30 to "10-ish." Both lunch and Sunday brunch start at 11:30 a.m.

The **Coonamessett Inn,** Jones Road at Gifford Street (tel. 548-2300), has a luxurious setting and meals to match. The dining rooms, done in colonial decor, overlook beautifully landscaped grounds and a pond. Prices for the traditional New England cooking are in the upper ranges, but the lobsters, scallops, and chowder are worth every dollar. Coonamessett Inn serves breakfast, lunch, and dinner daily throughout the year. There is entertainment in the evening, and a "coat and tie" dress code. This is a complete inn with accommodations in the main building, and in the attractive new additions.

If you prefer to be informal, the **Clam Shack,** at the corner of Clinton and Scranton Avenue, on the dock near the fishing charter boats, serves an excellent lobster roll and very good clam chowder (in paper cups). There are several fish selections too, and the lines are usually long. You can eat out on the dock or use the picnic-style tables inside the small dining room. Open from 11:30 a.m. to 8 p.m. daily.

Irish food and such trappings as an Irish singing group and a computer leprechaun show are the specialties of the **Century Irish Pub,** 29 Locust St. (tel. 548-0196), on the way to Woods Hole past where Rtes. 28 and 28A intersect. Open 4 p.m. to 1 a.m. May to October.

Try **David's Restaurant,** 553 Palmer Ave. (tel. 548-7313), for breakfast, brunch, and lunch. The thick deli sandwiches and garden salads are very good. And here's your chance to have New England–style johnny cakes made with stone-ground cornmeal for $3.50. David's is open seven days a week from 6:30 a.m. to "3:30ish."

The Pushcart Restaurant, famous in Boston's North End, has a branch at 339 East Falmouth Highway (tel. 548-5090), serving the same delicious food for which they're famous in Boston. From Memorial Day to Labor Day, they're open daily from 5 to 10 p.m. The rest of the year they're only open Thursday through Sunday.

Staying in Falmouth

Although Falmouth is a small town, there are several distinct areas—the harbor, Jones Pond, the oceanfront beaches along Nantucket Sound, the sheltered beaches in North Falmouth, and the Main Street section. Consider which would best meet your needs when making reservations.

IN TOWN. For the quiet charm of a colonial inn, we like the **Elm Arch Inn** on Elm Arch Way, Falmouth, MA 02540 (tel. 508/548-0133), a quiet little road off Main Street across from the public library. The white clapboard building with a gold eagle over the red front door, and the adjacent Richardson House, have 24 rooms, 12 with private bath and 12 with shared bath. All are individually decorated with antiques, primitive paintings, and handmade country quilts. Some beds have canopies and there's a trundle bed in one of the family rooms. Outdoors, there's a swimming pool, a large lawn, and a rustic, screened porch where guests can gather in the evening. Rates for accommodations are $40 to $50 for rooms with bath. Off-season (before July and after mid-September) rates drop as low as $38 for a double.

There's history, too, at the inn, which was built in 1812, and bombarded by a British frigate two years later. The dining room wall still shows the scar of the cannonball. Hosts Harry and Flossie Richardson are a wonderful source of knowledge on the history of the town.

ON THE HARBOR. The **Studio Motel,** 113 Falmouth Heights Rd., Falmouth, MA 02540 (tel. 508/548-1513), on Falmouth Harbor, is a cozy, quiet motel set back from the road. Since there are only 6 units, including some efficiencies, it's well booked in advance, especially the rooms with water views. It's secluded, yet within easy reach of the town, the beaches, and the cruise lines. Rates in season are $50 to $60 double, $65 for efficiencies. It's sheer delight to sit on the sunny, landscaped terrace and watch the boating activity in the harbor.

JONES POND AREA. The Jones Pond area is a quiet, country-like section set apart from the commercial areas of town. Two lovely hotels there are the Sheraton Falmouth and the Coonamessett Inn.

The **Sheraton Falmouth,** 291 Jones Rd., Falmouth, MA 02540 (tel. 508/540-2000, or toll free 800/325-3535), is a typical Sheraton hotel of 93 rooms in a very nice setting. There's a heated indoor swimming pool, and in summer a courtesy van takes guests to the local beaches (a good way to avoid the parking hassles). Rates for doubles are around $90 in season, but there are many package deals available (usually mid-week), which include breakfast and dinner allowances and will give you two nights for about the price of one. The special holiday prices are also good deals.

The **Coonamessett Inn,** Jones Road at Gifford Street, Falmouth, MA 02540 (tel. 508/548-2300) (see "Dining in Falmouth"), has comfortable rooms in the inn and 22 suites in the new units overlooking the pond and the landscaped grounds. Rates range from $100 to $115.

ON THE BAY. The **Sea Crest Resort and Conference Center,** Shore Road, North Falmouth, MA 02540 (tel. 508/548-3850), a complete resort hotel on Old Silver Beach, is very popular for weeklong or long-weekend vacations. Sea Crest features indoor and outdoor pools, a fitness center, four tennis courts, an ocean-view dining room, dancing and entertainment, and a children's day camp. All vacation plans include breakfast and dinner options. Modified American Plan as well as special holiday packages are available. Call 800/352-7175 in MA, 800/225-3100 in NH, NY, VT, RI, CT, or NJ for current rates.

Note: The **Falmouth Road Race,** which attracts some of the top runners in the world, is held in mid-August, and the town is usually very crowded. In recent years there have been close to 5,000 participants and 40,000 spectators! If you'd like to watch the race and stay in town for the weekend, make reservations early.

WOODS HOLE: From Falmouth to Woods Hole is just a short ride on Rte. 28. Ride down to see the Woods Hole Oceanographic Institute (although very little of it is open to the public) or to take the ferry to Nantucket or Martha's Vineyard. It's almost worth missing the ferry to dine at the **Landfall Restaurant,** on the wharf (tel. 548-1758). The food is excellent, the view spectacular, and prices for lunch and dinner are moderate.

And if you do miss the ferry and want to stay over in Woods Hole, the **Nautilus Motor Inn,** P.O. Box 147, Woods Hole, MA 02543 (tel. 508/548-1525), makes a good stopoff for the night, or longer. It's air-conditioned, comfortable, pleasantly located overlooking the harbor, and has a swimming pool and tennis courts plus award-winning formal gardens. Rates are $86 to $102 for doubles, mid-June through Labor Day. Lower off-season. One of the Cape's finest restaurants, **The Dome** (tel. 548-0800), is there too. This circular restaurant topped by a 54-foot geodesic dome was built by architect-philosopher Buckminster Fuller. The Dome serves breakfast and dinner from April into October.

ENTERTAINMENT ON THE CAPE: You have a choice of three well-known playhouses on the Cape: the **Cape Cod Melody Tent,** in Hyannis at the West Main Rotary (tel. 775-9100), has a season of musical theater and big-name variety shows from June to September; the **Falmouth Playhouse,** off Rte. 151 (tel. 563-5922), has established stars doing the summer circuit; and the **Cape Playhouse,** on Rte. 6A in Dennis (tel. 385-3911), has been famous for many years for its fine productions. In the same complex is the Playhouse Restaurant (where you might meet the stars of the shows) and the Cape Cinema which has a famous Rockwell Kent mural on its ceiling.

The kids will love the dolphin shows in West Yarmouth and West Brewster (you will too). In Yarmouth on Rte. 28, the **Aqua Circus of Cape Cod** (tel. 775-8883) is open daily February to December from 9:30 a.m. to 9 p.m. in season, and 9:30 a.m. to 5 p.m. off-season. There are five dolphin and sea lion shows daily, aquatic exhibits, a petting zoo, and piano-playing ducks and dancing chickens. At **Sealand,** on Rte. 6A in West Brewster (tel. 385-9252), the trained dolphins perform six times daily from 9:30 a.m. to 7:30 p.m. during the summer (other months, 10 a.m. to 4 p.m.). You can bring a lunch to their Marine Park and watch the sea lions and otters in the outdoor pools. There's also a restaurant on the grounds that features a hot and cold buffet.

CHATHAM: Chatham is overlooked by many tourists, but the little town at the elbow of the Cape, with water on three sides, is "the real Cape Cod." It has long, sandy beaches, beautiful ponds and old homes, and a mile-long shopping center on Main Street. A great spot for photographers, Chatham has the Cape equivalent of Rockport's Motif #1, a picturesque fishing shack on Barn Hill Road off Rte. 28; a 95-year-old red-and-yellow Victorian depot with a bright-red caboose in back; and a lighthouse at the south end of Main Street. And in Chase Park you can find one of the nation's few authentic 18th-century working windmills—**Godfrey Windmill**—where the miller grinds corn when the wind is right.

Monomoy Island, an eight-mile stretch of unspoiled barrier beach offshore, is a national wildlife preserve with excellent surf fishing. Calmer waters at Oyster Pond attract families with children.

Check with the Chatham Chamber of Commerce in the tiny white-and-green cottage on Main Street for the times of such local events as the Festival of Arts in August and the weekly band concerts.

ORLEANS: Orleans, at the entrance to the Lower Cape, is roughly mid-way between Hyannis and Provincetown, where Rtes. 6, 6A, and 28 meet. Within the Cape Cod National Seashore, it has both saltwater and freshwater beaches, including the spectacular **Nauset Beach** on the North Atlantic side with rolling dunes and top surfing in a specially designated area, and **Skaket Beach** on Cape Cod Bay, a gently sloping warm-water beach great for children—and their parents. There are also several freshwater ponds in the inland areas of town. Orleans is also a choice location for sports fishing. Striped bass, bluefish, bluefin tuna, flounder, and mackerel are abundant.

Staying In Orleans

The **Governor Prence Motor Inn,** at the intersection of Rte. 6A and Rte. 28 in the center of Orleans, MA 02653 (tel. 508/255-1216), is an attractive inn with large, comfortable guest rooms decorated in colonial style and parking at each unit. The big solar-heated outdoor pool is located in a rose garden surrounded by pine trees, and picnic tables with grills are available for guests. Rates change seasonally with double-occupancy prices for summer at $68; spring and fall at $44; and early spring at $38. (The mailing address for the Governor Prence is P.O. Box 127, Orleans, MA 02653.)

Dining in Orleans

For dinner in Orleans, try **Capt. Linnell House,** a short mile from the junction of Rtes. 6A and 6 (tel. 255-3400), an excellent restaurant in a restored, clapboarded antebellum mansion with old-fashioned gardens and wisteria-covered columns; or the **Barley Neck Inn,** Main Street (tel. 255-6830), an 18th-century captain's house with a reputation for fine food. Try **Cooke's,** Rt. 28 (tel. 255-5518), for good fish platters, sandwiches, and burgers at reasonable prices. Eat in the restaurant or on the terrace.

Shopping in Orleans

One of our favorite shopping places on the whole Cape is **Tree's Place,** Rte. 6A at Rte. 128 (tel. 255-1330). There's a wonderful selection of ceramic tiles, pottery, jewelry, tartans, art, and sculpture—all top-quality merchandise in all price ranges. Tree's Place is open seven days a week from 9:30 a.m. to 5:30 p.m.

When natives say, "It's for the birds," they're probably referring to **Bird Watcher's General Store,** 37 Route 6A (tel. 253-6974), which carries a full line of items for bird lovers, ranging from 50 varieties of bird feeders, bird bath heaters, and binoculars to bird T-shirts, bookmarks, and giftwrap. The store is open year round from 10 a.m. to 5 p.m., Monday through Saturday; and also Sunday from 9:30 a.m. to 5 p.m. from Memorial Day to Labor Day.

CAPE COD NATIONAL SEASHORE: In a great victory for conservationists and ecological groups, many of the beaches and forestlands of the Cape have been designated part of the Cape Cod National Seashore, protected from commercial encroachment and carefully watched over by the National Park Service. If you are at all interested in nature, natural history, and the beauty and preservation of the Cape Cod area—and particularly if you have youngsters in tow—take part in the many programs offered by the Seashore. The two places to get started are at the **Salt Pond Visitor Center** in Eastham, on Rte. 6, and at the **Province Lands Visitor Center,** high up on Race Point Road in ·Provincetown. The Eastham center is the busier, with a small natural history museum on the grounds, picnic and bicycling areas, and evening programs several times a week in the amphitheater. The Province Lands Visitor Center also has evening programs, plus an observation roof from which you'll get striking vistas of dune and forest and sea. Both centers are starting points for numerous self-guided or guided tours through the fascinating forest, swamp, and marshland trails of the Cape. (There are special paths for the blind.)

This is a great area for cyclists. The five-mile loop through sand dunes and a beach forest starting at the Province Lands Visitor Center is a good family trail as it is not too hilly for children. There is a two-mile trail at the Salt Pond Visitor Center, and another at the Pilgrim Heights Center in Truro which follows the route taken by the Pilgrims when they explored the area in 1629. Maps are available at the information centers. Joggers compete with the cyclers for space on the trails, but the best place for jogging is at Nickerson State Park on Rte. 6A in Brewster.

Note: This is surfing territory too, with special sections set aside at Coast Guard Beach, Marconi Beach, and Head of the Meadow Beach in Eastham and Truro.

PROVINCETOWN: P-town, as the regulars call it, is perhaps

the best-known spot on Cape Cod. First came the Indians, camping where the town hall now stands and barbecuing the wild boar that used to roam the forests. Then came the Pilgrims, who made their first landing here; then the Portuguese fishermen, who still go down to the sea in ships (come in June, if you can, to see the festive "Blessing of the Fleet"); then in the '20s, the artists and writers and actors and assorted free souls who make it, even today, America's Left Bank on the seashore, Greenwich Village transplanted to the waterfront, and a longtime favorite resort area of both the American and international gay community. Eugene O'Neill and Edna St. Vincent Millay and Edmund Wilson and Hans Hoffman and Robert Motherwell are some of the names associated with Provincetown, all attracted by its old clapboard houses, narrow, winding streets, a profusion of flowers, a salt tang to the breeze, and a laissez-faire spirit in the air.

Provincetown today still has its art colony, but at the height of the summer there's scarcely room for artists to take a pencil out of their pockets, let alone set up an easel. **Commercial Street,** in the center of town, is packed tight with shoppers and strollers, their erratic passage constantly interrupted by cars struggling up the one-way street to get to the beaches at the tip of the Cape. On scores of wave-lashed wharves, vacationists sit at "nautical" bars and restaurants sampling the local seafood, served by scores of college kids who relish the chance of a job in a resort where there are so many young people. If you crave peace and quiet, come to P-town before July 4 or after Labor Day, or else stay away from the middle of town (the east and west ends of town are relatively quiet). But if you want to be part of the most exciting scene on the Cape, this is your place.

Note that Provincetown is one of the few vacation areas on the Cape—or anywhere, for that matter—where you can get along perfectly well without a car. The town beach, the local grocery and drugstores, scores of restaurants, shops, whatever, can easily be reached on foot, and you won't have to hunt for those hard-to-come-by parking spaces.

Sightseeing and Shopping

You can hardly miss seeing the **Pilgrim Monument,** a 252-foot granite shaft built in 1910 to honor the first landfall of the Pilgrims in the New World and the signing here of the *Mayflower* Compact. It now houses a fascinating museum containing a miniature memorial to playwright Eugene O'Neill. There's a fine view of the Cape from the top of the tower (open daily in season; call 487-1310 for off-season hours). Be forewarned, it's a long hard climb by stairs and ramps. Admission is charged.

The **Provincetown Heritage Museum,** at 36 Commercial St., as its name suggests, records the heritage of the town from its artists to its fisherfolk. The paintings on display represent a cross-section of artists in Provincetown since 1899. There is a recreated dune shack, the world's largest indoor half-scale model of a fishing schooner, and many antique exhibits. The museum is open daily from 10 a.m. to 6 p.m. Admission is charged.

You can buy the Historical Society's "Walking Tour Guides" here. They only cost 25¢ and they tell you what to look for as you walk through the town. You can walk from one end to the other in less than an hour without stops. It might take all day or more if you check all the wonderful things in town.

Art is part of Provincetown's raison d'être, and you'll see plenty of it here, from sidewalk portrait painters to major exhibitions. The **Provincetown Art Association and Museum,** 460 Commercial St., has been part of the scene since 1914, with exhibitions by established and emerging artists. The Art Association offers lectures, artists' films, art classes and demonstrations, and works by local artists sold in their museum shop. Open daily, May to October; otherwise, only on weekends. The **Group Gallery** (tel. 487-0275) features artists who live and work on the outer Cape at its loft at the Provincetown Tennis Club at 286 Bradford St. Hours are 11 a.m. to 1 p.m. and 6 to 9 p.m. (Or call for an appointment.) And there are many commercial galleries throughout

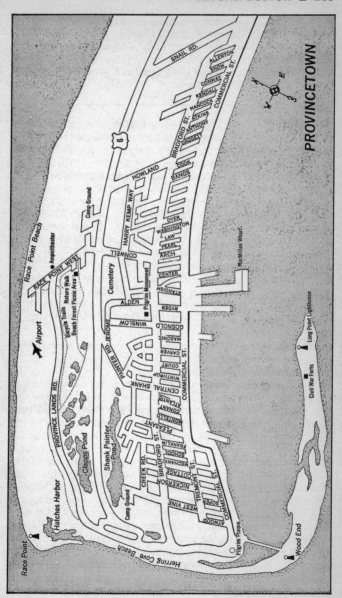

PROVINCETOWN

town. (Check the *Provincetown Advocate* or the P-town Chamber of Commerce for listings of current shows.)

The **Provincetown Chamber of Commerce** publishes a wonderful guide to the town. Check with them at 307 Commercial St., at MacMillan Wharf (P.O. Box 1017, Provincetown, MA 02657; tel. 508/487-3424).

THAR SHE BLOWS!: The newest summer "event" off the Massachusetts capes (Cape Cod to the south and Cape Ann to the north) is whale-watching. Specially chartered boats, often with naturalists aboard, take passengers out to sea to watch as the whales follow their migratory paths from Provincetown to Newfoundland—surfacing, spouting, and leaping out of the water almost on cue for the cameras clicking over the ship's rails. Humpback, finback, and minke whales, some of them 50 to 60 feet long, are among the migrating mammals. Several nonprofit organizations sponsor whale watches including the Boston Museum of Science, Science Park, Boston; New England Aquarium, Atlantic Avenue, Boston; Greenpeace New England, 286 Congress St., Boston; and the Web of Life Outdoor Education Center, Plymouth. These trips are usually in April to mid-October, and require reservations well in advance of sailing. Many of the local captains take out trips from Provincetown and Plymouth, spring through fall.

Provincetown Miscellany

We doubt that you'll run out of things to do in Provincetown. During the day you'll probably be at the town beach or else drive out to the better ocean beaches: **Race Point** and **Herring Cove** in Provincetown, or **Head of the Meadow** in nearby North Truro. Herring Cove has small waves; Race Point and Head of the Meadow have the long rolling breakers. (There is a daily parking fee, or you can buy a season pass.) The sports-minded can bike, sail, fish, play tennis or golf, or ride horseback through the beach forest, across the dunes, and along the ocean at designated National Seashore areas. There are several playgrounds for kiddies too.

What to do at night? No problem, just walk along Commercial Street, looking in at the shops, perhaps sitting down in front of Town Hall to watch the bizarre, outlandish, utterly absorbing passing parade. For something more organized, catch a movie at one of the local cinemas, or an art opening at a gallery. There are plenty of bars, both gay and straight. Among the straight bars are

Ciro and Sals, Kiley Court, and the **Cellar Bar** at Inn at the Mews, 359 Commercial St., both of which are crowded and busy; and **Downstairs at Plain and Fancy,** 334 Commercial St., quiet enough to carry on a conversation. **Back Street** in the Gifford House, 9 Carver St. (for men), and **The Pied Piper,** 193 Commercial St. (for women), are the most popular gay bars.

Most of the hotels feature entertainment in the lounges or restaurants and there are several dance bars. **Captain John's,** on Shankpainter Road, has the "Saturday Night Fever" crowd every day in the week. The local characters, including the fishermen, congregate at the **Old Colony Tap,** 323 Commercial St.

Whatever else you do, don't miss a ride on one of P-town's famous **beach taxis,** a gentle roller-coaster trip up and down the giant dunes. It's unique to this part of the world, and if you take it at sunset, you'll be treated to a windblown ride along the beach at Race Point, finally to watch a brilliant sun sink into the Atlantic—the only place you can see this on the East Coast.

Or drive your own car to Race Point and join the throng of sunset buffs watching the day fade away into the ocean.

Staying in Provincetown

The **Masthead,** 31-41 Commercial St., Provincetown, MA 02657 (tel. 508/487-0523), is a neatly kept cluster of apartments, cottages, and motel units on well-tended lawns with 450 feet of private beach. The waterfront sundeck, the lovely plantings, and warmly furnished units make this a distinctive spot. During the season, cottages and apartments are rented on a weekly basis for $695 to $1048, motel rooms are available for $65 to $110 daily, and prices go down in spring and fall. The Masthead is open all year, and has free deep-water moorings and launch service.

A perfect hideaway is the charming **Land's End Inn,** 22 Commercial St., Provincetown, MA 02657 (tel. 508/487-0706), perched atop Gull Hill at the tip of Provincetown's West End. Hidden from the street, it was once the summer "bungalow" of a wealthy Boston merchant; and the original woodcarvings and stained glass are still there, along with beautiful antiques and plants that flourish in the sunlit rooms. The panoramic view of Cape Cod is spectacular, especially from the octagonal Tower Room. This is a place to relax, read, and listen to red-bearded innkeeper David Schoolman's collection of classical music (no TV here). It's as popular in winter as in summer, so reservations well in advance are a must. In season, doubles are $56 to $94; efficiency apartments are $82 to $90. Lower rates in spring, fall, and winter, with doubles at $53 to $89 and efficiencies at $79 to $86. Some rooms can accommodate up to four people, and there is a $15-a-day charge over the doubles rate for each additional person. A complimentary continental breakfast is served on the breakfast porch each morning (the cinnamon toast is delicious). And there is plenty of parking available for guests.

Our own "special little place" in Provincetown is **Hargood House,** 493 Commercial St., Provincetown, MA 02657 (tel. 508/487-1324), in the quiet East End of town. Featured in *House Beautiful* for its architecture and decor, it consists of 17 waterfront and water-view apartments, beautifully appointed with antiques, decorator accessories, and personal touches everywhere, even including dishwashers. They are really little homes away from home and could comfortably be lived in for a whole summer. Hal Goodstein and Bob Harrison, the hospitable owners, are always on hand to see that everything functions smoothly—and it does. There's a back garden right on the beach, comfortable patio furniture for relaxing as you watch the ocean lash up against the pilings —and interesting people to talk to. The regulars here consist of Boston and New York professionals who don't mind paying a little extra for the charm and convenience. The apartments rent for $570 to $1,020 a week for two, including maid service, depending on size and location. Only weekly rentals are available from July 2 to Labor Day, but out of season (Hargood House is heated and open year round) they will take a two-day minimum. Off-season daily rates are $62 to $116, for two persons. Christmas on the Cape, anybody? Write well in advance for reservations.

Up in the East End is the **White Horse Inn,** 500 Commercial St., Provincetown, MA 02657 (tel. 508/487-1790), popular with many European visitors who've discovered its special charms: a backyard and garden with hibachi, beach rights to the bay across the street, and individually decorated rooms and public areas filled with original artworks and antiques. Paintings abound in every nook and cranny. Innkeeper Frank D. Schaefer also has studio apartments with kitchens; these are really lovely artist's or writer's studios, and could happily be lived in for a long summer. In season, rates are $30 to $50; less off-season. Reserve in advance, please.

Close to the center of town, **Somerset House,** 378 Commercial St., Provincetown, MA 02657 (tel. 508/487-0383), is a long-established guesthouse and one of the nicest in town. It's located just across the street from the beach with a front piazza (New England–ese for porch) for people-watching, and a lovely garden carefully landscaped by owner Jon Gerrity, who also carefully chooses the classical music he puts on the stereo for his guests. The century-old house is attractively maintained, filled with plants, the walls hung with paintings, some of the rooms with Victorian marble-topped furniture, others splashingly modern, all with modern tile baths and enclosed stall showers. Rates vary according to room size and location, but cost $40 to $70 for singles, $45 to $75 for doubles; prices drop, September to June, when a few attic rooms are available at $26 to $35. Advance reservations are advised for specific rooms in season, but you'll probably always be able to find something here, including a two-bedroom apartment at $550 per week. Limited private parking is available, and public parking is nearby.

One block away from Commercial Street, **Sunset Inn,** at 142 Bradford St., Provincetown, MA 02657 (tel. 508/487-9810), is a very appealing guesthouse with modest rates. John Gavin, the friendly owner, creates a warm atmosphere here; he serves his guests coffee out in the big backyard and patio in the morning. The 20-odd rooms are clean and comfortable, some with private bath, and go for about $38 to $58. Sunset Inn is heated, and off-season rates are very low: about $24 to $38, anywhere in the house. The crowd runs to people in their 20s and 30s, including families, who appreciate the big porches and the sundeck upstairs too. Reservations advised.

TOP FAMILY CHOICES. Kalmar Village, Provincetown, MA 02657 (tel. 508/487-0585), is a good choice for families. Kalmar is a cottage colony located right on its own 400-foot private beach, a cluster of 30 cottages, plus a motel. Not only is it *at* the beach, but there is also a heated pool that the kiddies love and a laundromat that makes life easy for mom. The two- and three-room cottages are furnished with everything for easy vacation living, from maid service to toasters. In high season, expect to pay around $550 to $650 a week, less in spring and fall.

Asheton House, 3 Cook St., Provincetown, MA 02657 (tel. 508/487-9966), in the East End, is really two early-19th-century whaling captains' houses, with lovely colonial gardens, water views, and decks from which to watch the Provincetown sunset. Inside are seven rooms and one apartment, each exquisitely furnished with antiques—French, English, American, and continental. In season, rates are $39 to $74, and a three-room, fully equipped apartment is $585 per week. Complimentary continental breakfast is served.

If you prefer resort-type accommodations to a guesthouse, try the **Holiday Inn,** Rte. 6A, Shore Rd., Provincetown, MA 02657 (tel. 508/487-1711), which has big-hotel amenities with small-hotel friendliness. All rooms have two double beds, color cable TV, direct-dial phones, and individually controlled heat and

AC. During the day the action centers around the large outdoor pool with poolside cocktail bar and barbecue. In the evening, it moves to the Whaler Lounge with its live entertainment and dancing. Rates vary according to view and season. High season, early July through August, is $82.50 to $99 for one or two persons. (Don't worry about driving your car into town and parking. There's a town bus at the door of the hotel that goes to the pier, with stops along the way.)

Dining in Provincetown

For the full flavor of Provincetown—the ocean, the nautical atmosphere, the seafood—we like the **Flagship,** 463 Commercial St. (tel. 487-1200). Jutting out over the water and built almost entirely of driftwood and ship salvage, it's crowded with nautical trimmings—anchors, ship's bells, ropes, and wheels. The two bars up front are actually halves of old fishing dories, and they're flanked by a large fireplace and open hearth. Try to sit by the windows and watch the sun set or the moon rise while dining on the likes of paella valenciana, scallops française, or the fish of the day, always an excellent choice. Lobster Louisiana, a house specialty, features a sauce of heavy cream, wine, and shrimp stock. Entrees range from $10 to $15. Dinner is served from 6 p.m. every evening. Piano music from 9 p.m. until closing in season.

For more than 25 years, **Ciro and Sal's,** 4 Kiley Court (off Commercial Street, about the 400 block; tel. 487-9151), has been a famous P-town landmark for excellent Italian food in intimate surroundings. Originally just a charming grotto with flickering candles atop tables and hanging chianti bottles, it's now expanded into additional light and airy upstairs rooms. (But it's still crowded, so phone ahead for a reservation.) Pasta dishes start around $9 for the plainest varieties, and go up for the exotic fare, such as fettuccine alla romano. Most other entrees—veal, chicken, fish in various manifestations—are in the $10 to $18 range. Be sure to save room for one of the incredible desserts, such as lime pie or coeur à la crème. Open all year.

Franco's by the Sea, 429 Commercial St. (tel. 487-3178), is a high-style sleek dining room that has become the rage of the town with entrees in the $10 to $16 range. In an area known for good food, Franco Palumbo has established a superior northern Italian restaurant with gourmet cooking handled with pizazz. The traditional pasta dishes are prepared with flair, the veal is perfectly tender, and the pan-blackened Cajun fish and shrimp can be ordered in mild, medium, or hot versions. And it's hard to resist desserts such as "Brownie All the Way," smothered with hot fudge and whipped cream. The decor, reminiscent of the heyday of Hollywood, is deco-design, with pink-and-gray booths named for legendary Hollywood stars. Open for dinner daily between 5:30 and 11 p.m.

We also recommend **The Mews,** 359 Commercial St. (tel. 487-1500), and **Pepe's Wharf,** 373 Commercial St. (tel. 487-0670), for fine dining on the harborfront; **Napi's,** 7 Freeman St. (tel. 487-1145), for a moderately priced varied menu that includes some vegetarian dinners; and the **Lobster Pot,** 321 Commercial St. (tel. 487-0842), a very popular spot with the locals that gives good value for the money.

Try a breakfast or brunch with enough sustenance to last until dinner. Some good choices—which you can also rely on for fine meals at lunch and dinner later in the day—include **Gallerani's Café,** 133 Commercial St. (tel. 487-4433). From 8 a.m. until 2 p.m. you can get a light continental breakfast with freshly made croissants, or create your own omelet by adding as many ingredients (from a delicious group of 30) as you like. Nearby at 149 Commercial St., the **Cottage Restaurant** (tel. 487-9160) starts serving its huge three-egg omelets at 7:30 a.m. and has breakfast available till 3 p.m. **Café Edwidge,** 333 Commercial St. (tel. 487-2008), features fresh-fruit bowls, whole-wheat pancakes, homemade bread, delicious omelets, and home-fries from 8 a.m. to 1 p.m. in its attractive second-story dining room. **Pronto Restaurant,** at 315 Commercial St. (tel. 487-2318) in the center of town, also serves a good breakfast at reasonable prices. Pick a bright and beautiful morning for your breakfast on the upstairs deck at **Ocean's Inn,** 386 Commercial St. (tel. 487-0358), and check the activity in the harbor as you sip your coffee. Enjoy the ocean view from another vantage point at **Pucci's Harborside Restaurant,** 539 Commercial St. (tel. 487-1964), where brunch starts at noon. The banana pancakes and French toast with strawberries are delicious.

And if you want some "fast food," try **Mojo's** at 5 Ryder St. Extension (tel. 487-3140), at the foot of Macmillan Pier. They're famous for deep-fried foods—potatoes, clams, mushrooms—and everything else from a Kosher hot dog to a char-broiled chicken or a fish dinner.

WELLFLEET: From Provincetown take a drive to Wellfleet, summer home to shrinks from all over the country, and year-round home of the famous Wellfleet oyster. In contrast to P-town, Wellfleet is quiet and relaxing, with miles and miles of secluded ocean beaches, picturesque bicycle trails, and excellent art galleries.

There are many fine restaurants, and we've had some enjoyable meals at the nouvelle cuisine spot in town, **Aesops Tables,** Main Street, in Wellfleet Center (tel. 349-6450). Dinners go for about $10 to $19, and might include scallops with green sauce, chicken with lime, or medallions of veal with a mustard tomato sauce. Leave room for one of the unusual desserts, perhaps the "death by chocolate." Sunday brunch is very popular with its "eggs from the heart," salmon Benedict, and fresh fruit waffles.

For something less elegant, such as lobster in the rough (considered by some critics to be the best on the Cape) or steamed clams, the **Lobster Hutt,** Commercial Street (tel. 349-6333), is the place to go. The restaurant is in an old oyster shack—it's self-service, and very informal. And the seafood is all fresh from Cape waters. Open late May to late September.

If you plan on staying in Wellfleet, the **Inn at Duck Creeke,** Main Street, Wellfleet, MA 02667 (tel. 508/349-9333), is a guesthouse that reflects the old-fashioned charm of the town. The 20 rooms in this old sea captain's house built in the early 1800s are decorated antique-style with spool beds, Boston rockers, and cane-bottomed chairs. The inn has its own duck pond and views of a tidal creek and salt marsh. There are 25 rooms, 8 of them with shared baths. Rates are in the $50 to $75 range for private bath and $45 to $60 for shared bath, and include a continental breakfast. Open mid-May to mid-October. The adjoining **Sweet Seasons Restaurant** is a top choice for dinner, with entrees in the $10 to $17 range.

A good family restaurant, casual and reasonably priced, is the **Yum Yum Tree,** Rte. 6A, Wellfleet (tel. 349-9468), where there's a fresh juice bar, chicken and fish dishes, Portuguese bread, and good soups. Open from 11 a.m. to 9 p.m. Monday through Saturday, and from 8 a.m. to 9 p.m. on Sunday. During July and August breakfast is served daily from 8 a.m. to 11 a.m.

Note: Be sure to listen to the clock in the steeple of the First Congregational Church, which strikes on ship's time. See if you can figure out what time it is when the clock strikes "four bells."

CHAPTER IX

A STUDENT'S GUIDE TO BOSTON

□ □ □

Thousands of students arrive in Boston every year, bound for Harvard and MIT and Tufts and Simmons and Boston University and Boston College and a myriad other schools and colleges that have made the city one of the most exciting student gathering places anywhere.

WHERE TO STAY

First, of course, you need a place to stay, and that will be the hardest thing to find in town, unless you can afford the hotel rates. The best way is to know a student who is willing to make room for your sleeping bag (or whose roommate is out of town). Even if you don't know anyone, it's rather easy to make friends by mingling with the crowd at Harvard's Holyoke Center in Harvard Square or Boston University's meeting places at Kenmore Square and Sherman Student Union. Someone usually knows where there is a space for a visitor.

If, however, you prefer a more organized approach, there are the Ys, a youth hostel, and a variety of small hotels around the university areas. Let's begin with the Ys.

THE Ys: The **Central Branch YMCA,** 316 Huntington Ave., Boston, MA 02115 (tel. 617/536-7800), has attractive and modern accommodations. It now accepts both men and women. Rooms have maid service and color TV, and rates include use of a wide range of Y facilities—pool, gym, and weight room. There is also a cafeteria on the premises. Rates are $27 for a single room; some doubles are available at $40. Always a bargain, the YMCA is located about ten minutes from downtown Boston on the MBTA Green Line.

The **YWCA,** 7 Temple St. at Central Square, Cambridge, MA 02139 (tel. 617/491-6050), caters to college students and working women. There are two buildings and a heated pool. Guest rates are $35 per night for nonmembers, $30 for members, plus a refundable $10 key deposit. Private rooms with community bathroom, laundry, kitchen, lounge, and TV room are available for a four-week minimum stay. These rooms require application and reference forms.

The **Berkeley Residence Club of the YWCA,** well located at 40 Berkeley St., Boston, MA 02116 (tel. 617/482-8850), welcomes women of all ages. It's a lovely place, with a garden, drawing room, library, sewing room, cafeteria, and laundry facilities. Rates for transients are singles $29 per night, doubles $36 to $44. Resident accommodations for those staying at least four consecutive weeks include breakfast and dinner daily at $76, $89, and $95 per person per week.

AMERICAN YOUTH HOSTELS: The **Boston International Youth Hostel,** one of the largest youth hostels in the country, is at 12 Hemenway St., Boston, MA 02115 (tel. 617/536-9455), near the Museum of Fine Arts and handy to transportation. Sleeping arrangements for 150 persons are dormitory style, at $10 a night, and you bring your own sleep sack or rent one for $2. You may use the kitchen facilities if you wish. You must be a member to use the hostel. Membership is $10 for those 17 and under and $18 for foreign nationals. For all others, membership is $20.

SMALL HOTELS AND ROOMING HOUSES: In Brookline, **Longwood Inn,** 123 Longwood Ave., Brookline, MA 02146 (tel. 617/566-8615), offers comfortable accommodations at modest rates. Located in a residential area, it is near transportation on the Beacon Street and Riverside lines, close to the colleges and medical complex. This large Victorian guesthouse has 20 rooms. Singles rent for $35 to $44. Doubles are $38 to $46. Kitchen privileges, laundry facilities, and parking are included. Guests may also use the parlor and TV room. Weekly rates are available.

Nearby is the **Longwood Avenue Guest House,** 83 Longwood Ave., Brookline, MA 02146 (tel. 617/277-1620). The exterior is not distinguished, but inside the rooms are spacious, neat, and tastefully furnished with antiques. Guests share a small living room and kitchen, where they can use the refrigerator, make coffee or boil water, but not cook. Single rooms with private bath are $35 per night; with shared bath, $30. Doubles with shared bath are $40, with private bath $45. There is a color TV in the living room.

Almost hidden from the street by shrubbery, the **Kirkland,** 67 Kirkland St., Cambridge, MA 02138 (tel. 617/547-4600), is worth looking into since there are so few inexpensive transient accommodations only one block from Harvard Square. Travelers must have ID cards and all guests must follow the house rules, which include no visitors or pets in the rooms. Depending on whether you share one of the several bathrooms on the floor or have private facilities, singles run $25 to $45; doubles $45 to $55. There are family rooms for three to five people at $60 to $70.

Check out the bed-and-breakfast outfits too. Some of them might have rooms in your price range. If you choose a place in the suburbs, just make sure there's transportation nearby.

WHERE TO EAT

MARKET DISTRICT AND DOWNTOWN: That old Boston standby, **Durgin-Park,** 30 N. Market St., is still a find for inexpensive food, but only at lunchtime (evening prices have risen quite a bit lately). Get there between 11:30 a.m. and 2:30 p.m. for hearty meals. . . . And, of course, there's the **Fanueil Hall Marketplace** for all kinds of fast foods, but they're not cheap. . . . Check out the pushcarts in the Haymarket or walk over the North End for good, inexpensive Italian food. Have sheet pizza at the **Galleria Umberto Rosticceria,** 289 Hanover St., for 55¢ a piece. This type of bakery sheet pizza, along with a beverage, makes a tasty, inexpensive lunch. . . . Or have a regular pizza anywhere in town, especially at these North End places: **Francesco's,** 90 North Washington St.; **Regina's,** 11½ Thatcher St.; and the **European Restaurant,** 218 Hanover St. And you can also have a good inexpensive meal at the European. Buy Italian bread at **Drago and Sons,** 275 North St., and some cheese at **Al Capone Cheese Company,** 73 Salem St., with over 200 varieties, and make yourself a moveable feast.

In Boston's Downtown Crossing area, get cream cheese and bagel or a bagel sandwich at **Bruegger's Bagel Bakery,** 32 Bromfield St. Branches at Kenmore Square and Harvard Square. . . . Uptown at 310 Stuart St., **Flash's Snack & Soda Restaurant** serves good breakfasts at very reasonable prices. It's right behind the Greyhound Terminal on St. James Street.

Some of the government buildings at **Government Center** have cafeterias open to the public where you can get a good meal for around $3 in pleasant surroundings. They don't have signs advertising the fact, so ask around: The cafeteria at the John F. Kennedy building is one of the best.

Down in Boston's Chinatown, you'll have no trouble finding inexpensive lunches and dinners. Try the **Chinatown Mall,** 44-46 Beach St., on the second floor for real Chinese food—no tourist stuff. Several little restaurants serve inexpensive meals from 11 a.m. to 9:30 p.m. daily. **King Wah,** 29 Beach St., has good specialties, and most of the places have their menus posted outside so you can check the values. . . . **Oceanic Chinese Restaurant,** 91 Massachusetts Ave., has authentic Cantonese food at reasonable prices, with many seafood items, including whole fishes. Also noodle dishes, poultry, and beef. Open seven days from 11 a.m. to 2:30 p.m. Luncheon specials cost $2.75 to $3.25.

Mississippi's, 484 Commonwealth Ave. at Kenmore Square, features overstuffed sandwiches, a fresh salad bar, and homemade soups and desserts from $4 to $6. Hours are Monday through Friday from 11:30 a.m. to 11 p.m. and weekends from noon to 11 p.m.

Looking for barbecued spareribs? The most reasonably priced are at **Ma Dixon's Diner,** 478 Blue Hill Ave., Roxbury. **Chef's,** 604 Columbus Ave., in the South End, famous for soul food, has hearty, moderately priced ribs. And **Hoodoo** at the Rathskellar, 528 Commonwealth Ave., is a favorite with the college crowd.

If you've got wheels, ride out to the **Hilltop Steak House,** 855 Broadway, Saugus (tel. 233-7700), for your steak. (Look for the life-size steer statue out front.) Figure around $10 with the makings of another meal in your doggie bag. It's informal, noisy, and crowded. Be prepared to wait an hour or more for your table.

And in town, **Newbury's Steak House,** 94 Massachusetts Ave., has some good deals on steak, especially at lunch.

In the Beacon Hill/Back Bay area, try the **Paramount Restaurant,** 44 Charles St., with an excellent souvlaki. . . . **Chiu's Garden,** 757 Boylston St., across from the Prudential Center, may have some of the best Chinese food bargains (and some of the best food) in town. Weekday luncheon specials include soup.

The Cambridge area offers just about anything you want in food. We've listed just a few of the places preferred by the local students—those we've found to give both good food and good value. (See coffeehouse listings, also.) **The Border Café,** 32 Church St., Harvard Square, overflows every evening with a young adult crowd clamoring for Cajun and Mexican food in a tavern-like atmosphere. It's casual, inexpensive, and very tasty.

Open daily for dinner. Lunch is served Sunday through Thursday.
. . . Maybe your mother told you never to eat by hand, but it's okay at **Asmara,** the African restaurant at 714 Massachusetts Ave. You dip into a large communal platter, and scoop up your chicken, lamb, or beef with a traditional East African bread. . . . **Elsie's,** 71A Mt. Auburn St., is a Cambridge institution, usually open from 11 a.m. to 1 a.m., where everyone goes for roast beef sandwiches on a bulkie roll with onions and Russian dressing, or a TD (turkey delight). Another cholesterol nightmare is Fresser's Delight, a combination of hot pastrami, roast beef, brisket, and coleslaw.

If you want to expand your food horizons, there's **Kebab-N-Kurry,** 30 Massachusetts Ave., Boston, for some of the best Indian food with some of the spiciest sauces.

FOOD WITH A HARVARD ACCENT: One of the best places to eat cheaply and well is at the university-subsidized dining halls, usually open to nonstudents for lunch only. Harvard's dining rooms are not your basic college cafeterias: many have rich wood paneling and golden chandeliers, and serve excellent, even gourmet food at unbelievably low prices. The **Kennedy School of Government** is the best place for breakfast. Fresh-squeezed orange juice, bagels, eggs, and breakfast specials help start off your day; there are luncheon specials as well. For an elegant and extensive menu, try the **Cronkhite Graduate Center,** 6 Ash St., beyond the Loeb Drama Center. For the best view, sit near one of the large glass windows which open onto a grassy courtyard. There is even waitress service! The luncheon buffet is fantastic. For international cuisine we like the **Center for International Studies,** on Cambridge Street, next to the modern School of Design. We sampled some excellent moussaka and fried polenta, with two vegetables and bread. **Harvard Divinity School's Refectory,** 47 Francis Ave., has some of the best homemade soups in the area. You must also sample the brownies—simply divine! **Conroy Commons,** at the Graduate School of Education, Longfellow Hall on Appian Way, is a pub with beer and wine, as well as breakfast and luncheon specials. Open 7:30 a.m. to 8 p.m.

NIGHTLIFE

MUSIC: Try to get "rush seats" for the **Boston Symphony,** Friday afternoon and Saturday night, September through April.

They're $5.50, on sale at 9 a.m. on Friday and at 5 p.m. Saturday —there's always a long line. Try to attend one of the "open rehearsals." Second-balcony seats for Pops concerts (April through June) cost $9 and Esplanade concerts in July are free.

Free Concerts

Isabella Stewart Gardner Museum, 280 The Fenway, offers soloists and chamber music in a Venetian palazzo, Tuesday at 6 p.m. and Thursday at 12:15 p.m. (also on Sunday at 3 p.m.), except July and August. Student and faculty concerts are given at the **New England Conservatory of Music,** 290 Huntington Ave. (tel. 262-1120), October through May, and most are free. **Berklee College of Music,** 1140 Boylston St. (tel. 266-1400), offers pop, rock, and jazz at its campus and also at Berklee Performance Center, 150 Massachusetts Ave. Most of the colleges have some free concerts and recitals.

THEATER AND LECTURES: Tickets for the Broadway-bound shows are expensive, but there's more than enough to see at the colleges. You can count on good productions at the **Loeb Drama Center** at Harvard, home of the American Repertory Theater; **Tufts Arena Theater** in Medford; **Spingold** at Brandeis; and Boston University, MIT, and Emerson. The **Boston Repertory Theater** gives good performances and charges low fees. Free summer performances are given from time to time in various parts of the city, including Copley Square. Check the newspapers. You can attend a lecture free at **Ford Hall Forum,** one of America's most famous platforms, if the house has not been sold out by 7:45 of a Sunday or Thursday night. Call Ford Hall Forum (tel. 437-5800) for specifics.

FILMS: Our Boston nightlife chapter has all the information, but if you want something different, try **China Cinema** in Chinatown. There are free films at the **Boston Public Library** and many suburban libraries. The colleges also have film series, often quite low priced with your student ID. There are several art and repertory theaters, including: **The Coolidge Corner Moviehouse,** 290 Harvard St., Brookline (tel. 734-2501); the **Brattle Theater,** 40 Brattle St., Cambridge (tel. 876-6837); and **Somerville Theater,** 55 Davis Sq., Somerville (tel. 734-2501). Since the scene changes so often, check the "Calendar" section of the Boston *Globe* or the "Weekend" section in the Boston *Herald* for current happenings.

SINGLES BARS: In the "where-to-go" listings in the newspapers, singles bars are often dubbed "lounges." Same thing! We've listed some of the best ones in Chapter VII, but here are a few that are especially student oriented: **T.T. the Bear's,** 10 Brookline Ave., Cambridge; and the **Rat,** 528 Commonwealth Ave., at Kenmore Square, Boston, are for the rock 'n rollers. **Ryles,** 212 Hampshire St., Cambridge, covers the jazz scene; and **Western Front,** 343 Western Ave., Cambridge, is a reggae dance club. **Hong Kong,** 1236 Massachusetts Ave. (over the restaurant), is the hottest drinking spot in Harvard Square. The Scorpion Bowl, a communal bowl with fruit juices and liquor, is one of the bar's most popular drinks. Open until 2 a.m.

COFFEEHOUSES: If your choice is a coffeehouse, there are many to choose from. See our Boston Nightlife section (Chapter VII) for listings. And look for Italian coffeehouses listed in Boston Sights.

Index

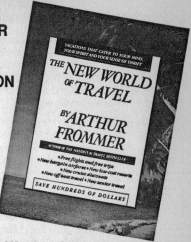

NOW, SAVE MONEY ON ALL YOUR TRAVELS!
Join Frommer's™ Dollarwise® Travel Club

Saving money while traveling is never a simple matter, which is why, over 27 years ago, the **Dollarwise Travel Club** was formed. Actually, the idea came from readers of the Frommer publications who felt that such an organization could bring financial benefits, continuing travel information, and a sense of community to economy-minded travelers all over the world.

In keeping with the money-saving concept, the annual membership fee is low—$18 (U.S. residents) or $20 U.S. (Canadian, Mexican, and foreign residents)—and is immediately exceeded by the value of your benefits which include:

1. The latest edition of any TWO of the books listed on the following pages.

2. A copy of any Frommer City Guide.

3. An annual subscription to an 8-page quarterly newspaper *The Dollarwise Traveler* which keeps you up-to-date on fastbreaking developments in good-value travel in all parts of the world—bringing you the kind of information you'd have to pay over $35 a year to obtain elsewhere. This consumer-conscious publication also includes the following columns:

> **Hospitality Exchange**—members all over the world who are willing to provide hospitality to other members as they pass through their home cities.
>
> **Share-a-Trip**—requests from members for travel companions who can share costs and help avoid the burdensome single supplement.
>
> **Readers Ask . . . Readers Reply**—travel questions from members to which other members reply with authentic firsthand information.

4. Your personal membership card which entitles you to purchase through the club all Frommer publications for a third to a half off their regular retail prices during the term of your membership.

So why not join this hardy band of international Dollarwise travelers now and participate in its exchange of information and hospitality? Simply send $18 (U.S. residents) or $20 U.S. (Canadian, Mexican, and other foreign residents) along with your name and address to: Frommer's Dollarwise Travel Club, Inc., Gulf + Western Building, One Gulf + Western Plaza, New York, NY 10023. Remember to specify which *two* of the books in section (1) and which *one* in section (2) above you wish to receive in your initial package of member's benefits. Or tear out the next page, check off your choices, and send the page to us with your membership fee.

FROMMER BOOKS
PRENTICE HALL PRESS
ONE GULF + WESTERN PLAZA
NEW YORK, NY 10023

Date_____

Friends:
Please send me the books checked below:

FROMMER'S™ $-A-DAY® GUIDES
(In-depth guides to sightseeing and low-cost tourist accommodations and facilities.)

☐ Europe on $30 a Day	$14.95	☐ New Zealand on $40 a Day	$12.95
☐ Australia on $30 a Day	$12.95	☐ New York on $50 a Day	$12.95
☐ Eastern Europe on $25 a Day	$12.95	☐ Scandinavia on $50 a Day	$12.95
☐ England on $40 a Day	$12.95	☐ Scotland and Wales on $40 a Day	$12.95
☐ Greece on $30 a Day	$12.95	☐ South America on $30 a Day	$12.95
☐ Hawaii on $50 a Day	$13.95	☐ Spain and Morocco (plus the Canary Is.)	
☐ India on $25 a Day	$12.95	on $40 a Day	$13.95
☐ Ireland on $30 a Day	$12.95	☐ Turkey on $25 a Day	$12.95
☐ Israel on $30 & $35 a Day	$12.95	☐ Washington, D.C., & Historic Va. on	
☐ Mexico (plus Belize & Guatemala)		$40 a Day	$12.95
on $25 a Day	$13.95		

FROMMER'S™ DOLLARWISE® GUIDES
(Guides to sightseeing and tourist accommodations and facilities from budget to deluxe, with emphasis on the medium-priced.)

☐ Alaska	$13.95	☐ Cruises (incl. Alask, Carib, Mex, Hawaii,	
☐ Austria & Hungary	$14.95	Panama, Canada, & US)	$14.95
☐ Belgium, Holland, Luxembourg	$13.95	☐ California & Las Vegas	$14.95
☐ Brazil	$14.95	☐ Florida	$13.95
☐ Egypt	$13.95	☐ Mid-Atlantic States	$13.95
☐ France	$14.95	☐ New England	$13.95
☐ England & Scotland	$14.95	☐ New York State	$13.95
☐ Germany	$13.95	☐ Northwest	$13.95
☐ Italy	$14.95	☐ Skiing in Europe	$14.95
☐ Japan & Hong Kong	$13.95	☐ Skiing USA—East	$13.95
☐ Portugal, Madeira, & the Azores	$13.95	☐ Skiing USA—West	$13.95
☐ South Pacific	$13.95	☐ Southeast & New Orleans	$13.95
☐ Switzerland & Liechtenstein	$13.95	☐ Southwest	$14.95
☐ Bermuda & The Bahamas	$13.95	☐ Texas	$13.95
☐ Canada	$13.95	☐ USA (avail. Feb. 1989)	$15.95
☐ Caribbean	$13.95		

FROMMER'S™ TOURING GUIDES
(Color illustrated guides that include walking tours, cultural & historic sites, and other vital travel information.)

☐ Australia	$9.95	☐ Paris	$8.95
☐ Egypt	$8.95	☐ Thailand	$9.95
☐ Florence	$8.95	☐ Venice	$8.95
☐ London	$8.95		

TURN PAGE FOR ADDITIONAL BOOKS AND ORDER FORM.

FROMMER'S™ CITY GUIDES

(Pocket-size guides to sightseeing and tourist accommodations and facilities in all price ranges.)

☐ Amsterdam/Holland	$5.95	☐ Montreal/Quebec City	$5.95
☐ Athens	$5.95	☐ New Orleans	$5.95
☐ Atlantic City/Cape May	$5.95	☐ New York	$5.95
☐ Boston	$5.95	☐ Orlando/Disney World/EPCOT	$5.95
☐ Cancún/Cozumel/Yucatán	$5.95	☐ Paris	$5.95
☐ Dublin/Ireland	$5.95	☐ Philadelphia	$5.95
☐ Hawaii	$5.95	☐ Rio (avail. Nov. 1988)	$5.95
☐ Las Vegas	$5.95	☐ Rome	$5.95
☐ Lisbon/Madrid/Costa del Sol	$5.95	☐ San Francisco	$5.95
☐ London	$5.95	☐ Santa Fe/Taos (avail. Mar. 1989)	$5.95
☐ Los Angeles	$5.95	☐ Sydney	$5.95
☐ Mexico City/Acapulco	$5.95	☐ Washington, D.C.	$5.95
☐ Minneapolis/St. Paul	$5.95		

SPECIAL EDITIONS

☐ A Shopper's Guide to the Caribbean	$12.95	☐ Motorist's Phrase Book (Fr/Ger/Sp)	$4.95
☐ Beat the High Cost of Travel	$6.95	☐ Paris Rendez-Vous	$10.95
☐ Bed & Breakfast—N. America	$8.95	☐ Swap and Go (Home Exchanging)	$10.95
☐ Guide to Honeymoon Destinations		☐ The Candy Apple (NY for Kids)	$11.95
(US, Canada, Mexico, & Carib)	$12.95	☐ Travel Diary and Record Book	$5.95
☐ Manhattan's Outdoor Sculpture	$15.95	☐ Where to Stay USA (Lodging from $3	
		to $30 a night)	$10.95

☐ Marilyn Wood's Wonderful Weekends (NY, Conn, Mass, RI, Vt, NH, NJ, Del, Pa) $11.95
☐ The New World of Travel (Annual sourcebook by Arthur Frommer previewing: new travel trends, new modes of travel, and the latest cost-cutting strategies for savvy travelers) $12.95

SERIOUS SHOPPER'S GUIDES

(Illustrated guides listing hundreds of stores, conveniently organized alphabetically by category)

☐ Italy	$15.95	☐ Los Angeles	$14.95
☐ London	$15.95	☐ Paris	$15.95

GAULT MILLAU

(The only guides that distinguish the truly superlative from the merely overrated.)

☐ The Best of Chicago (avail. Feb. 1989)	$15.95	☐ The Best of New England (avail. Feb.	
☐ The Best of France (avail. Feb. 1989)	$15.95	1989)	$15.95
☐ The Best of Italy (avail. Feb. 1989)	$15.95	☐ The Best of New York	$15.95
☐ The Best of Los Angeles	$15.95	☐ The Best of San Francisco	$15.95
		☐ The Best of Washington, D.C.	$15.95

ORDER NOW!

In U.S. include $1.50 shipping UPS for 1st book; 50¢ ea. add'l book. Outside U.S. $2 and 50¢, respectively. Allow four to six weeks for delivery in U.S., longer outside U.S.

Enclosed is my check or money order for $_____

NAME _____

ADDRESS _____

CITY _____ STATE _____ ZIP _____